The Psychology of
Terrorism Fears

THE PSYCHOLOGY OF TERRORISM FEARS

Samuel Justin Sinclair

and

Daniel Antonius

OXFORD
UNIVERSITY PRESS

OXFORD
UNIVERSITY PRESS

Oxford University Press, Inc., publishes works that further
Oxford University's objective of excellence
in research, scholarship, and education.

Oxford   New York
Auckland   Cape Town   Dar es Salaam   Hong Kong   Karachi   Kuala Lumpur   Madrid
Melbourne   Mexico City   Nairobi   New Delhi   Shanghai   Taipei   Toronto

With offices in
Argentina   Austria   Brazil   Chile   Czech Republic   France   Greece   Guatemala   Hungary
Italy   Japan   Poland   Portugal   Singapore   South Korea   Switzerland   Thailand
Turkey   Ukraine   Vietnam

Copyright © 2012 by Oxford University Press, Inc.

Published by Oxford University Press, Inc.
198 Madison Avenue, New York, New York 10016
www.oup.com

Oxford is a registered trademark of Oxford University Press, Inc.

Library of Congress Cataloging-in-Publication Data

Sinclair, Samuel J., 1975-
  The psychology of terrorism fears / Samuel Justin Sinclair and Daniel Antonius.
    p. cm.
  Includes bibliographical references and index.
  ISBN 978-0-19-538811-4 (hardback : alk. paper)   1. Terrorism—Psychological aspects.
2. Terrorism—Prevention.   I. Antonius, Daniel. II. Title.
  HV6431.S5333 2012
  303.6'25019—dc23   2011039851

9 8 7 6 5 4 3 2 1

Printed in the United States of America on acid-free paper

This is for my loves: Tate, Mr. Pants, Reesey Peesey, Lu, and Maggie—I love every minute of being with you.

— Samuel Justin Sinclair

For Beth, M.J., and RyRy—Thank you for all the fun.

— Daniel Antonius

Foreword

Despite the fact that engaging in activities designed to produce "terror" in others has been a part of human life for centuries, only in the post-9/11 era has it become a topic attracting the attention of many prominent psychologists and psychiatrists. That is not to say that there has not been earlier theorizing and research. There has been a steadily increasing rate of thinking about the topic coinciding with the steadily increasing use of terrorism by national liberation and resistance movements in the post-World War II time period. In particular, after the 1967 Arab–Israeli war, bombings targeting general civilian populations and then, more recently, the emergence of the suicide bomber as a tool to kill civilians added particular impetus to the study of this topic.

Not surprisingly, the initial focus of much of the research was directed at understanding the psychology of the terrorist. What combination of predisposing personal characteristics and momentary situational conditions would lead to an individual committing a terroristic act? The body of research that emerged has been highly informative and has disabused scholars of many common myths. Individual terrorists are not particularly economically deprived and tend to come from families that are above average in socioeconomic status. The research suggests that situational factors, peer groups, and organizational psychological processes play important roles in channeling young people into terrorist acts while individual socioeconomic factors do not.

While the political oppression of a population with whom one identifies and their economic disadvantages may engender the anger that sets the stage for terrorism against the oppressing population, these characteristics can be found in those who engage in terrorism and those who do not. Research has now shown that associations with other like-minded peers and segregation from out-group peers is an important additional factor. It promotes group cohesion and a desire to act for the in-group. Then, if the leaders of the revolt create the appropriate organizational mechanisms, they can channel the anger of youth into terrorist acts by attending to certain well-developed psychological principles (e.g., make participation appear to be highly selective and honorific; cement in-group cohesion; demand public commitment, which will make disengagement difficult and enhance self-beliefs in the cause; place the individual on a track with no choice points). Still, research shows that some individuals are more susceptible to succumbing to these forces and following the path to the terrorist act than are others.

All of this research has advanced our understanding of the causes of terrorism, but it has also highlighted the dearth of existing research on the psychological reactions that victims and potential victims of terrorism experience. A number of scholars have attempted to fill this void by extending the existing research on psychopathology and on post-traumatic stress to explain psychological reactions to terrorism. However, the analogy is flawed. Post-traumatic stress theorizing has been based on the canonical case of an individual, usually a direct victim or a relative of a victim of a highly stressful event, who experiences serious and lasting psychological consequences as a result of the highly stressful event. This paradigm may apply well to soldiers' experiences in wars, to accident victims or victims of domestic violence, to children who observe horrific violence, and to other similar experiences. However, terrorism, whether organized by a state (e.g., mass bombing of civilian populations), organized by a politically motivated underground organization, organized by a small angry group of youth, or organized by single individuals, has the direct purpose of making a population experience anxiety and fear in the future. An additional purpose of terrorism is often to force the state whose population is threatened to react violently and therefore to increase the total atmosphere of fear and anxiety. This is quite a different paradigm than the usual post-traumatic stress paradigm, and the need for research on the psychological effects of terrorism on both the targeted populations and the terrorist supporters is crystal clear. This current book is a welcome and highly needed step in this direction.

In the opening chapter of this book the authors cogently argue that most of the existing body of research on outcomes of terrorism, while providing valuable information, has failed to adequately describe or explain the fear and terror that the general population experiences as a consequence of terrorism and in anticipation of possible future terrorism. The key outcome of concern is what the authors denote as "anticipatory fear," which they argue can have both short- and long-term deleterious psychological consequences. After reviewing the existing literature in Chapter 2, the authors elaborate on the construct of "anticipatory fear" in Chapter 3. In many respects this is the crux of the book. While paying due respects to what I consider the poorly named "terror management theory" (Pyszczynski, Soloman, & Greenberg, 2003), the authors develop a theoretical perspective that draws substantially from Seyle's (1956) stress response theory, cognitive consistency theory (Festinger, 1957), learning and habituation theory (Abramson, Seligman, & Teasdale, 1974), risk appraisal theory (Slovic & Peters, 2006), and most importantly cognitive-behavioral theory (Beck, 1976). Terror management theory is really a theory simply of how people think and behave when their own mortality is made salient that has been applied after the fact to the effects of terrorism. On the other hand, the cognitive-behavioral theory of the psychological impact of terrorism that is developed by the authors of this book represents a large step forward toward understanding the unique elements of psychological responses to terrorism. They view the complex set of processes that occur when a terroristic event is seen as likely as operating automatically, which makes derailing the processes difficult. And once fear is activated, the fearful feel a need to bond more closely with their in-group and consequently to derogate and act more aggressively toward the perceived out-group responsible for the terror.

Building on this theoretical perspective, the authors use the rest of the book to provide valuable insights into the negative psychological consequences that derive from the anticipatory fear that terrorism produces, the kinds of warning strategies that might minimize long-term anticipatory fear, and the kind of moderating variables that might explain individual differences in reactions to terrorism. All in all this is a wonderful exposition of the knowledge we have, the knowledge we don't have but should try to acquire, and the psychological theory that best explains how people react.

As an aggression researcher who grew up trying to understand what determined whether an organism faced with threat responded with "flight" or "fight," and who has focused on resolving the issue with cognitive information processing explanations, I am impressed with how much the same principles that have been around in psychology for a long time can be applied again with an information processing model to understand the psychological reactions to the threat of mass terrorism. This is a notable achievement for this book. In addition, I find reasons for optimism in the kinds of understanding that grow out of this book. For example, while the "fight" response to terrorism threats could lead to misdirected aggression, it more likely can serve as a protective factor against the more psychologically damaging "flight" response and chronic fear reaction.

The more one thinks about such issues, the more one also must wonder what beliefs terrorists themselves have about these issues. Overall, I think that even very intelligent terrorist masters (and many are very intelligent) are generally pretty poor intuitive psychologists. As long as terrorism has been around, the directors of terrorism have seemed to believe that they could bring states or opposing people to their knees with fear—yet it is has seldom happened. The mass civilian bombings of World War II did not bring societies to their knees; the suicide bombings of the Middle Eastern wars have not brought society to their knees; and it is unlikely that even nuclear terrorism could in the future bring a state or society to its knees. The psychological responses, as this book illustrates, are too complex and humans are too good at finding ways to cope with anticipatory fear. The bigger danger is that societies may transform themselves in ways that make life less pleasant for most of us in order to deal with these kinds of fears.

L. Rowell Huesmann
Ann Arbor, Michigan
February 2011

Acknowledgments

We have many people to thank for making this book a reality. As such, we would each like to take a moment to express our gratitude to some people who have been particularly kind to us as we have set about this project.

Samuel Justin Sinclair:
I would first like to thank my family (Tatum, Cole, Reese, Lucy, and Maggie) for filling me up and making me whole. I just don't think any of this would be meaningful or worthwhile without you to share it. I want to say thank you to my parents, Hilary and Wayne, and my brother Ross for motivating and driving me. Finally, I also want to acknowledge the Monteyne family, who over the past decade has become my surrogate family (thanks to Mama Roe for her sauce and love, also).

There have also been many teachers and mentors I have been privileged to have in my life over the past decade, who, aside from helping me evolve professionally and think more critically about what I do, have become very close friends and feel like family. Specifically, I want to express my deep appreciation to Drs. Mark Blais and Kim Bistis for being my friends first and mentors second—I have learned and continue to learn an incredible amount from you both, and feel lucky to have you as my teachers. I also want to thank Alice LoCicero for giving me the direction and support to pursue my passions. Thanks to Barbara Gandek and John Ware, who, in addition to being incredibly kind to me as I struggled with my ill son, opened up a whole new world of statistics and numbers, and helped me to see things around me in more complicated ways.

I want to acknowledge my friends and colleagues at the Massachusetts General Hospital and Harvard Medical School, and specifically my posse at the Psychological Evaluation and Research Laboratory (the *PEaRL*). I feel incredibly lucky to work with a group of people who are much smarter than me, but also equally passionate and just plain fun. Coming to work each day and being around all of you is just awesome. Specifically, thank you to Mark Blais, Sheila O'Keefe, Kim Bistis, Michelle Jacobo, Dennis Norman, Michelle Stein, Caleb Siefert, Jenelle Slavin-Mullford, Iruma Bello, Annie Gupta, and Maren Nyer.

I must also acknowledge the friends and colleagues I have met along the way through the Society for Terrorism Research (STR)—who have continued to believe this is important work and who have given significantly of themselves to make this process meaningful. Following on this, I want to acknowledge and express my deep appreciation to the many international partners with whom we have had the good fortune to collaborate and learn from over the course of this process. When I first set about constructing STR, I had no idea the power and positive force this would create in my life—and I am honored and humbled to have had the chance to know and learn from you.

My appreciation also extends to Beth Davidson, Nicola Jones, Janet Remmington, and Glyn Lavers at Taylor and Francis & Routledge Publishing, who have helped us launch our peer-refereed journal, *Behavioral Sciences of Terrorism and Political Aggression* (see www.informaworld.com/BSTPA). Throughout this process, we have been very lucky to work within such a committed and talented community of people who see this as necessary and important work. As we enter our third year of publishing, we would like to say thank you to all of the reviewers, associate editors, and others who have made this a successful process. In many ways, this process has inspired the work contained within this book, and we are profoundly grateful to all of you.

I have deep gratitude to Lori Handelman at Oxford University Press, our original editor for the book, for initially believing the idea was important but also for her enormous help in developing the structure for it. I am also especially thankful to our new editor, Abby Gross, for challenging us throughout this process and giving us the support we needed to make this see the light of day. Thank you also to Joanna Ng, who has been incredibly kind and patient with us as we have stumbled our way through this (and asked a gazillion questions). Finally, I would like to express my deep appreciation to Drs. Randall Marshall and L. Rowell Huesmann for honoring us by writing the Foreword and Introduction to this volume. We look up to you in many ways and are profoundly humbled that you would share this with us.

Lastly, I would like to specifically thank my good friend Daniel Antonius, who, aside from contributing significantly to produce this book, has helped give me perspective on a lot of personal and professional matters over the past few years. Daniel has also brought an energy and passion into my life in many different ways, and more than anything makes this process feel worthwhile and fun. I feel lucky to have you as my colleague and friend, and sometimes look at you as my alter ego—Marshall Mathers to my Slim Shady.

Daniel Antonius:

I would like to start by thanking my co-author Samuel "Justin" Sinclair for inviting me to participate in this book project. Without him, this book would never have become a reality. I first got to know Justin in 2006 and it did not take long before I realized our shared interest in the psychological sciences of aggression, political violence, and terrorism. Since then, we have had hundreds of conversations, either over the phone or at meetings, sometimes several times a day, in which we have discussed issues related to terrorism and political violence. Often, these conversations would turn to our shared interests in addressing what we consider to be lacking in the field—the current gap in scientific knowledge of the psychological aspects of fear and how it specifically in its varied forms relates to terrorism and trauma. Both Justin and I perceive this to be one of the more intriguing questions for which we, as scientists and academics, are still looking for answers. Thus, when he asked me to embark on this project and to be a co-author, there was no hesitation and only immediate acceptance. This book presents our conversational journey over the past several years, where we have discussed papers, articles, theories, research, etc., that relates to the terrorism fears. This has been, personally speaking, an absolutely fascinating journey, as well as a tremendous learning experience. Not only has Justin been an inspiration throughout this process, but he has also become truly one of my dearest friends—Thanks Slim, for the invitation and your friendship!

I would also like to acknowledge the Society for Terrorism Research, which Justin introduced me to in 2007. Through my involvement with this organization, both as a board member and an editor for the newsletter, and through collaborations with its members and affiliates, I have been able not only to establish some great friendships, but also to develop my own knowledge base on theoretical constructs and empirical research related to terrorism as an interdisciplinary field. I would specifically like to mention the rewarding project of getting off the ground and co-editing (with Justin) the journal *Behavioral Sciences of Terrorism and Political Aggression* (Taylor & Francis), which is published in collaboration with the Society for Terrorism Research.

A special mention goes to my always-supportive work environment at Institute for Social and Psychiatric Services—Research, Education, and Services (InSPIRES) at New York University School of Medicine. They are the ones that have to deal with me on a daily basis. In particular, thank you to Dolores Malaspina for all the inspiration and support from Day 1, Mary Perrin for always being there to listen to me through thick and thin, Mark Opler for being the only other male (you are much more important than you think!), Sue Harlap for setting me straight, and Karine Kleinhaus for all the help when needed, as well as the rest of the bunch for putting up with me.

There are also two other people that I would like to acknowledge, who have in different and unique ways been inspirational to me in preparing this book. One of these is Maki Haberfeld at John Jay College for Criminal Justice, who I have had the fortune to know for over 10 years. Our numerous discussions on terrorism, counter-terrorism, violence, and other related topics have greatly affected my views on terrorism and science in general. The other person is Adam Brown, who since the first day I met him in graduate school at the New School for Social Research to this day has continued to keep me updated on the latest scientific developments in trauma research.

I would also like to echo Justin in thanking the editors in helping to prepare this book, as well as Drs. Huesmann and Marshall for writing the Foreword and Introduction for this book. Lastly, I would like to thank my family in Norway, Denmark, and the United States for all your (much needed) daily support and encouragement

—Thank You!

Samuel Justin Sinclair, Ph.D.   Daniel Antonius, Ph.D.
Boston, Massachusetts   New York, New York

Contents

The Psychology of
Terrorism Fears

Introduction

Randall D. Marshall

"He who is always prepared for the worst grows old early."
Søren Kierkegaard (1941)

Any productive exchange of ideas requires some common ground upon which to begin. This excellent book begins with a review of the meanings evoked by the dialectic of terror in our age. To put it briefly, terrorism may be said to be the deliberate targeting of innocents in the conduct of war. It is the context of war—a violent and organized conflict between nations, states, or parties in the service of some larger objective—that sets terrorism apart from murder and accidents.

An act of terrorism is in essence an attempt to manipulate the human fear of mortality. The rare individual who has transcended his fear of death is immune to its effects. Thus, the larger psychological, moral, and even spiritual contexts of terrorism fears are those related to the human response to the inevitability of death. To the behavioral scientist, what is problematic and deserving of study about the *response* to terrorism is the way it can radically distort fear perception out of proportion to the actual threat, and thus provoke extreme behavioral and emotional collective responses. This also sets it apart from study of the normal stress response, in that it links the stress response to a specific category of stimuli (various kinds of terrorist threats) that evoke the biological and social responses to fear and anxiety.

Sinclair and Antonius succeed in this book with their ambitious agenda to pull together important emerging and maturing concepts and data in the field of terrorism studies. The proliferation of original research, theoretical articles, and books on terrorism since Sept. 11, 2001, makes it fitting and even necessary to take stock at the

10-year anniversary. And, beyond all our expectations in the months after 9/11, the 10-year hiatus of attacks on U.S. soil, despite years of a "war on terror" in which the United States' declared enemies in this war have shown they can strike here, gives us the emotional and intellectual luxury of more objective analysis, at a distance from the searing emotions of those early days and months following 9/11 in the United States. Of course, the threat and actuality of terrorist attacks is much greater at present in many other countries, and Sinclair and Antonius draw from the international literature to avoid a purely U.S.-centric viewpoint. In fact, Sinclair and Antonius contribute substantively to the field through this book by sketching with such clarity the broad outlines of a rapidly evolving international multidisciplinary exchange of ideas.

This book is an in-depth review of the many scholarly approaches to understanding the *effects* of terrorism on its intended victims, and what has been learned so far. It does not address the causes of terrorism or its potential solutions, as that is a different (though inevitably related) area of inquiry. Although the book is grounded in a humanistic clinical perspective, it moves well beyond the traditional limitations of the language and modes of clinical science and epidemiology. Perhaps because the primary emphasis after 9/11 was on the construction and evaluation of a public health response to the epidemic of 9/11-related mental health problems, mental health heuristics tended to dominate such research. In retrospect, however, those models' limitations are obvious, and Sinclair and Antonius' discussion of the literature places 9/11 in its rightful broader context. Many researchers in the first months and years were exclusively focused on the language of symptom and sign (e.g., counting PTSD symptoms), when much more profound, multivocal, sociocultural phenomena related to fear and anxiety were manifesting across the United States.

Fear as an emotion is the natural consequence of a perceived threat. It shades into anxiety as the risk is de-centered, made vague ("what is it?") or less localizable ("where is it?"). We argued that the well-documented widespread reactions to 9/11 could not be understood by traditional mental health models, but could be better understood instead by the concept of relative risk appraisal, within Slovic's framework as a dreaded and unknown risk carrying high signal potential (Marshall et al., 2007). Anxiety and depressive symptoms among vulnerable persons not directly exposed to 9/11, wildly exaggerated fears in the general public of being harmed by terrorist attacks, racist attacks, and avoidance of air travel in the months afterward are all consistent with this explanatory model. Perhaps a more effective public policy would make use of the work of researchers and scholars in this area. As Sinclair and Antonius point out, terrorism is primarily psychological warfare, and so effective strategies for minimizing its damaging effects can be crafted only from an accurate understanding of the psychology of fear and threat. The goal is, put clearly, to reduce the level of terrorism threat appraisal in the general public so that effective protective actions (if there are any) can be taken by ordinary individuals without undue and maladaptive fear. A simple analogy: Public education programs are designed to promote healthy vigilance among drivers, seat belt use, and safe driving habits, not to instill counterproductive and distracting fear in the minds of drivers. This may be extremely difficult—to respond to the prospect of a terrorist attack in the way that we would to the prospect of a fatal car accident—but nonetheless these models offer maps for achieving this perspective. There are individuals with driving phobias who require treatment, but in general the vast majority of individuals manage the risks of driving without maladaptive levels of fear.

The authors' discussion of the arms race is particularly notable. They point out that fear can lead to both aggressive and avoidant responses. And since both are equally meaningful and understandable reactions (to borrow from Jaspers [1963]), the Cold War debates proceeded in endless circles as if only one (war) or the other (avoidance of war) were predictable responses to nuclear threat. They point out that similar circular quandaries in the field of terrorism research can be avoided when we accept that the field itself is unavoidably ambiguous, value-laden, and morally and politically charged. And surely a dialog about intentionally inflicted harm and death that was somehow purged of moral implications would in itself be intrinsically inhumane.

The authors' scholarly review of current trends and milestones in terrorism studies is notable for both its breadth and its accessibility to the nonspecialist reader. If each model is considered a heuristic in relation to the field of terrorism studies, then Sinclair and Antonius are highly proficient in their uses. There is also an unusually balanced fluency with the strengths and weaknesses of each model, ranging across the experience-near cognitive-behavioral models to the more sociological and even philosophical disciplines. They present in particular an in-depth discussion of fear-related cognitive schema that should be useful to students and even consumers of cognitive-behavioral therapy services, and a lucid appreciation of Pyszczynski's work, which re-introduces for the field an ages-old wisdom about the effects of mortal awareness on consciousness.

They also do not shy away from critical analysis of the many failed institutional attempts at managing—or perhaps exploiting?—the psychological impact of 9/11. The science of risk communication has much to offer public policy on these matters, chiefly because our current model is, to put it bluntly, so contrary to the desired effect, so ineffective, and even harmful to some sectors of the public. Sinclair and Antonius provide an excellent up-to-date review and emphasize the critical component that is so obvious and yet has been so strikingly absent from governmental risk communication: that it is essential to take into account the public's likely responses to national-level warnings. To be continually preparing for the worst is in fact an unhealthy and counterproductive way to live. It is in effect to live focused on one's future death, which is a kind of *foreshortening* of life's focus, or "to grow old early."

Fear and anxiety are relatively well-understood emotions, with well-understood behavioral and psychological responses, and the science of risk communication and threat appraisal has also come to maturity in the last couple of decades, anchored in the groundbreaking work of Slovnic and others. Sinclair and Antonius leave the reader much better educated about the latest research findings that should be informing the future work of scholars, journalists, and public officials. General readers will also find it enlightening, and perhaps even personally beneficial, since, to quote Jenny Holzer, the multimedia artist: "Categorizing fear is calming."

REFERENCES

Holzer, J. *Truisms* (1977–1979), from the Venice Installation.

Jaspers, K. (1963). *General psychopathology* [English translation]. Chicago: University of Chicago Press.

Kierkegaard, S. (1941). *Fear and trembling* and The sickness unto death. Princeton: Princeton University Press.

Marshall, R. D., Bryant, R., Amsel, L., Cook, J., Suh, E. J., & Neria, Y. (2007). The psychology of ongoing threat: Relative risk appraisal, the September 11, 2001 attacks, and terrorism-related fears. *American Psychologist, 62*(4), 304–316.

1 A Psychology of Fear

"The only thing we have to fear is fear itself—nameless, unreasoning, unjustified, terror which paralyzes needed efforts to convert retreat into advance."
Franklin D. Roosevelt

"You gain strength, courage, and confidence by every experience in which you really stop to look fear in the face. You must do the thing which you think you cannot do."
Eleanor Roosevelt

The events of September 11, 2001, represent the worst attacks on United States soil since the horrific events of Pearl Harbor, December 7, 1941. In the days and weeks that followed, people were witness to an entire airline industry being shut down, streaming images of planes flying into the World Trade Center towers in New York City and the buildings collapsing, and the beginnings of a national and international debate around what was to occur next. In total, the death toll of 9/11/2001 approached three thousand, although the emotional fallout has continued to manifest in many other significant ways.

However, unlike the events of Pearl Harbor, there was no clear perpetrator of the attacks in the form of a government or state, and the United States was instead forced to declare war on a complicated network of groups that was unified only in terms of the focus of their violence. Some have argued these networks were and are also unified in terms of their radical ideology and religious interpretation of Islam, although we as the authors of this book do not know this to be globally true (i.e., for all of these interconnected groups) and are not prepared to oversimplify what is likely a very complex dynamic. As researchers on violence in general, we have come to know that the reasons people become violent are complicated and usually reflect a convoluted interaction between a person and his or her environment. That is to say, people become violent for many, many reasons, and the probability of violence varies significantly across individuals, groups, and contexts. Thus, to simplify violence as being the sole product of one's ideology, in our minds, distorts the truth.

In response to the national outcry for retaliation and vengeance, former President George W. Bush launched attacks in October 2001 on the existing Taliban government in Afghanistan, who was known at the time to have been supportive of Osama bin Laden and Al Qaeda at large. However, many realized deep down that the Taliban was not immediately responsible and eventually the targets of American wrath shifted. The psychological and emotional impact of the 9/11/2001 attacks was surpassed only by the complex threat environment that ensued, where fears about what was to come next dominated public and governmental discourse.

In the aftermath of 9/11/2001, many turned to the mental health field to better understand both the psychology of those committing these acts of violence as well as the psychological impact of terrorism. Interestingly, and perhaps even ironically, many behavioral scientists concurrently began making similar remarks about the dearth of research that existed on the psychology of mass-terrorism. As if opening the floodgates completely, the research in this area exploded in the months and years that followed. We now know much more than we did about how acts of terrorism and political violence affect people psychologically. In general, this research reflected what people believed to be true—that is, that in the days, weeks, and months that followed, people were more anxious, traumatized, depressed, and generally distressed as a result of the attacks.

Given the excellent work by North and colleagues (1999, 2002) and others, we have also had the opportunity to compare the effects of 9/11/2001 to other terrorist attacks that have occurred on United States' soil, including those on the Alfred P. Murrah Federal Building in Oklahoma City, Oklahoma. In addition, we have had the opportunity to evaluate this body of work with other research on terrorism that has been conducted in Israel and elsewhere over the past decade (Bleich, Gelkopf, & Solomon, 2003; Njenga, Nicholls, Nyamai, Kigamwa, & Davidson, 2004; Rubin, Brewin, Greenberg, Simpson, & Wessely, 2005; Rubin, Brewin, Greenberg, Hughes, Simpson, & Wessely, 2007). As a result, the larger science on the psychological impact of terrorism has grown considerably, and we are in a much better position now to anticipate the effects of terrorism and respond as an integrated mental health field to terrorist attacks as they occur. This work is summarized in greater depth in Chapter 2.

However, in short, several prominent data trends have emerged across this large body of research. These include (1) the pattern of immediate increases in rates of psychiatric disorders and general levels of distress following an act of terrorism; (2) the greater relative impact in populations directly exposed, but also the significant residual impact felt outside of the epicenter; and (3) the longitudinal pattern of reduction in psychological distress over time in most populations (perhaps with the exception of those immediately affected, such as those in lower Manhattan). As is discussed in greater detail in Chapter 2, similar patterns were identified in Israel during and after the Second Intifada at the beginning of the millennium; in Madrid, Spain, in 2004 following the March 11 bombings on their transit system; and in the United Kingdom following the June 2005 attacks on the London subway system.

As researchers in this area of psychological science, we had some trouble understanding these findings. Although qualitative in nature and based in large part on our own personal observations of what was happening around us—in the cities of Boston (SJS) and New York City (DA), where we work and reside—these data trends seemed to mask the sense of fear and worry about the future that many people appeared to have about terrorism. In short, there seemed to be something missing within these scientific studies, as if only a portion of the story were being told. Terrorism had become the "boogeyman" that everyone was worried about and trying to avoid but could not seem to pinpoint with any precision. Thus began a new endeavor to study the psychology of terrorism fears, which in our estimation is *truly* the underlying psychology of terrorism itself.

In 2007, Marshall and colleagues published what we consider to be the seminal work on this topic. In the article, they discussed the psychological impact of terrorism but then went on to talk about how existing mental health paradigms do not provide adequate models for understanding this phenomenon. For example, they discussed current post-traumatic stress disorder (PTSD) models in terms of a "bull's eye" phenomenon, where those immediately exposed to a traumatic event are more susceptible to PTSD sequelae. However, in the case of 9/11/2001 they talked about how many people across the United States and internationally were adversely affected and even met most clinical criteria for PTSD, despite their lack of proximity to New York City, Washington, D.C., or Pennsylvania.

Marshall and colleagues (2007) discussed a variety of factors that may have contributed to this process, including both the role of media in vicariously traumatizing an entire population, as well as the notion of *relative risk appraisal* and complex array of factors that influence how people perceive risk around them. Towards the end of their monograph, they discussed the concept of fear as being an independent and significant vulnerability in the general population—standing apart from more conventional and clinical models of psychopathology.

Since the events of 9/11/2001, researching and understanding this very complex concept of fear has become a primary focus in our academic lives. As we have set about this process, we have come to agree in many ways with Marshall and colleagues (2007) that existing mental health frameworks are inadequate when studying both the short-term and longer-term effects of terrorism, and that *fear*—as distinct from discrete clinical disorders or syndromes—is a construct that plays a significant role in the psychology of terrorism and something that needs to be better understood. As Marshall and colleagues (2007) point out, fear likely represents an underlying vulnerability in the general population, above and beyond specific clinical disorders. In the age of technology and immediate access to information, fear is also fueled within people by a complex array of factors, such as immediate access to information through the Internet, a constant stream of media reporting on the issues, and greater connectivity (and thus direct and/or indirect exposure).

GENERAL THESIS

The basic thesis of this book is several-fold. First, we would argue that research on the psychological impact of terrorism in the past decade has provided for a robust body of literature on the short- and medium-term psychological impact of terrorism. While the majority of this research has focused on the events of 9/11/2001, it has also inspired researchers from across the globe to more systematically and exhaustively assess the psychological impact of terrorism internationally. Further, this body of research has not only evaluated the impact generally for those within a given population, but has also assessed these effects across specific subgroups of people who may be more vulnerable to the deleterious effects of terrorism—such as children, the elderly, those directly exposed, those with pre-existing psychiatric vulnerabilities, and so forth.

Second, we would submit that the majority of this science has used more conventional and clinically based models of psychopathology (e.g., the *Diagnostic and Statistical Manual of Mental Disorders* [DSM-IV]; American Psychiatric Association, 2000), which in our opinion only tells part of the story—and, ironically, perhaps *not* the most relevant part. Overall, these research models and data trends suggest a general reduction in discrete clinical disorders and psychological symptoms associated with the 9/11/2001 attacks over time. Some have argued that by 6 to 12 months following the attacks, these rates essentially returned to those seen prior to 9/11/2001, suggesting a general trend towards recovery and normalcy.

Third, and following this last point, we contend that these models have done very little to describe how people have been fearful or even "terrorized" as a result of terrorism, and are incomplete, and inadequate frankly, when assessing the psychological impact of terrorism. Indeed, as Marshall and colleagues (2007) noted, conventional psychopathology frameworks such as the DSM-IV are likely insufficient by themselves in understanding the full psychological fallout from terrorism, particularly in studying phenomena such as fear. We concur with Marshall and colleagues (2007) in this assessment, and throughout the rest of this book we present an argument as to why.

Over the course of this volume, we argue that anticipatory fear and worries about what is to come can also have serious and deleterious effects. As is discussed in greater detail in later chapters, some, including the former President of the American

Psychological Association, Dr. Philip Zimbardo, have even gone so far as to formally label this phenomenon a pre-traumatic stress syndrome (Zimbardo, 2003a, 2003b) as it relates to the American color-coded terror alert system. In contrast to clinical disorders such as PTSD, which manifest in the aftermath of a traumatic event to which a person is exposed, Zimbardo argues that other factors (such as the implementation of terror alert systems, frequent and nonspecific alerts issued by governments across the globe, and the constant media streaming of threat information) have all generated a significant amount of anticipatory anxiety about future threat. In a very basic way, this is at the crux of terrorism—in other words, to instill fear as a means of achieving some other end.

Given this thesis, the purpose of this volume is also manifold. In Chapter 2, we hope to present a comprehensive summary of the latest research on the psychological effects of terrorism, most of which is drawn from science that was disseminated over the past decade, since 9/11/2001. We then compare these broad findings to research that was conducted following the 1995 attacks on Oklahoma City, as well as investigations into the psychological impact of international terrorism—all as a means of elucidating with greater precision how terrorism affects people psychologically. These clinical constructs (e.g., PTSD, depression, anxiety, etc.), which are almost exclusively the focus of psychological research on terrorism, are then differentiated from the more general concept of fear—which we would argue is qualitatively different and the core psychological weapon underlying acts of terrorism.

In Chapter 3, we begin to present our primer on fear in general and with respect to terrorism specifically, and discuss a variety of theoretical paradigms that are useful in understanding fear as a dynamic process. Toward these ends, Chapter 3 presents an array of frameworks for understanding how people experience fear cognitively and affectively, as well as ways in which they actively engage various coping mechanisms as a means of buffering themselves against this underlying anxiety. Terror Management Theory (TMT; Pyszczynski, Soloman, & Greenberg, 2003; Pyszczynski, Motyl, & Abdollahi, 2009), in particular, is one theory that has received considerable attention in the social sciences following the 9/11/2001 attacks, and is presented as a primary model for better understanding why and how people fear terrorism, as well as why people engage culture and community to fend off an overriding sense of threat and existential terror. Cognitive-behavioral theory (Beck, 1976; 1979) is also discussed as a model for understanding how specific terrorism fears manifest in people from a cognitive standpoint, and the subsequent impact this has on emotional and behavioral process.

Chapter 4 extends much of what is presented in the previous two chapters and presents empirical data from a variety of different scientific and polling sources, which document how fear has manifested in the general population—separate from more conventional models of psychopathology—as well as how fear has affected people in negative ways. This chapter first discusses how fear differs in quality from clinical constructs such as PTSD, which has been the primary focus of most behavioral science research investigations, and extends this by talking about how fear leads people to make significant changes in their lives. Finally, Chapter 4 presents new empirical frameworks for measuring fear and its impact, which provide benchmarks from which to make meaningful comparisons as to magnitude. The Terrorism Catastrophizing Scale (TCS; Sinclair & LoCicero, 2007, 2010; Sinclair, 2010) is presented as one assessment framework for pursuing these ends.

Chapter 5 reviews these data in the context of the new threat environment in which we all live and discusses ways of crafting and disseminating communications to the general public in a manner that enhances effectiveness and reduces panic. In this chapter, we also discuss the effectiveness of the United States' color-coded terrorist alert system, which was implemented shortly after the 9/11/2001 attacks. In the years following the attacks, some have argued that the frequent warnings from our government regarding the terrorism threat we face only served to prime people's fears about impending threat. Over time, these fears morphed into frustration and even apathy, all of which has undermined the original intended message. At the very least, the meaning of the original communication becomes distorted and misinterpreted in many ways, and is thus ineffective as originally intended. Given this, Chapter 5 seeks to provide new frameworks for threat communication, given what we know and what is presented in Chapters 1 through 4.

Chapter 6 presents the opposite side of the coin—that of psychological resilience in the context of threat. Thus far, the book has centered on the issue of fear, and how people are vulnerable to and affected by fears of future terrorism. In contrast, the purpose of Chapter 6 is to present research suggesting that in the face of these kinds of threats, there is a wide spectrum of individual reactions, and that many people remain unaffected psychologically and are able to negotiate their lives as they otherwise would. Psychological science has come a long ways in terms of identifying factors that reinforce coping, recovery, and resilience in the face of adversity and/or external threat, and this chapter will begin to unpack some of the complexity surrounding this construct and psychological equanimity in the context of risk.

Finally, Chapter 7 discusses ways in which these findings can be useful to those tasked with responding to the general public following disasters such as terrorist attacks, as well as models for effectively communicating warning and managing these situations prospectively. This chapter also talks about how health care workers and others (including those directly affected) can negotiate these dynamics moving forward—both in terms of identifying risk factors for people at greater risk, and promoting health and recovery (and even resilience) following these sorts of disasters.

DEFINING TERRORISM

Prior to launching into a book about terrorism and fear, it is first necessary to operationally define the variables being studied. This is especially true here given the degree to which terms such as "terrorism" have been debated and scrutinized by various academics and laypeople alike. Some have suggested that using terms like "terrorism" is pejorative and impedes the scientific process, as there is no commonly accepted meaning of the term. Others have posited that "One person's terrorist is another's freedom fighter," highlighting the problems of differential and/ or relative meaning across groups of people. Even the United Nations has struggled with defining terrorism in a way that is mutually acceptable by all member-states over the past decade, and has consistently run into the same sorts of difficulties as they set about this process.

A recent special issue of the journal *Behavioral Sciences of Terrorism and Political Aggression* (2011 Issue 2; www.informaworld.com/BSTPA) was exclusively devoted to the definitional dilemmas surrounding the use of terms such as "terrorism" in academic discourse. Based on a symposium of papers presented in 2009 at the third annual conference of the Society for Terrorism Research and the Coloquios Internationales sobre Cerebro y Agresión in Belfast, Northern Ireland, this special journal issue presented a different set of perspectives on the advantages and disadvantages of using terms such as "terrorism" in scientific inquiry. As attendees to this symposium, we can both attest to the fact that this discussion was interesting and lively, and useful for purposes of discussion here!

In this special issue, Bryan, Kelly, and Templer (2011) presented the argument for the "failed paradigm of terrorism" and initially reviewed an array of definitions used by various leaders in the field, which differ along key dimensions. For example, some definitions distinguish between state-sponsored and non-state–sponsored terrorism and perpetrators of terrorism, while others do not. Further, some separate out violence that is perpetrated within the context of war, versus violence that occurs in its absence. Finally, some definitions focus almost exclusively on the underlying psychological dimensions and intentions of the actor (i.e., to instill fear within a particular group as a vehicle for effecting some form of political or social change), while others focus more on the explicit characteristics of the act (violence aimed at noncombatants to affect some sort of external reality). As Bryan and colleagues argued with great clarity, the result is a highly inconsistent set of definitions—on which to, among other things, wage war.

Bryan and colleagues (2011) pointed out that while many within the terrorism studies community argue that implicit within the terrorist act is the underlying communication to some larger entity or group, the same could be argued with respect to any form of violence. If this is true, then why use the term "terrorism" in lieu of "violence," or some other word that is less pejorative and politically loaded? Following on this, these authors pointed out that while many terrorism studies scholars appear to focus on noncombatants and/or civilians as being the primary targets, the term is applied to many situations that do not fall within these parameters—such as the 1983 bombings of the U.S. Marine Corps barracks in Beirut, Lebanon. The group Islamic Jihad ultimately took responsibility for these attacks, although reports have varied. However, many have assumed this group was "terrorist" in nature, as labeled by the United States' government, and thus many have considered and labeled it an act of "terrorism."

Finally, in reviewing various definitions of terrorism, Bryan and colleagues (2011) focused on terrorism expert Bruce Hoffman's observation that "on one point, at least, everyone agrees: 'Terrorism' is a pejorative term." They suggest that this is perhaps the most "alarming" aspect of using the term at all, as an entire field is built upon a pejorative and "politically loaded term." The resulting science is thus based on an underlying phenomenon that is known to vary by group, differs in terms of the operational definition across academic disciplines, and means very different things to different people. Assuming as they do that the term is socially constructed and politically laden, using terms such as "terrorism" may even further the agendas of some groups in power while limiting those in weaker positions— thus maintaining the status quo. As Guess (2011) discussed in his study of language and terrorism (within this same *BSTPA* special issue on terrorism), people manifest very different emotional and perceptual reactions to terms that are often used inter-changeably—including "suicide terrorist," "martyr," "Islamic martyr," "suicide bomber," and "volunteer." Given these findings, one could see how even subtle semantic differences in regards to how these terms get used in political discourse may have significant psychological and perceptual effects.

Rapin (2011) went on to argue that the process of defining terrorism has become circular in ways, where terrorism is any act to instill "terror"—however this term is defined. He argues that for this to be true, there must be some way of evaluating whether acts of terrorism truly instill terror within some target group. Interestingly, he moved a bit away from the assumption that terrorism must have as a prerequisite the assumption that instilling terror is the primary intention, and focused instead on whether terrorism actually terrifies people. Based on his review of the literature, Rapin (2011) appears to argue that this is not the case—that is, that terrorism does not instill *terror*, itself seen as a more extreme variant of anxiety or worry. As a result, the term is a misnomer and is contradictory in many ways.

In his rebuttal, Jackson (2011) conceded that the term "terrorism" has been crit-icized *ad nauseam* along three key dimensions. First, he agreed that many see the term as pejorative and politically laden, designed to support the status quo within the government and media elite. The term is then used as a means of maintaining and manipulating power for those in positions of advantage. Second, Jackson dis-cussed how the term "terrorism" is very much a rhetorical construct rooted within the social and cultural dimensions of the times, which also vary markedly across time and people. As Jackson (2011, p. 117) himself noted, "In other words, the term terrorism is an empty signifier; we cannot know the thing itself, only the way in which it is discursively constructed through language usage and social practices." Finally, because of the former two criticisms, Jackson pointed out the irony that the term now includes as part of its definition the very fact that it is contested and lacks consistency in terms of meaning across groups.

Taking these criticisms into consideration and responding to the position made by Bryan and colleagues (2011) in particular, Jackson (2011) then proceeded to argue that these facts should *not* preclude attempts at defining the term. In proposing a new field of "Critical Terrorism Studies," Jackson argued that all forms of academic and scholarly inquiry have been rooted within particular historical and cultural contexts—all of which affect the process and outcome of such inquiry. With respect to the issue of terrorism, the same is true, and rather than abandoning the task of defining the phenomenon, effort should be put towards better elucidating and understanding the concept within historical context.

As a means of going about this, Jackson (2011) then discussed four common misconceptions of terrorism that bog down academics in their struggle for clarity: (1) civilians and/or noncombatants are the intended targets, which themselves are value-laden terms; (2) victims are chosen "randomly" and are "innocents" within a larger group or society that is the target of some coercion; (3) one of the primary goals of terrorism is to be spectacular and public in nature—for purposes of creating instability within a population as a means of affecting some change within the organized power structure; and (4) terrorism is an "illegitimate" form of violence perpetrated by non-state actors alone, and that states are exempt from this category. In presenting these misconceptions, Jackson then went on to argue how they keep academics mired within the perpetual exercise of redefining something that is inherently multi-definitional, and preclude people from focusing on the underlying characteristics that are generally consistent when considering whether some event is terrorism—which thus prevents any sort of meaningful definition of the term.

In presenting these common objections and places where academics and others alike seem to get hung up in perpetual debate, Jackson (2011) then presented a new definition of terrorism that focuses almost exclusively on the underlying intention of the act itself—distancing itself both from specific targets and politically laden terms, which have seemed to derail these discussions in the past. Specifically, Jackson (2011, p. 123) proposed the following definition for the term "terrorism":

Terrorism is violence or its threat intended as a symbolically communicative act in which the direct victims of the action are instrumentalized as a means of creating a psychological effect of intimidation and fear in a target audience for a political objective.

For purposes of this book, we acknowledge the many problems with using terms such as terrorism but also agree with Dr. Jackson that this should not preclude efforts to define and understand and ultimately to empirically test theories related to this category of violence. We further agree with Dr. Jackson that it is not the specific target or particular qualities of the perpetrator that underlie the definition of terrorism, but rather the intentions behind the act, where some target is both intentionally and instrumentally used as a means of affecting some political change by way of fear and intimidation. Given this, and as a means of achieving some degree of consistency in terms of an operational definition of "terrorism" for this volume, we refer the reader to the above definition proposed by Jackson (2011).

FEAR IN RECENT HISTORICAL CONTEXT

At a recent lecture given by the first author at a university in Boston on the topic of terrorism and fear, a student raised his hand and argued that this phenomenon is not new. He went on to efficiently discuss the many other periods in human history where fear was both rampant in the population and used for political gain. Specifically, he discussed the Cold War era and our race for nuclear weapons with the former Soviet Union and Eastern bloc of nations, and how fear of nuclear annihilation was a common focus of people's anxieties and worries. In many ways, this student made very good points. There have been many periods in history where fear and worry have been significant, and this should be acknowledged in the context of what is to follow in subsequent chapters. If for no other reason, it is important to root fear in a historical context as a means of both learning from the past and building our knowledge in more complex ways moving forward.

Recent history is replete with examples of fear. In the late 1940s to the late 1950s, Sen. Joseph McCarthy from Wisconsin began stoking fears of communism and subversion at the beginning of the U.S. Cold War with the former Soviet Union by asserting that a great many members of Congress and the government were secret communist spies. As a result of these accusations, many in government circles began fearing for their political (and personal) futures and the coming accusations they would have to weather, while many outside government worried that their government had come under the control of a hostile nation. Ultimately, McCarthy was censured by the government and became politically impotent, although not before he injected a significant amount of fear and even paranoia into our political process.

Another incident within the past half-decade that comes to mind is the Cuban missile crisis of 1962, which occurred when the former Soviet Union moved nuclear weapons to the shores of Cuba, just a few miles from the southern coast of the United States. President Kennedy and his advisors were then tasked with negotiating with the Soviet government for the removal of all weapons, and in many people's minds nuclear war hung in the balance. Then-Secretary of Defense Robert McNamara was noted to have remarked, "I thought I might not see another Saturday night" (Finkelstein, 1994, p. 91). Although this immediate conflict lasted 13 days, the public was privy to only roughly a week (Smith, 2003). In his interesting analysis of public opinion polling during this period, Smith (2003) found that 59% of the general public felt that the Cuba situation was a serious threat to world peace at the time, and approximately one third to one half believed there was "much danger" of a world war. Roughly 12% reported having made changes to their regular daily activities as a result of the Cuban missile crisis, and roughly one third of people polled said that people they spoke to about this crisis were "very worried" about the situation.

Following on this theme of anxiety about nuclear war, Newcomb (1986) published a study in the *Journal of Personality and Social Psychology* where he evaluated roughly 700 young adults (approximately 19 to 24) who grew up in the nuclear era in terms of their level of worry and anxiety about nuclear war. Results suggested that increased nuclear anxiety was associated with depression, substance abuse, feelings of powerlessness and purposeless in life, and less life satisfaction. Findings also demonstrated that gender had an effect, with more women than men reporting nuclear concerns and fears of the future. In a follow-up study by Rabow, Hernandez, and Newcomb (1990), many of these results were replicated and additional findings demonstrated that Swedish students expressed less concern and fear about nuclear issues than their American counterparts—which would lend initial support to the notion that people in the immediate areas affected or targeted experience greater levels of fear and anxiety.

In his seminal work on the psychology of avoiding nuclear war, Blight (1987) made a number of arguments that have clear parallels with today's issues surrounding terrorism. He began his monograph by discussing the "groundswell of interest among psychologists in issues related to nuclear policy and nuclear war" (Blight, 1987, p. 12) and went on to remark about the explosion of articles and books, and even courses being taught on the subject—similar to what we do in Chapter 2 with respect to modern terrorism. Speaking to the issue of fear and the arms race specifically, Blight (1987, p. 14) referred to the observation made by fellow psychologist Charles Osgood that "Using a method one might call fear assessment Osgood attributed the rising risk of war to deep fear and tension caused by continued participation in the arms race." Fear in this context was seen as a potential catalyst for war, while other psychologists, including Thomas Schelling, believed war would be *prevented* by this fear. Regardless of who was absolutely correct, the issue of fear took center stage in terms of how the nuclear arms race was negotiated, and some believe it stood at the crux of the concept of "mutually assured destruction," the notion that fear of mutual extinction by nuclear war kept the superpowers (the United States and Soviet Union) from using these weapons at all.

A more recent and perhaps relevant phenomenon in the technological sense that caused widespread fear was the Y2K bug, which many worried would occur as computer systems made the transition from the year 1999 to 2000. In essence, this situation had to do with basic computer programming systems that used two-digit numbers to specify time in years (i.e., "76" for 1976). No one knew what would happen when this number system reset to "00," and anxiety abounded about whether computer systems would simply shut down and airplanes would begin falling from the sky as a result of failed computer aviation systems.

To evaluate people's responses to this potential threat, Aspinwall, Sechrist, and Jones (2005) interviewed roughly 700 people in the months leading up to Y2K and found that levels of worry were significant and that worry predicted both damage estimates and level of preparation (seen in this study as a coping strategy). Quigley (2005) subsequently argued that it was this fear and anxiety being expressed in the media that influenced the governments of the United States and United Kingdom to prepare and respond with greater force initially—as a means of controlling public opinion. Ultimately, the computer systems made the transition into the new millennium without any significant problems, although not before some were calling for widespread panic.

CONCLUSIONS

The basic premise of this book is that although rates of psychopathology normalize in the months and years that follow terrorist incidents, there is evidence to suggest that fears about future threat continue to affect people in significant ways. These fears affect where people live and work, how they vote in elections and make decisions about political discourse, who they interact with socially, and how they prepare themselves for the future. Aside from altering many other aspects of life, the 9/11/2001 attacks have also called attention to the fact that our current frameworks for assessing the psychological impact of terrorism are inadequate and incomplete, and require revision—as a means of better understanding the impact of fear and anticipatory threat. We join our colleagues, notably Marshall and associates (2007), in suggesting that further revision is necessary in terms of the models we use to understand large-scale disasters, such as terrorism.

This book is meant to be an initial attempt at accomplishing this goal, with a focus on terrorism *fears* and the impact that is felt above and beyond whether people meet a certain number of clinical criteria for a discrete psychological disorder. While useful, this latter approach is overly simplistic and perhaps blurs the true effects of terrorism—which at its core is a psychological weapon. Following on this, we further hope to use this preliminary work to begin to present new models for managing and communicating this risk moving forward. We acknowledge that many prior attempts to do this (e.g., implementing the color-coded alert system, making nonspecific reports about impending threat, etc.) have been largely unsuccessful and have perhaps even done more to enhance fear, frustration, and in some cases apathy—all of which run counter to the initial intention of the message. Finally, we also hope to present a framework for resilience that draws on an already substantial body of research into why and how some people remain immune from the more detrimental effects of trauma exposure. With respect to the issue of terrorism specifically, we hope to present a clearer framework for how to keep people healthy following disasters.

This book is meant to be an initial push for future research on the subject of terrorism and fear. We hope that our colleagues and academics alike engage with us in challenging and refining these ideas and working towards a more complicated and integrated behavioral science of terrorism. We believe this process must be interdisciplinary and international in nature, and must integrate knowledge from a broad array of scientific disciplines. Our ultimate goal is twofold: (1) to better understand the complex process by which some people enter down a path where the end result is violence against others and (2) to understand and eventually anticipate the psychological consequences of terrorism, and to be able to respond quickly and effectively. We hope that this book is the first step in what will likely be a long and winding staircase.

REFERENCES

American Psychiatric Association. (2000). *Diagnostic and statistical manual of mental disorders—Fourth edition—text revision.* Washington, D.C.: American Psychiatric Association.

Aspinwall, L. G., Sechrist, G. B., & Jones, P. R. (2005). Expect the best and prepare for the worst: Anticipatory coping and preparations for Y2K. *Motivation and Emotion, 29,* 357–388.

Beck, A. T. (1976). *Cognitive therapy and the emotional disorders.* New York: Basic Books.

Beck, A. T. (1979). *Cognitive therapy of depression.* New York: The Guilford Press.

Bleich, A., Gelkopf, M., & Solomon, Z. (2003). Exposure to terrorism, stress-related mental health symptoms, and coping behaviors among a nationally representative sample in Israel. *Journal of the American Medical Association, 290,* 667–670.

Blight, J. G. (1987). Toward a policy-relevant psychology of avoiding nuclear war. *American Psychologist, 42,* 12–29.

Bryan, D., Kelly, L., & Templer, S. (2011). The failed paradigm of "terrorism". *Behavioral Sciences of Terrorism and Political Aggression, 3,* 80–96.

Finkelstein, N. H. (1994). *Thirteen days/ninety miles: The Cuban missile crisis.* New York: Simon and Schuster.

Guess, D. (2011). Suicide terrorism: Exploring Western perceptions of terms, context, and causes. *Behavioral Sciences of Terrorism and Political Aggression, 3,* 97–115.

Jackson, R. (2011). In defence of terrorism: finding a way through a forest of misconceptions. *Behavioral Sciences of Terrorism and Political Aggression, 3,* 116–130.

Marshall, R. D., Bryant, R. A., Amsel, L., Suh, E. J., Cook, J. M., & Neria, Y. (2007). The psychology of ongoing threat: Relative risk appraisal, the September 11 attacks, and terrorism-related fears. *American Psychologist, 62,* 304–316.

Newcomb, M. D. (1986). Nuclear attitudes and reactions: Associations with depression, drug use, and quality of life. *Journal of Personality and Social Psychology, 50,* 906–920.

Njenga, F. G., Nicholls, P. J., Nyamai, C., Kigamwa, P., & Davidson, J. R. (2004). Post-traumatic stress after terrorist attack: psychological reactions following the US embassy bombing in Nairobi: Naturalistic study. *British Journal of Psychiatry, 185,* 328–333.

North, C. S., Nixon, S. J., Shariat, S., Mallonee, S., McMillen, J. C., Spitznagel, E. L., & Smith, E. M. (1999). Psychiatric disorders among survivors of the Oklahoma City bombing. *Journal of the American Medical Association, 282,* 755–762.

North, C. S., Tivis, L., McMillen, J. C., Pfefferbaum, B., Cox, J., Spitznagel, E. L., Bunch, K., Schorr, J., & Smith, E. M. (2002). Coping, functioning, and adjustment of rescue workers after the Oklahoma City bombing. *Journal of Traumatic Stress, 15*, 171–175.

Pyszczynski, T., Motyl, M., & Abdollahi, A. (2009). Righteous violence: Killing for God, country, freedom, and justice. *Behavioral Sciences of Terrorism and Political Aggression, 1*, 12–39.

Pyszczynski, T., Solomon, S., & Greenberg, J. (2003). *In the wake of 9/11/2001: The psychology of terror.* Washington, D.C.: American Psychological Association.

Quigley, K. F. (2005). Bug reactions: Considering US government and UK government Y2K operations in light of media coverage and public opinion polls. *Health, Risk, & Society, 7*, 267–291.

Rabow, J., Hernandez, A. C. R., & Newcomb, M. D. (1990). Nuclear fears and concerns among college students: A cross-national study of attitudes. *Political Psychology, 11*, 681–698.

Rapin, A. J. (2011). What is terrorism? *Behavioral Sciences of Terrorism and Political Aggression, 3*, 161–165.

Rubin, G. J., Brewin, C. R., Greenberg, N., Hughes, J., Simpson, J., & Wessley, S. (2007). Enduring consequences of terrorism: 7-month follow-up survey of reactions to the bombings in London July 7, 2005. *British Journal of Psychiatry, 190*, 350–356.

Rubin, G. J., Brewin, C. R., Greenberg, N., Simpson, J., & Wessley, S. (2005). Psychological and behavioral reactions to the bombings in London on July 7, 2005: cross sectional survey of a representative sample of Londoners. *British Journal of Psychiatry.* Retrieved Dec. 1, 2010, from http://www.bmj.com/content/331/7517/606.abstract.

Sinclair, S. J. (2010). Fears of terrorism and future threat: Theoretical and empirical considerations. In D. Antonius, A. D., Brown, T. Walters, M. Ramirez, & S. J. Sinclair (Eds.), *Interdisciplinary analyses of terrorism and aggression,* (pp. 101–115). Cambridge, England: Cambridge Scholars Publishing.

Sinclair, S. J., & LoCicero, A. (2007). Anticipatory fear and catastrophizing about terrorism: Development, validation, and psychometric testing of the Terrorism Catastrophizing Scale (TCS). *Traumatology, 13*, 75–90.

Sinclair, S. J., & LoCicero, A. (2010). The Terrorism Catastrophizing Scale (TCS): Assessing the ongoing psychological impact of terrorism. In L. Baer & M. Blais (Eds.), *Handbook of clinical rating scales and assessment in psychiatry and mental health* (pp. 278–285). Boston: Humana Press.

Smith, T. W. (2003). The Cuban missile crisis and U.S. public opinion. *Public Opinion Quarterly, 67*, 265–293.

Zimbardo, P. (2003a). *Overcoming terror.* Retrieved February 2004 from http://www.brucekluger.com/PT/PT-OvercomingTerror-JulAug2003.html

Zimbardo, P. (2003b). *The political psychology of terrorist alarms.* Retrieved February 2004 from http://www.zimbardo.com/downloads/2002%20Political%20Psychology%20of%20Terrorist%20Alarms.pdf

2 The Psychological Aftermath of Terrorism

A Current State of the Science

"*The oldest and strongest emotion of mankind is fear.*"
H. P. Lovecraft

"*Sleep with one eye open, gripping your pillow tight. Exit light, enter night. Take my hand, we're off to Never NeverLand.*"
Metallica

Research on the psychological impact of terrorism exploded following the September 11, 2001, attacks in New York City, Washington, D.C., and Pennsylvania. Although the context for such a rapid generation and dissemination of science was unfortunate, the resulting field has evolved considerably and we now know much more about the impact terrorism has on people's lives than we did prior to these events. Speaking to this proliferation in research, Ranstorp (2009) pointed out that in 2001 there were roughly 100 articles appearing in mainstream academic journals associated with terrorism (per the Social Sciences Citation Index, which is a large repository of academic/scientific sources), compared to approximately 2,300 articles in 2007. Also, some have noted that since 9/11/2001 there has been a 300% increase in peer-refereed papers focused on issues of terrorism and political violence (Lentini, 2008).

Although this emerging literature has examined a wide range of topics associated with terrorism from a myriad of professional disciplines, numerous studies have begun to unpack the complexity underlying the mental health effects of terrorist violence specifically. In a recent issue of the journal *Behavioral Sciences of Terrorism and Political Aggression,* Jhangianai (2010) reported that between 2001 and 2006 approximately 1,000 articles emerged that focused on the psychological effects of terrorist attacks specifically, based on a keyword search in the PsycINFO and PsycARTICLES databases, compared to 75 published articles prior to 2001. The reasons for this are likely complex.

Some have argued that the 9/11/2001 attacks affected both national (United States) and international communities in ways that differed from other attacks or disasters because of the role the media played in displaying the events from that day over and over again (Ahern, Galea, Resnick, & Vlahov, 2004; Marshall, Bryant, Amsel, Suh, Cook, & Neria, 2007; Jhangiani, 2010). Within the United States specifically, normal television broadcasting essentially ceased for several weeks, and even on sports channels, such as ESPN, where one would expect to find the baseball game for that evening, it was instead a constant media stream playing and replaying the 9/11/2001 attacks over and over again with intermittent news updates and dialog between "experts."

Marshall and colleagues (2007), as briefly mentioned in Chapter 1, discussed how the psychological impact of terrorism following 9/11/2001 did not fit neatly within existing mental health paradigms for those living in the United States. Specifically, they discussed how traumatic experiences typically affect those most proximal to the event, and that the magnitude of effect dissipates as one achieves greater distance. They use the metaphor of the "bull's eye" to illustrate the concept, where people in the center (i.e., those most proximal) experience the most negative outcomes psychologically and physically. Aside from the role of media, others have also suggested that the magnitude of attacks in terms of lives lost, damage done (in terms of immediate dollar costs, scope of the physical destruction, and longer-lasting economic damage), and the subsequent amount of uncertainty that ensued all have played a significant role in terms of the psychological toll on the general population. The purpose of this chapter is to summarize the large body of research that has been disseminated post-9/11/2001 and to compare it to other terrorist attacks both within the United States and internationally.

OVERALL TRENDS IN PSYCHOLOGICAL IMPACT FOLLOWING THE 9/11/2001 ATTACKS

The vast majority of research that has been disseminated since 9/11/2001 has focused inordinately on rates of post-traumatic stress disorder (PTSD), as defined by the American Psychiatric Association (APA, 2000), both in the areas directly exposed as well as in the general population. PTSD is a clinical diagnosis given to individuals following a traumatic event who must meet certain criteria for a diagnosis. These include that a person (1) is directly exposed to an event that threatens death or harm to himself or herself or people close to him or her and (2) experiences symptoms of intrusive ideation (e.g., re-experiencing the event through flashbacks or dreams, etc.), engages in increased avoidance of situations and/or people that remind him or her of the traumatic event, and manifests increased anxiety and/or arousal (e.g., hypervigilance, elevated feelings of fear, irritability, etc.) (APA, 2000).

For a diagnosis of PTSD to be made, these symptoms must be consistently present for at least one month following the event and must cause clear distress and functional impairment, such as difficulties at work, in relationships, attending school, and other major life domains. According to the *Diagnostic and Statistical Manual of Mental Disorders* (DSM-IV-TR) (APA, 2000), the *lifetime* prevalence rate is roughly 8% in the general population. This means that approximately 8% of people in the general population will develop PTSD over the course of their lives as a function of exposure to some traumatic event.

This distinction is important to make for several reasons. First, the majority of studies that have been disseminated since 9/11/2001 have evaluated psychiatric symptoms in relation to this event specifically, as opposed to over the course of a lifetime. Thus, to say that 5% to 10% of people developed symptoms of PTSD as a result of 9/11/2001 (*as one discrete point in time*) is significant, given that these numbers would be expected over the course of a lifetime. These criteria are also important to recognize clinically because many of the studies to have emerged since 9/11/2001 examined only clusters of these symptoms and were not reporting on rates of PTSD *per se*. For example, acute stress disorder (ASD; APA, 2000) is another clinical term that has received attention more recently following terrorist attacks. ASD is similar to PTSD, although it manifests within several days following a traumatic event and lasts up to 4 weeks. If symptoms persist after 4 week, a PTSD diagnosis is then made. The implication is that PTSD is a more chronic and longer-lasting disorder, whereas ASD is more acute and limited in duration.

In addition to PTSD and ASD, research on the mental health effects of terrorism after 9/11/2001 has also reported on general mood (e.g., depression) and anxiety symptoms, substance abuse, suicide, and rates of prescription drug use—all of which is summarized below. Further, risk factors for negative mental health outcomes following traumatic events have been evaluated exhaustively, as well as factors that have been shown to produce positive outcomes (Jhangiani, 2010). Finally, this body of research has begun to evaluate many of these factors across time, assessing both the immediate and longer-term psychological effects of terrorism, and have done so in the general population and across different cross-sections of communities varying in terms of exposure to the traumatic event. The present chapter will summarize these trends as they exist currently, with the caveat that new science continues to evolve and emerge in these areas, and thus may change over time.

Immediate Psychological Impact of the 9/11/2001 Attacks

Laugharne, Janca, and Widiger (2007) recently conducted a meta-review of the relationship between PTSD and terrorism in the United States, and reported that there was both a clear and immediate spike in PTSD sequelae following the 9/11/2001 attacks, which was followed by a resolution in symptoms at roughly 6 to 12 months following the attacks. Independent reviews conducted by Lee, Isaac, and Janca (2002) and Friedman, Hamblen, Foa, and Charney (2004) also suggest that approximately one third of people directly exposed to a terrorist attack will likely develop symptoms of clinically significant distress, including PTSD and ASD. Trends in PTSD and other forms of psychopathology have been studied at the population level and in regions directly affected by terrorism. Studies have shown elevated rates of distress in both groups immediately following an attack, and prolonged elevations in the latter over time.

The first and most widely cited study to emerge following the 9/11/2001 attacks was conducted by Schuster and colleagues (2001) and used a large random sample of United States adults to evaluate the overall degree of stress in the general population three to five days following the events. They reported that 44% of the general population reported one or more acute symptoms of stress/anxiety, 90% reported at least some degree of stress, and people across the country (and not just those in and around New York City, Washington, D.C., and Pennsylvania) also reported elevated rates of stress.

Other studies found similar spikes in distress following the 9/11/2001 attacks, both in the general population and in groups directly exposed to the attacks. For example, Galea and colleagues (2002) assessed rates of PTSD specifically in the weeks following 9/11/2001 in a large sample of 1,008 people living south of 100th Street in Manhattan and found that 7.5% reported symptoms consistent with PTSD and 9.7% reported symptoms consistent with depression. PTSD symptoms were assessed using a semi-structured interview adapted from the Diagnostic Interview Schedule for PTSD. As would be expected, those living closer to the site of the attacks reported a higher (20%) rate of PTSD symptoms, supporting the notion that direct exposure has greater psychological impact.

Similarly, in a large national study conducted 1 to 2 months following the 9/11/2001 attacks, Schlenger and colleagues (2002) evaluated rates of PTSD symptoms in a representative sample of 2,273 United States adults. Using slightly different data-collection methods, which included administering the PTSD Checklist and Brief Symptom Inventory as psychometric tools for gauging rates of psychopathology, they reported that the prevalence of "probable PTSD" was approximately 4% in the general population, compared to 11.2% in New York City, 2.7% in Washington, D.C., and 3.6% in other metropolitan areas sampled. Further, they found that direct exposure, female sex, and the amount of time watching television coverage of the attacks were associated with elevated PTSD rates.

Silver and colleagues (2002) conducted a similar epidemiologic study 9 to 23 days following the 9/11/2001 attacks, using a large national probability sample of 2,729 adults obtained from the Internet. Using the Stanford Acute Stress Reaction Questionnaire and Impact of Life Events Scale—Revised, which was adapted to be specific to the 9/11/2001 attacks, they were able to then approximate rates of likely PTSD by coding people according to DSM-IV criteria. In contrast to the study by Schlenger and colleagues (2002), Silver and colleagues (2002) reported that 17% of people nationally reported symptoms consistent with PTSD 1 to 2 months following the attacks, but this declined to 5.8% at a 6-month follow-up.

Summary of the Immediate Psychological Impact of the 9/11/2001 Attacks

Overall, despite employing slightly different research methodologies, which likely explain at least in part the variability in findings, these studies illustrate several key patterns: (1) rates of PTSD and other disorders increased well above the established base rates in the U.S. population immediately after the 9/11/2001 attacks and (2) while direct exposure was associated with elevated rates of distress and symptomatology, there was also a significant impact manifest within the broader population. As noted above, the DSM-IV (APA, 2000) reports the lifetime prevalence rate of PTSD to be 8% in the general community. This means that roughly 8% of people across the United States will meet criteria for PTSD *at one point in their life or another* following exposure to one or more traumatic events. The above studies illustrate that many in the United States came close to or exceeded these prevalence rates following the 9/11/2001 attacks specifically—at one discrete point in time.

That being said, it is also important to point out that there is a difference between making a clinical diagnosis (upon which the APA statistics are based) versus screening large numbers of people for self-reported symptoms, and thus it would be expected that the rates may differ as a result. Further, these rates should also be considered in the context of methodological differences for assessing these constructs, where some studies involved semi-structured interviews and others used varied self-report instruments.

Longer-Term Psychological Impact of the 9/11/2001 Attacks

While the above studies illustrated the immediate psychological impact of the 9/11/2001 attacks, several very powerful longitudinal studies have emerged over the past 5 to 10 years documenting the longer-term psychological impact of terrorism in the general population. Overall, this research has shown that while rates of general stress and PTSD declined over time following 9/11/2001, significant cross-sections of the population have experienced ongoing stress and anxiety, especially those populations directly exposed to the attacks. Figure 2.1 illustrates trends in general stress and PTSD symptoms over time in several large national (U.S.) samples that were evaluated in the weeks and months following the 9/11/2001 attacks.

For example, as noted above, Schuster and colleagues (2001) conducted a national survey of Americans to assess for general symptoms of stress and anxiety

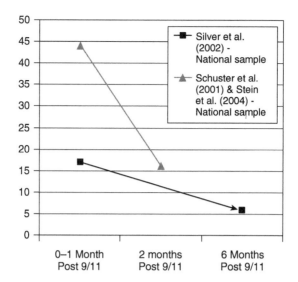

FIGURE 2.1 Percentage reporting general distress and PTSD symptoms in two large U.S. samples following the Sept. 11, 2001, terrorist attacks.

and found that roughly 44% of the sample reported at least one symptom of "substantial distress." Stein, Elliot, Jaycox, Collins, Berry, Klein, and Schuster (2004) then conducted a follow-up survey with 395 members of this original sample (71% response rate) and re-assessed rates of psychiatric distress several months following their original measurement period in September (between November 9 and 28, to be exact). As Stein and colleagues (2004) noted, although 44% of the sample reported one or more symptoms of psychological distress immediately following the attacks, roughly 16% displayed persistent distress over time. Further, among those reporting persistent distress, 65% reported occupational disturbance as a result, 24% reported ongoing avoidance of public places, and 38% reported using alcohol or medications to relax and feel better. This study seemed to suggest that there was a vulnerable subset of people within the larger group who were more predisposed to longer-term negative outcomes.

This pattern of decline over time was also a central finding by Silver and colleagues (2002), who evaluated rates of PTSD over time in the general population (i.e., at 1 to 2 months and then again at 6 months following the attacks). As noted above, they reported a decline of roughly 17% to 5.8% between these two time periods. Niles and colleagues (2003) reported similar rates of decline in a sample of Vietnam veterans, suggesting that even previous traumatic experience may not affect the longitudinal course of PTSD symptoms over time. That being said, it is important to note that the study by Stein and colleagues (2004) assessed more global symptoms of distress and reported the overall percentage of people reporting any symptoms, as opposed to the studies by Silver and colleagues (2002) and Niles and colleagues (2003)—the latter of which evaluated more focal symptom clusters (i.e., PTSD). As a result, it would be expected that the latter would be lower as a function of more criteria needing to be met for classification.

Supporting the notion that rates of psychopathology began to normalize over time and achieve baseline rates seen prior to 9/11, Richman, Cloninger, and Rospenda (2008) conducted a large, multi-wave study in which they assessed a variety of psychological and psychosocial variables between 1996 and 2005 in a large Midwestern sample. Among other factors, they measured rates of depression, anxiety, hostility, somatization, and PTSD between these two time points and found very little difference across all of the variables studied; in fact, average PTSD and anxiety scores were slightly higher in 1996 than 2005.

Similarly, DeLisi and colleagues (2003) evaluated rates of PTSD in a large sample of Manhattan residents 3 to 6 months after the 9/11/2001 attacks and found that roughly 56% of participants reported at least one severe or two mild or moderate symptoms of PTSD during this timeframe. That being said, these researchers also reported that symptom endorsement decreased as time went on, and that very few people reported increases in alcohol or drug consumption as a result of the 9/11/2001 attacks. Risk factors for PTSD included being female, living closer to the attacks, and losing occupation, residence, or family members and/or friends.

Along these lines, Liverant, Hofmann, and Litz (2004) conducted a local study in Boston following the 9/11/2001 attacks and evaluated both rates of distress and coping styles at 2 and then again at 4 months following the attacks. They reported that while initial anxiety levels were significantly elevated at the first measurement, they declined markedly over time. Further, they reported that a chronic tendency to focus on the attacks and vent emotions was associated with longer-term anxiety.

Seo and Torabi (2004) conducted a national study evaluating the degree to which people continued to report general symptoms of distress and PTSD 10 to 12 months after the 9/11/2001 attacks and found that 5% to 8% of people reported symptoms consistent with PTSD and 50% continued to *experience elevated fears of personal safety*. These rates are generally consistent with those reported by Silver and colleagues (2002) and suggest that (1) the rate of decline in symptoms of psycho-pathology happened rapidly following the attacks and (2) a vulnerable subset of those in the population will continue to experience more chronic symptoms of stress and PTSD.

Salib (2003) analyzed the rate of suicides and homicides in England and Wales in the 12 weeks before and after the 9/11/2001 attacks to see if the events had any significant impact on these trends. While suicide rates decreased in both men and women following the attacks, homicide rates were static. As Salib (2003) points out, events such as 9/11/2001 may even serve to strengthen group cohesion and reduce levels of suicide as a function of greater social integration and connection. It is somewhat unclear why these trends were not observed with homicide rates, however.

Overall, the vast majority of longitudinal research conducted following the 9/11/2001 attacks suggests a general decline in distress and rates of psychopathology over time, a trend also identified by Laugharne, Janca, and Widiger (2007) in their meta-review of the post-9/11/2001 literature. That being said, it is also important to point out here that despite this decline in distress over time, many of these samples were experiencing significant rates of distress associated with one event (9/11/2001) even 6 months following the attacks. Further, these longer-term elevations in psychiatric symptoms are comparable to lifetime prevalence rates for disorders such as PTSD in the general population. Thus, although a general pattern of decline was noted consistently across a series of research studies, the general impact in the population continued to be clinically significant.

Effects of Terrorism on Children

Numerous studies have also emerged since 9/11/2001 assessing the psychological impact of terrorism on children, and overall the results of these studies have been mixed. For example, Henry, Tolan, and Gorman-Smith (2004) evaluated rates of parent- and child-related symptoms, including depression, anxiety, and general feelings of safety, and found no significant differences in any of these factors before and after 9/11/2001. However, the degree to which parents reported monitoring their family and general beliefs about family were found to have increased following the 9/11/2001 attacks.

In a similar study, Hoven and colleagues (2005) conducted a study among New York City children in grades 4 through 12 and assessed rates of psychopathology using the Diagnostic Interview Schedule for children in the 6 months following the 9/11/2001 attacks. In contrast to the findings by Henry and colleagues (2004), Hoven and colleagues (2005) reported that approximately 29% of the 8,236 children sampled likely met criteria for at least one psychiatric disorder, with agoraphobia accounting for the greatest percentage (~15%). Approximately 11% of the children sampled also likely met criteria for PTSD. However, unlike the study by Henry and colleagues (2004), which had the advantage of being able to compare rates of distress before and after 9/11/2001, the percentages of children screening positive for these disorders in the latter study exceed established base rates and are considered to be clinically significant.

In a comparable study conducted by Phillips, Prince, and Schiebelhut (2004), which evaluated children from the Washington, D.C., area 3 months following the 9/11/2001 attacks, results showed significant emotional impact and heightened distress among children as reported both by parents and children. Similarly, Pfefferbaum, Stuber, Galea, and Fairbrother (2006) conducted a large survey study of adolescents in the New York area 6 to 9 months following the 9/11/2001 attacks and found that roughly 12.6% likely met criteria for PTSD and 26% were considered to have sub-threshold PTSD. The manifestation of panic attacks specifically was also found to be strongly associated with subsequent PTSD sequelae.

General behavior problems in children following the 9/11/2001 attacks have also been studied by a number of researchers, with some interesting and perhaps counter-intuitive trends emerging. For example, Stuber, Galea, Pfefferbaum, Vandivere, Moore, and Fairbrother (2005) assessed parent ratings of problematic behaviors in their children all residing in New York at 11 months before the attacks and at 4 and 6 months after the attacks. They found that behavior problems decreased immediately following the attacks, when compared to pre-9/11/2001 levels, but ultimately returned to pre-attack levels by 6 months post-9/11/2001. The authors suggest that this may reflect "a dampened behavioral response or a decreased sensitivity of parental assessment to behavioral problems," which makes it difficult to identify children who are at risk.

Effects of Terrorism on College Students

Some research has emerged looking at college students in the aftermath of 9/11/2001, with overall trends mirroring those seen in the general population. For example, in their study of Midwestern college students several months after 9/11/2001, Cardenas, Williams, Wilson, Fanouraki, and Singh (2003) reported that 5.9% of students displayed symptoms consistent with PTSD. Similarly, several days after 9/11/2001, Murphy, Wismar, and Freeman (2003) evaluated rates of PSTD and other forms of psychological distress in an African-American college student population not directly exposed to the attacks and reported that 5% of their sample likely had PSTD. In addition, a considerable percentage of people reported general stress symptoms and concerns about their family members and friends in the military.

Effects of Terrorism on Service Professionals

It would be expected that the psychological impact of terrorism may be more pronounced in certain populations uniquely exposed to these sorts of traumatic events, such as flight attendants and airline personnel, rescue workers, and others involved in the "helping" professions (e.g., clergy, mental health professionals, etc). This hypothesis is driven by the assumption that these specific groups of people may be more exposed to reminders of the trauma, and in ways may be more vulnerable to vicarious traumatization. In a study examining this effect, Lating, Sherman, Everly, Lowry, and Peragine (2004) assessed the psychological reactions to 9/11/2001 among 26,000 American Airlines flight attendants in June 2002 and found that approximately 18% reported symptoms indicative of PTSD. Those living alone and those who were unmarried were most at risk, while years of service and age were not related to outcome. These rates also fall well above rates seen in the general population (as described above), which would suggest that they represent a more vulnerable cross-section of the population—as would be expected given the nature of their profession relative to the attacks.

Following on this, Kramer and colleagues (2003, 2004) evaluated a large sample of disaster-relief workers from the World Trade Center site using a variety of interview and survey methods over time, and while not originally the intent of the study, they were able to assess variations in psychological functioning in a small sub-sample of workers who reported their symptoms daily. As a result, the effects of alterations in the Department of Homeland Security's Color Coded Terror Alert System were able to be evaluated longitudinally. During the study period, there were nine changes in the alert system between "Yellow: Elevated" and "Orange: High." These researchers found that between certain time periods, especially in 2003, increases in the alert levels were associated with greater reported levels of depression and anxiety, as would be expected.

Others have studied the impact of the 9/11/2001 attacks on people working in the "helping professions," including those in the clergy and mental health fields. Roberts, Flannelly, Weaver, and Figley (2003) assessed the phenomenon of "compassion fatigue" among those in the clergy (defined using the Compassion Satisfaction and Fatigue Test) and found that many of those queried experienced significant fatigue. While proximity to the attacks and length of time showed no relationship to compassion fatigue, the specific agency used to volunteer did have a significant effect. In a similar study of psychologists, Eidelson, D'Alessio, and Eidelson (2003) reported that practitioners experienced significant changes in both positive and negative emotions following the 9/11/2001 attacks, with greater movement towards positive experience, and that those most proximal to the attack sites experienced the most change.

Use of Psychotropic Medications and Mental Health Services Following the 9/11/2001 Attacks

A number of interesting studies have evaluated trends in prescription drug use following the 9/11/2001 attacks. The results of these studies have been somewhat mixed, due in part to the populations studied. For example, Druss and Marcus (2004) used two large pharmacy databases in their study, which documented rates of psychotropic prescription claims before and after 9/11/2001. They evaluated the rates of increases in overall prescriptions, new prescriptions, and daily prescription doses nationally and in Washington, D.C., and New York City specifically. Both nationally and in Washington, D.C., there were no changes in any of these trends, but in New York City, there was an increase in dosages for existing prescriptions from 13.6% in 2000 to 16.9% in 2001. This difference in trends was considered statistically significant and is consistent with the elevated rates of psychiatric conditions in those areas directly affected by terrorism. It is somewhat unclear why there were no changes in Washington, D.C., which was also affected by the attacks. This may reflect differences in terms of the magnitude of the attacks themselves—there was far greater physical destruction and lives lost in New York versus

Washington on that day. Regardless, this is something for future research to clarify.

Boascarino, Galea, Adams, Ahern, Resnick, and Vlahov (2004) evaluated use of mental health services and medications among New York residents in the 4 to 5 months following the 9/11/2001 attacks and found that rates of both dropped compared to rates 2 months following the attacks. This again points to a normalizing trend over time. That being said, 7.6% and 7.7% of the sample reported using mental health services and taking medications 4 months after the attacks, respectively, and both previous traumatic experience and a history of depression predicted use of both kinds of services. African-American and Hispanic participants, and those who were younger and without health insurance, were *less* likely to seek out either service. Among other things, this may reflect the issue of access to different kinds of psychiatric and other medical services, and the fact that some groups may be more disadvantaged in this respect.

In another large study of Manhattan residents, DeLisi and colleagues (2003) reported that only 1.4% were receiving psychotropic medications and 11.3% were involved in psychotherapy or another form of counseling following the 9/11/2001 attacks. While there are no clear pre-attack benchmarks with which to compare these findings, they would suggest an ongoing propensity for people to seek psychiatric care in the aftermath of terrorism.

A prior psychiatric history has also been noted as a risk factor for negative mental health outcomes following terrorist attacks. For example, Franklin, Young, and Zimmerman (2002) conducted a study comparing the psychological functioning of psychiatric patients already receiving services versus that of general medical patients in the aftermath of the 9/11/2001 attacks. They found that, despite no differences in exposure to the attacks, psychiatric patients reported significantly greater rates of PTSD symptoms (33%) compared to general medical patients (13%). This likely reflects an underlying and preexisting vulnerability that some groups may have for negative mental health outcomes, which are expressed differentially in the context of some traumatic stimulus.

Summary

Overall, while the psychological impact of terrorism in the general population has been seen to immediately spike and then steadily decline over time across a number of studies, the focal impact in certain cross-sections of the population was more variable. While university students were seen to exhibit rates of distress that were comparable to the general population, research on younger children was somewhat more mixed—with some research suggesting little effect and other studies indicating considerable impact. As would be expected, other populations, including those in the airline and recovery industries, were also somewhat *more* affected than the general population, and those tasked with providing mental health and other services were also found to be vulnerable to "compassion fatigue" and elevated rates of stress. Mirroring the overall decline in general symptoms of distress nationally following 9/11/2001, use of mental health services also appeared to return to pre-disaster rates as early as 4 to 6 months following the 9/11/2001 attacks overall, but this was not consistent across certain subgroups of people who may have more difficulty accessing these services.

IMPACT OF TERRORISM AND STRESS ON PHYSICAL HEALTH

There is a considerable body of literature indicating a direct mind–body relationship, where physical and mental health are seen as intertwined. Depending on the direction of this relationship, a wide array of both positive and negative outcomes can result. For example, increased stress and anxiety have been found to correlate highly with medical conditions, including hypertension and high blood pressure. High stress and anxiety have also been associated with conditions such as headaches, fatigue and low energy, rapid heart rate, and elevated perspiration. With respect to the issue of terrorism specifically, preliminary research has suggested direct links between psychological well-being and physical/medical health status.

For example, using a national probability sample of adults in the United States, Holman, Silver, Poulin, Andersen, Gil-Rivas, and McIntosh (2008) evaluated the relationship between acute stress reactions to the 9/11/2001 attacks specifically and physician-diagnosed cardiovascular problems at 1, 2, and 3 years following the attacks. Astoundingly, they reported that acute stress reactions were associated with a 53% increase in cardiovascular problems over the 3 years, even after controlling for premorbid health conditions. Further, they noted that elevated stress associated with the 9/11/2001 attacks predicted increases in rates of hypertension and other heart problems at 1- and 2-year follow-up periods, and that ongoing terrorism fears predicted heart problems at 2 and 3 years.

In a similar study, Gump, Reihman, Stewart, Lonky, and Darvill (2005) evaluated whether the stress associated with the 9/11/2001 attacks affected cardiovascular response to acute stress tasks in a small group of children. They report that compared to pre-9/11/2001 levels, there was a significant increase in stroke volume and cardiac output to acute stress tasks following the 9/11/2001 attacks. This would suggest a direct association between stress reactions to terrorist events and alterations in underlying physiology, as was hypothesized by the researchers.

In a different approach to assessing this relationship, Fagan, Galea, Ahern, Bonner, and Vlahov (2003) evaluated whether PTSD was associated with increases in somatic complaints, including asthma-related conditions, in a large sample of New York adults 6 to 9 months following the 9/11/2001 attacks. As hypothesized, they found a significant relationship between PTSD and asthma symptoms, as well as rates of people seeking care in the emergency room for these health problems.

Similarly, Adams and Bosacarino (2005) evaluated 2,368 individuals sampled randomly from the New York City area and assessed whether there was an association between exposure to the attacks and self-reported physical and mental health (as measured by the SF-12 Health Survey). While there was a clear and significant association between exposure and poorer mental well-being (as would be expected), the relationship between exposure and physical health status was weak. This pattern of findings fits with the existing literature that shows a very clear impact in terms of psychological functioning, although it is less clear in terms of its impact on general health.

Finally, Reissman and colleagues (2004) conducted an extraordinary study where they evaluated 15 of the 16 adult survivors of the 2001 anthrax attacks on the general US population, which was conducted through the American postal system. Results showed that those directly affected reported significantly more physical health symptoms, psychological distress, and poor quality of life compared to the general population. This provides further evidence supporting both the physical and mental health effects of being directly exposed to terrorism, particularly bioterrorism.

INTERNATIONAL RESEARCH ON THE IMPACT OF TERRORISM

Terrorism is an international problem, despite the increased attention it has received in the United States following the 9/11/2001 attacks. With the spate of attacks that have occurred since 9/11/2001 in Bali (2002), Madrid (2004), Beslan (2004), London (2005), and Mumbai (2008), among others, a considerable body of international research has emerged assessing the psychological impact of terrorist attacks on various populations. Although the literature surrounding these attacks continues to emerge and is somewhat limited relative to the body of research that was generated following the 9/11/2001 attacks, the overall rates of those immediately affected and declining rates of distress over time are generally consistent with what was reported in the United States following 9/11/2001. These trends would indicate some degree of reliability both in terms of the rates of people affected and longitudinal patterns over time. The following section summarizes this important body of research.

March 11, 2004, Attacks on Madrid

Miguel-Tobal and colleagues (2006) reported that in a random sample of Madrid residents queried 1 to 3 months following the March 11 train bombings, there were elevated rates of PTSD (2.3%) and depressive symptoms (8%) associated with these attacks specifically. Similarly, Miguel-Tobal, Vindel, Iruarrizaga, Ordi, and Galea (2005) noted that roughly 11% of residents reported symptoms that would meet diagnostic criteria for a panic attack, with women reporting these symptoms 2.2 times greater than men. The authors went on to note that while the rates of PTSD were somewhat lower than those reported in the United States following 9/11/2001, the rates of increased depression were similar. Further, they questioned whether the magnitude of attacks in terms of lives lost and physical destruction resulted in the differing rates of PTSD. Vazquez, Perez-Sales, and Matt (2007) found similar rates of PTSD in a large sample of 503 Madrid residents queried 18 to 25 days following the attacks, although they noted that rates varied as a function of the methods used (PTSD rates ranging from 3.4% to 13.3%).

In slight contrast, Munoz, Crespo, Perez-Santos, and Vazquez (2004) reported that in the second week following the March 11 attacks in Madrid, roughly half of their convenience sample reported symptoms consistent with depression, and of these 17% evidenced deterioration in their functioning that was considered to be clinically significant (e.g., affected their occupational, social, educational functioning, etc.). They also reported that roughly half of the sample endorsed symptoms of acute stress. Using a somewhat different approach, Conejero and Extebarria (2007) evaluated the emotional well-being of 1,807 residents of Spain (representing seven autonomous regions of the country) and found significant levels of sadness, anger, disgust, contempt, and fear both at 1 week and 2 months following the March 11 attacks. Overall, emotional reactions were seen to improve over time, and personal emotions were moderated by level of national identification with Spain (i.e., the greater the national identification, the lesser the negative affect).

In a study of patients presenting to the emergency room for injuries sustained in Madrid on March 11, Fragus and colleagues (2006) followed a sub-sample of 56 residents over time and surveyed them at 1 and 6 months after March 11. Several interesting findings emerged. First, a significant portion of the sample reported symptoms consistent with PTSD at both time points, which is consistent with other studies demonstrating larger effects in populations directly exposed to terrorism. Second, PTSD symptoms were relatively consistent across time points (41.1% at 1 month and 40.9% at 6 months). This latter finding is also consistent with other research suggesting that the psychological effects of terrorism may persist in groups of people immediately affected.

July 7, 2005, Attacks on London

Following the London attacks, the same immediate spikes in general distress followed by a partial resolution in symptoms were reported. For example, in a large sample of 1,010 residents living in London who were queried 11 to 13 days following the July 7 attacks on the subway system, approximately 31% of participants reported "substantial stress" using the same survey methodology (i.e., asking questions about more general stress, as opposed to discrete psychopathology) employed by Schuster and colleagues (2001) following the 9/11/2001 attacks (Rubin, Brewin, Greenberg, Simpson, & Wessely, 2005). Also, 32% of these participants reported they intended to travel less frequently. These researchers further noted that difficulty contacting friends and family, being a Muslim, and thinking that you could have been killed or injured were associated with elevated levels of distress. That being said, only 1% of this sample reported that they required professional help to manage their symptoms.

Rubin, Brewin, Greenberg, Hughes, Simpson, and Wessely (2007) then conducted a follow-up study where they were able to re-assess 574 of these original respondents 7 months later. As has been noted in other populations affected by terrorism, "substantial stress" levels dropped from 31% to 11%, and reductions in travel decreased from 32% to 19% at 7 months following the July 7 attacks. Of note, only degree of exposure to the attacks predicted which of the people in the sample would exhibit more persistent negative reactions.

The "Troubles" in Northern Ireland

Several large studies have emerged out of Northern Ireland over the past few decades documenting the psychological impact of political violence in that country. For example, Luce, Firth-Cozens, Midgley, and Burges (2002) queried a large sample of health services staff following the Omagh car bombing in August 1998 and found that staff who witnessed the trauma both professionally (i.e., working with those affected) and personally presented with the most elevated rates of PTSD and general distress. The authors used these data to support their argument that response personnel are not necessarily immune to the effects of trauma, and in ways may be more vulnerable. In a more positive vein, the authors noted that roughly two thirds of those affected by the event sought some form of help, and those with the most elevated symptoms were the most likely to seek professional services.

Following on this, McDermott, Duffy, and McGuinness (2004) discussed the psychological effects of the Omagh car bombing on youths and adolescents who were directly exposed to the attacks and who were referred to the authors' Community Trauma and Recovery Team within the few years following the incident. Of those referred, a significant portion reported symptoms consistent with PTSD (47%), depression (13%), and other forms of anxiety (3%). Demonstrating the significant comorbidity issue, approximately 15% of the sample met criteria for more than one psychiatric diagnosis. Hayes and Campbell (2000) reported similar elevations and rates of comorbidity in a small sample of 26 relatives whose family members were victims of the "Bloody Sunday" terrorist attack in 1972. Overall, these results again display how those directly affected by terrorism are at increased risk for negative outcomes, and further suggest that PTSD is not likely to be the only form of psychopathology present. These data have major implications for how practitioners respond to terrorist attacks, and the need for comprehensive assessment procedures to evaluate a broad array of psychological domains.

Curran (1988) published a study in the *British Journal of Psychiatry* that documented a variety of psychiatric outcomes in Northern Ireland in the years between

1969 and 1987 (a period considered to have elevated upheaval and political violence). In his review of the data, Curran reported that there was *no* significant change in hospital admissions, psychotropic medicine use, and suicide rates. Curran went on to discuss the methodological problems with this approach, however, and reported on a number of factors that may have influenced these findings, including, among other things, non-reporting and denial. Also, Curran's study involved surveying general Northern Ireland society, whereas many of the studies above involved the study of those directly affected.

Second Intifada Attacks on Israel

Bleich, Gelkopf, and Solomon (2003) were among the first to conduct a large-scale study of the psychological impact of terrorism in Israel during the Second Intifada. Specifically, they conducted a telephone survey between April and May 2002 in Israel following 19 months of semi-consistent terrorist attacks on buses and transit systems, marketplaces, and general communities. They assessed rates of traumatic stress using the Stanford Acute Stress Reaction Questionnaire, among other measures, and found that roughly 16% of the sample had been directly exposed to an attack and 37% had a friend or family member who had been directly exposed. Of those who participated in the study, roughly 9.4% met criteria for PTSD, and approximately 77% reported at least one traumatic-stress–related symptom.

Gelkopf, Solomon, Berger, and Bleich (2008) evaluated longer-term psychological outcomes in a large Israeli sample composed of a Jewish majority and Arab minority, between 19 and 44 months following the beginning of the Second Intifada in Israel, which began in roughly 2000. Although rates of PTSD and other outcomes were similar between the two groups 19 months following the beginning of the terrorist attacks, the Arab group tripled in terms of the percentage manifesting PTSD symptoms, while the Jewish group decreased slightly over time. The authors discussed these findings in the context of how groups may differ in terms of their reactions to terrorism as a function of the underlying sociopolitical landscape. With respect to this situation specifically, the Arab group may have had the double burden of being exposed to the attacks and then being placed under heightened scrutiny because of cultural and other (e.g., phenotypic) factors.

This finding was replicated in another large-scale Israeli study by Hobfoll, Canetti-Nisim, Johnson, Palmieri, Varley, and Galea (2008). These researchers assessed rates of PTSD within large Jewish ($N = 1,117$) and Arab ($N = 394$) samples of people living in Israel between August and September 2004. Results suggested higher rates of PTSD in the Arab (18%) versus the Jewish (6.6%) sample, although it is important to again point out that these rates either approach or exceed lifetime prevalence rates for PTSD in both groups, as outlined in the DSM-IV (APA, 2000), and are clinically significant. Across both samples, predictors of PTSD included greater resource loss.

Unlike the 9/11/2001 attacks, which occurred at one point in time, the situation in Israel was ongoing and the quality of violence was more chronic in nature. Further, the number of people who were directly exposed to a terrorist attack or who reported having a friend or family member directly exposed was distinct from other contexts reported thus far and may yield a different quality of impact over time. In her seminal work on this issue, Terr (1991) discussed the differences between type I and II trauma, and how chronic, ongoing traumatic experiences, as opposed to single isolated traumatic events, may manifest differently in affected people.

As discussed in greater detail in Chapter 3, Van der Kolk (1987, 1996) demonstrated how people exposed to repeated and more chronic trauma may change physiologically over time, as evidenced by lower levels of cortisol (which is associated with the body's response to stress) and reduced hippocampal volume. Because of the body's inability to maintain a high state of alert or stress over time, the response to repeated traumatic experiences also changes from one of acute/poignant stress to more chronic and persisting (but at points sub-acute) stress and exhaustion. This may explain the somewhat higher rates of PTSD and general distress after 19 months in the United States as opposed to other countries such as Israel, where there has been more of an unremitting and persisting dynamic of terrorism for a longer time.

Some have suggested that terrorism and other man-made catastrophes differ, in terms of the psychological toll they inflict on people, from either natural disasters or accidents that did not involve some form of purposeful violent act. In a study by Shalev and Freedman (2005), also conducted in Israel, terrorist attack survivors and motor vehicle accident survivors were compared with respect to psychological functioning. Results generally supported the above hypothesis and demonstrated that survivors of terrorist attacks had significantly higher rates of PTSD (38%) than motor vehicle accident survivors (19%), which is consistent with the notion that intentional disasters (as opposed to those that occur naturally or more randomly) result in more negative psychological outcomes (Schlenger et al., 2002).

Finally, Thabet and Vostanis (2002, p. 390) evaluated a sample of Palestinian children who had experienced ongoing armed conflict in the Intifada between 1987 and 1993 and reported that many (41%) had "moderate to severe post-traumatic stress reactions" and high rates of behavioral problems (27%). In a follow-up study, Thabet, Abed, and Vostanis (2002) studied a sample of 91 children exposed to home bombardment, comparing them to 89 controls, and found that the former group had higher rates of post-traumatic reactions (59%) than the latter (25%).

Effects of Terrorism in France

Large-scale epidemiological studies have also been conducted in France, where terrorism affected the country in the middle to late 1990s. For example, Verger,

Dab, Lamping, Loze, Descaseaux-Voinet, Abenhaim, and Rouillon (2004) conducted a large retrospective study evaluating a sample of 228 French citizens who had been directly exposed to a series of bombings, most of which occurred in various Metro stations and were ultimately attributed to Islamist terrorist groups. They reported that 31% of the sample experienced PTSD.

1998 Attacks on the U.S. Embassy in Nairobi, Kenya

In a similar study by Njenga, Nicholls, Nyamai, Kigamwa, and Davidson (2004), a large sample of 2,883 native Kenyans was evaluated in the aftermath of the 1998 attacks on the US embassy in Nairobi. Using a structured questionnaire that matched DSM-IV criteria for PTSD, the authors reported that roughly 35% of the sample met criteria for PTSD 1 to 3 months following the attacks. As has been noted in other research on terrorism trauma, direct exposure, female sex, marital status (and being unmarried), financial problems, and low education were all associated with elevations in PTSD.

Pfefferbaum, North, Doughty, Gurwitch, and Fullerton (2003) evaluated the psychological impact of the 1998 embassy bombings in Nairobi, focusing on children specifically. Following on the findings presented above, these researchers introduced the issue of prior traumatic experience (e.g., death, illness, crime, natural disasters, etc.) as being a major risk factor for manifesting post-traumatic reactions following the embassy bombings. This highlights how traumatic experience can at times become cumulative in quality, and in and of itself can be a risk factor for future negative outcomes.

PSYCHOLOGICAL IMPACT OF THE OKLAHOMA CITY BOMBINGS

Another factor to consider when assessing the psychological impact of terrorism is whether the quality of the perpetrator matters in terms of subsequent impact. For example, would distress levels vary as a function of the perpetrator being domestic (and thus similar in terms of culture) and acting alone (e.g., Timothy McVeigh) versus international and acting as a collective (e.g., Osama bin Laden and Al Qaeda)? That is to say, would people be more "terrorized" knowing that a global cadre of unknown people was targeting them, versus a single individual who was from the United States?

Prior to the 9/11/2001 attacks, the most serious act of terrorism that had been perpetrated on U.S. soil was the Oklahoma City bombing on April 19, 1995. North, Nixon, Shariat, Mallonee, McMillen, Spitznagel, and Smith (1999) were the first to systematically assess mental health outcomes for victims of the bombings, who were part of a confidential list that was maintained by the Oklahoma Department of Health. These researchers screened for a number of psychiatric conditions as

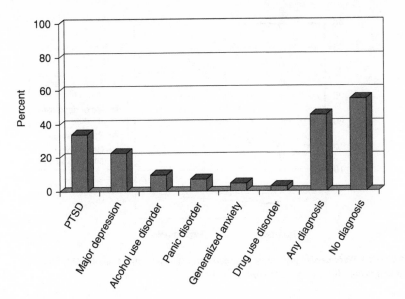

FIGURE 2.2 Percentage of post-disaster psychiatric conditions following the Oklahoma City bombing (North et al., 1999).

outlined in the DSM-III (APA, 1987) (i.e., major depression, panic disorder, generalized anxiety disorder, alcohol use disorder, drug use disorder) using the Diagnostic Interview Schedule (DIS), both before and after the bombing.

Two interesting trends emerged from this study. First, following the attacks roughly 34% of the sample screened positive for PTSD and 45% screened positive for at least one of the psychiatric disorders assessed. As has been noted by other studies across various settings, female gender, direct exposure, and premorbid psychiatric disorders predicted post-disaster rates of psychopathology. Further, there was a large prevalence of post-disaster psychiatric conditions, including major depressive disorder (23%), panic disorder (7%), generalized anxiety disorder (4%), alcohol use disorder (9.4%), and drug use disorder (2.2%). See Figure 2.2 for further detail. Second, the rates of all of these disorders increased significantly after the attack, providing further support for how terrorist attacks negatively affect people psychologically (see Fig. 2.3 for these trends).

North, Tivis, McMillen, Pfefferbaum, Cox, Spitznagel, Bunch, Schorr, and Smith (2002) conducted a follow-up study to evaluate the psychological effects of the Oklahoma City bombing on 181 people who served as rescue and recovery workers following the disaster. All participants were sampled within the 27 months following the attacks. Results showed that 13% of those sampled experienced PTSD reactions following the attacks; although this was significantly lower than the rate in the preceding study of those directly exposed to the attacks, it was still well above established baseline rates for the disorder in the general population. Perhaps most significantly, post-bombing alcohol use disorders were associated with greater functional impairment and poorer mental health outcomes.

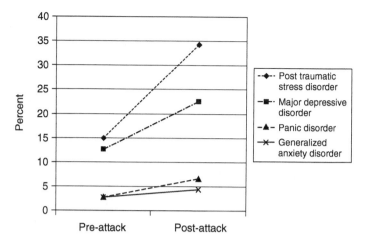

FIGURE 2.3 Percentage of psychiatric disorders before and after the Oklahoma City bombing among people directly exposed (North et al., 1999).

The results of these research studies suggested that terrorism takes a significant psychological toll on those affected and this does not appear to vary significantly as a function of the individuals or groups responsible. However, these latter studies focused only on populations most proximal to the event (i.e., those living and working in Oklahoma City), and thus more national/global estimates are unavailable for comparison. As a result, it is not possible to answer this question completely.

EFFECTS OF TERRORISM ON SUBSTANCE ABUSE TRENDS

Numerous studies have been conducted post-9/11/2001 assessing the degree to which rates of alcohol and drug abuse disorders have changed, both in the general population and in groups of people directly exposed to terrorist attacks. For example, in a large study of Manhattan residents, DeLisi and colleagues (2003) found no significant increase in reported alcohol use patterns following 9/11/2001. In contrast, Richman, Wislar, Flaherty, Fendrich, and Rospenda (2004) evaluated the effect of the 9/11/2001 attacks on alcohol use trends in a large multi-wave study of Midwestern residents and found a significant increase in use for women, although not for men. The authors also found a significant interaction between work-related stress and distress associated with the 9/11/2001 attacks, which consequently led to increases in alcohol use.

In a powerful follow-up study, Richman, Cloninger, and Rospenda (2008) conducted a multi-wave longitudinal study in which they evaluated a variety of factors, including psychological distress and substance use, at six different time periods. As hypothesized, they reported that negative beliefs about and fears of terrorism in 2003 predicted general psychological distress and negative alcohol use outcomes in 2005, after controlling for a host of sociodemographic factors, which included pre-9/11/2001 drinking patterns. Taken together, the results of this study would support the unique negative impact of terrorism on substance abuse patterns over time.

Forman-Hoffman, Riley, and Pici (2005) assessed smoking trends in 462 residents of Washington, D.C., who were involved in a research protocol comparing different methods for dosing nicotine inhalers. As such, the researchers were able to measure smoking rates following the 9/11/2001 attacks and compare them to baseline rates, which were assessed before 9/11/2001. They found that average smoking rates increased only slightly following the attacks, but that increases in smoking were significantly related to PTSD symptoms. In a parallel study, Adams, Boscarino, and Galea (2006) evaluated alcohol use trends in a large New York City sample at 1 and 2 years following the attacks. They found that while binge-drinking was associated with partial PTSD, alcohol dependence was associated with severity of PTSD and depression, and poor mental health status.

Vlahov, Galea, Ahern, Resnick, and Kilpatrick (2004) evaluated rates of substance use in two large samples of Manhattan residents at 1 and 6 months following the 9/11/2001 attacks. Results showed that 30.8% of the former and 27.3% of the latter reported increased use of alcohol, cigarettes, and marijuana. However, when compared over time, while rates of alcohol and cigarette use declined between 1 and 6 months, rates of marijuana use increased somewhat. Perhaps most striking, there were no differences in rates of substance use between groups of people directly exposed to the attacks versus those who were not, which may provide further support for the generalized psychological impact in Manhattan overall.

North and colleagues (1999) found the opposite pattern of decreases in alcohol and drug abuse disorders (determined via structured interview methods) in a large sample of people directly exposed to the Oklahoma City bombing. Rates were compared before and after the attack; post-disaster interviews were conducted on average 6 months following the incident. They reported that the percentage of people meeting criteria for alcohol use disorders declined from 28.7% before the attack to 9.4% after the attack. Similarly, trends in drug use disorders in this sample decreased from 9.4% to 2.2%. See Figure 2.4 for more detail on these trends.

ROLE OF THE MEDIA IN EXACERBATING TRAUMATIC IMPACT

Many have suggested that the unique quality of trauma and distress associated with the 9/11/2001 attacks is due, at least in part, to the role played by media in perpetually re-exposing people to the events of that day (Marshall et al., 2007). More recently, studies have begun to emerge supporting this belief. For example, Ahern, Galea, Resnick, Kilapatrick, Bucuvalas, Gold, and Vlahov (2002) conducted a large survey of New York residents in the 1 to 2 months following the 9/11/2001 attacks and found that people who repeatedly viewed images of people falling from the

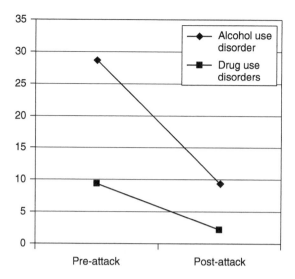

FIGURE 2.4 Percentage of alcohol and drug use disorders before and after the Oklahoma City bombing among people directly exposed (North et al., 1999).

World Trade Towers were significantly more likely to experience symptoms of PTSD (17.4%) and depression (14.7%) than those who had not (6.2% and 5.3% respectively).

Similarly, Ahern, Galea, Resnick, and Vlahov (2004) conducted a study 4 months after the 9/11/2001 attacks and evaluated the relationship between television viewing and endorsement of PTSD symptoms among 2,001 people from New York. As hypothesized, they found a significant association between the amount of television viewed in the 7 days following 9/11/2001 and reported PTSD symptoms, supporting the proposition that the media played a significant role in the subsequent manifestation of psychopathology in the weeks and months following the attacks. They reported that those in the top third of television viewing had roughly 2.3 greater odds of meeting criteria for PTSD than those in the lower third.

Jarolman and Sisco (2005) evaluated rates of PTSD symptoms in two groups of participants from New Jersey: (1) people who were directly and individually exposed to the 9/11/2001 attacks and (2) people who watched the events unfold on television. In further support of the vicarious traumatic effect of witnessing terrorism through the media, there were no statistically significant differences in PTSD symptoms between these two groups. There were also no gender effects noted, although the older participants tended to report more elevations in symptoms than the younger participants.

Marshall and colleagues (2007) more recently discussed how national rates of PTSD and other psychological disorders that manifested as a consequence of the 9/11/2001 attacks do not fit neatly within existing mental health frameworks. They discussed how most models of impact employ a "bull's eye" framework where those more proximal to the event are more affected psychologically. In contrast, numerous studies (many of which are discussed above) have illustrated repeatedly the immediate and significant impact across the United States following the 9/11/2001 attacks. Marshall and colleagues (2007) discussed the issue of media exposure as being central to this phenomenon, where people in essence lived and relived the attacks through television and other media exposure, creating a vicarious exposure contagion effect. Further, as they pointed out, the rates of PTSD that were reported nationally following this one event either met or *exceeded lifetime prevalence* rates reported in the DSM-IV (APA, 2000). This highlights the significant impact of the 9/11/2001 terrorist attacks specifically, and the role that the media played in vicariously traumatizing the general population, thereby creating a sense of direct exposure.

CONCLUSION AND SUMMARY

The purpose of this chapter was to summarize the research literature assessing the psychological impact of the 9/11/2001 attacks and compare it to both the international research evaluating these trends in other countries affected by terrorism, as well as other terrorist attacks that have been perpetrated domestically. The majority of this research has focused on assessing specific clinical, psycho-diagnostic constructs such as PTSD and ASD. However, studies have also reported on more general symptoms of stress and anxiety, as well as mood difficulties (e.g., depression), substance use, and use of health services (e.g., psychotropic medications, psychotherapy, etc.). Finally, these studies have evaluated many different samples, including the general population, those directly exposed to terrorist attacks, children and adolescents, psychiatric patients, those with existing trauma histories, and those who vary in terms of their professional proximity to the attacks (e.g., those in the airline industry, recovery workers, those in the helping professions, etc.).

Overall, the research has indicated an immediate spike in general distress and specific PTSD/ASD symptoms across populations, which is then followed by a gradual resolution in distress and symptomatology over time. Some have suggested that the psychological impact fully resolves by 6 to 12 months following the attacks, although other studies contradict this finding. For example, when thinking about baseline rates for disorders such as PTSD and ASD, as outlined by the DSM-IV (APA, 2000), one needs to remember that these reflect *lifetime* prevalence rates—or percentages of people who experience these conditions at *any point* over the course of their lives. In contrast, many of the above-mentioned studies suggest that considerable numbers of people continue to experience clinically significant distress at 6 or more months, and this is in relation to *one discrete event*. So, while 5% to 8% of the population endorses most if not all symptoms of PTSD at 6 to 12 months after 9/11/2001, which falls slightly below the 8% lifetime prevalence rate for PTSD (APA, 2000), it reflects the reactions to *one* discrete event.

Specific populations are also at greater risk for negative outcomes, including those most proximal to the event physically (e.g., those living in the area affected by an attack, those tasked with recovery following an attack, etc.) and those in specific professional discipline (e.g., those in the airline industry, mental health, or clergy). Research has also suggested that large-scale acts of terrorism are associated with general increases in alcohol and drug use, and that people will significantly increase their use of various mental health resources. Finally, these trends generally appear to be consistent when considering the impact of domestic terrorist attacks (e.g., the Oklahoma City bombing) as well as in the international community. That being said, most of the international studies that have been conducted have focused more on the specific populations affected (e.g., those in London or Madrid) as opposed to the general population in that country, so a complete comparison is not possible.

REFERENCES

Adams, R. E., & Boscarino, J. A. (2005). Stress and well-being in the aftermath of the World Trade Center attack: The continuing effects of a community disaster. *Journal of Community Psychology, 33,* 175–190.

Adams, R., Boscarino, J., & Galea, S. (2006). Social and psychological resources and health outcomes after the World Trade Center disaster. *Social Science & Medicine, 62,* 176–188.

Ahern, J., Galea, S., Resnick, H., & Vlahov, D. (2004). Television images and probable post-traumatic stress disorder after September 11. *Journal of Nervous and Mental Disease, 192,* 217–226.

Ahern, J., Galea, S., Resnick, H., Kilpatrick, D., Bucuvalas, M., Gold, J., & Vlahov, D. (2002). Television images and psychological symptoms after the September 11 terrorist attacks. *Psychiatry-Interpersonal and Biological Processes, 65,* 289–300.

American Psychiatric Association. (1987). *Diagnostic and statistical manual of mental disorders- Third edition.* Washington, D.C.: American Psychiatric Association.

American Psychiatric Association. (2000). *Diagnostic and statistical manual of mental disorders-TR: Fourth edition.* Washington, D.C.: American Psychiatric Association.

Bleich, A., Gelkopf, M., & Solomon, Z. (2003). Exposure to terrorism, stress-related mental health symptoms, and coping behaviors among a nationally representative sample in Israel. *Journal of the American Medical Association, 290,* 667–670.

Boscarino, J. A., Galea, S., Adams, R., Ahern, J., Resnick, H., & Vlahov, D. (2004). Mental health service and psychiatric medication use following the terrorist attacks in New York City. *Psychiatric Services, 55,* 274–283.

Cardenas, J., Williams, K., Wilson, J. P., Fanouraki G., & Singh, A. (2003). PTSD, major depressive symptoms, and substance abuse following September 11, 2001 in a Midwestern university population. *International Journal of Emergency Mental Health, 5,* 15–28.

Conejero, S., & Etxebarria, I. (2007). The impact of the Madrid bombings on personal emotions, emotional atmosphere and emotional climate. *Journal of Social Issues, 63,* 273–287.

Curran, P. S. (1988). Psychiatric aspects of terrorist violence: Northern Ireland 1969–1987. *British Journal of Psychiatry, 153,* 470–475.

DeLisi, L. E., Maurizio, A., Yost, M., Papparozzi, C. F., Fulchino, C., Katz, C. L., et al. (2003). A survey of New Yorkers after the September 11, 2001 terrorist attacks. *American Journal of Psychiatry, 160,* 780–782.

Druss, B. G., & Marcus, S.C. (2004). Use of psychotropic medications before and after September 11, 2001. *American Journal of Psychiatry, 161,* 1377–1383.

Eidelson, R. J., D'Alessio, G. R., & Eidelson, J. I. (2003). The impact of September 11 on psychologists. *Professional Psychology: Research and Practice, 2,* 144–150.

Fagan, J., Galea, S., Ahern, J., Bonner, S., & Vlahov, D. (2003). Relationship of self-reported asthma severity and urgent health care utilization to psychological sequelae of the September 11, 2001 terrorist attacks on the world trade center among New York City area residents. *Psychosomatic Medicine, 65,* 993–996.

Forman-Hoffman, V., Riley, W., & Pici, M. (2005). Acute impact of the September 11 tragedy on smoking and early relapse rates among smokers attempting to quit. *Psychology of Addictive Behaviors, 3,* 277–283.

Fragus, D., Teran, S., Conejo-Galindo, J., Medina, O., Ferrando, E. S., Gabriel, R., & Arango, C. (2006). Posttraumatic stress disorder in victims of the March 11 attacks in Madrid admitted to a hospital emergency room: 6-month follow-up. *European Psychiatry, 21,* 143–151.

Franklin, C. L., Young, D., & Zimmerman. M. (2002). Psychiatric patients' vulnerability in the wake of September 11th terrorist attacks. *Journal of Nervous and Mental Disease, 190,* 833–838.

Friedman, M. J., Hamblen, J. L., Foa, E. B., & Charney, D. (2004). Fighting the psychological war on terrorism. *Psychiatry, 67,* 123–136.

Galea, S., Resnick, H., Ahern, J., Gold, J., Bucuvalas, M., Kilpatrick, D., et al. (2002). Posttraumatic stress disorder in Manhattan, New York City, after the September 11th terrorist attacks. *Journal of Urban Health, 79,* 340–353.

Gelkopf, M., Solomon, Z., Berger, R., & Bleich, A. (2008). The mental health impact of terrorism on the Arab minority in Israel. A repeat cross-sectional study of Arabs and Jews. *Acta Psychiatrica Scandinavica, 117,* 269–380.

Gump, B. B., Reihman, J., Stewart, P., & Darvill, T. (2005). Terrorism and cardiovascular responses to acute stress in children. *Health Psychology, 6,* 594–600.

Hayes, P., & Campbell, J. (2000). Dealing with post traumatic stress disorder: The psychological sequelae of Bloody Sunday and the response of state services. *Research on Social Work Practice, 10,* 705–721.

Henry, D. B., Tolan, P. H., & Gorman-Smith, D. (2004). Have there been lasting effects associated with the September 11, 2001 terrorist attacks among inner-city parents and children? *Professional Psychology: Research and Practice, 5,* 542–547.

Hobfoll, S. E., Canetti-Nisim, D., Johnson, R. J., Palmieri, P. A., Varley, J. D., & Galea, S. (2008). The association of exposure, risk, and resiliency factors with PTSD among Jews and Arabs exposed to repeated acts of terrorism in Israel. *Journal of Traumatic Stress, 21,* 9–21.

Holman, E. A., Silver, R. C., Poulin, M., Andersen, J., Gil-Rivas, V., & McIntosh, D. N. (2008). Terrorism, acute stress, and cardiovascular health. *Archives of General Psychiatry, 65,* 73–80.

Hoven, C. W., Duarte, C. S., Lucas, C. P., Wu, P., Mandell, D. J., Goodwin, R. D., Cohen, M., et al. (2005). Psychopathology among New York City public school children 6 months after September 11. *Archives of General Psychiatry, 62,* 545–552.

Jarolman, J., & Sisco, H. (2005). Media effects on post-traumatic stress disorder and the World Trade Center tragedy. *Best Practices in Mental Health, 1,* 133–139.

Jhangiani, R. (2010). Psychological concomitants of the September 11, 2001 terrorist attacks: A review. *Behavioral Sciences of Terrorism and Political Aggression, 2,* 38–69.

Kramer, M. E., Brown, A., Spielman, L., Giosan, C., & Rothrock, M. (2004). *Psychological reactions to the national terror alert system.* Paper presented at the American Psychological Association's 2004 annual conference.

Kramer, M. E., Brown, A. D., Spielman, L., Giosan, C., & Rothrock, M. (2003). Psychological reactions to the national terror alert system. *The ID, 1*, 67–70.

Lating, J. M., Sherman, M. F., Everly, G. S., Lowry, J. L., & Peragine, T. F. (2004). PTSD reactions and functioning of American Airlines flight attendants in the wake of September 11. *Journal of Nervous and Mental Disease, 192*, 435–441.

Laugharne, J., Janca, A., & Widiger, T. (2007). Posttraumatic stress disorder and terrorism: 5 years after 9/11/2001. *Current Opinion in Psychiatry, 20*, 36–41.

Lee, A., Isaac, M., & Janca, A. (2002). Post-traumatic stress disorder and terrorism. *Current Opinions in Psychiatry, 15*, 633–637.

Lentini, P. (2008). Review essay—Understanding and combating terrorism: Definitions, origins, and strategies. *Australian Journal of Political Science, 43*, 133.

Liverant, G. I., Hofmann, S. G., & Litz, B. T. (2004). Coping and anxiety in college students after the September 11th terrorist attacks. *Anxiety, Stress, and Coping, 17*, 127–139.

Luce, A., Firth-Cozens, J., Midgley, S., & Burges, C. (2002). After the Omagh bomb: Posttraumatic stress disorder in health service staff. *Journal of Traumatic Stress, 15*, 27–30.

Marshall, R. D., Bryant, R. A., Amsel, L., Suh, E. J., Cook, J. M., & Neria, Y. (2007). The psychology of ongoing threat: Relative risk appraisal, the September 11 attacks, and terrorism-related fears. *American Psychologist, 62*, 304–316.

McDermott, M., Duffy, M., & McGuinness, D. (2004). Addressing the psychological needs of children and young people in the aftermath of the Omagh bomb. *Child Care in Practice, 10*, 141–154.

Miguel-Tobal, J. J., Cano-Vindel, A., Gonzalez-Ordi, H., Iruarrizaga, I., Rudenstine, S., Vlahov, D., & Galea, S. (2006). PTSD and depression after the Madrid March 11 train bombings. *Journal of Traumatic Stress, 19*, 69–80.

Miguel-Tobal, J. J., Cano-Vindel, A., Iruarrizaga, I., Gonzalez, H., & Galea, S. (2005). Psychopathological repercussions of the March 11 terrorist attacks in Madrid. *Psychology in Spain, 9*, 75–80.

Muñoz, M., Crespo, M., Pérez-Santos, E., & Vázquez, J.J. (2004). Presencia de síntomas de estrés agudo en la población general de Madrid en la segunda semana tras el atentado terrorista del 11 de Marzo de 2004. *Ansiedad y Estrés, 10*, 147–161.

Murphy, R. T., Wismar, K., & Freeman, K. (2003). Stress symptoms among African-American college students after the September 11, 2001 terrorist attacks. *Journal of Nervous and Mental Disease, 191*, 108–114.

Niles, B. L., Wolf, E. J., & Kutter, C. J. (2003). Post traumatic stress disorder symptomatology in Vietnam veterans before and after September 11. *Journal of Nervous and Mental Disease, 191*, 682–684.

Njenga, F. G., Nicholls, P. J., Nyamai, C., Kigamwa, P., & Davidson, J. R. (2004). Post-traumatic stress after terrorist attack: psychological reactions following the US embassy bombing in Nairobi: Naturalistic study. *British Journal of Psychiatry, 185*, 328–333.

North, C. S., Nixon, S. J., Shariat, S., Mallonee, S., McMillen, J. C., Spitznagel, E. L., & Smith, E. M. (1999). Psychiatric disorders among survivors of the Oklahoma City bombing. *Journal of the American Medical Association, 282*, 755–762.

North, C. S., Tivis, L., McMillen, J. C., Pfefferbaum, B., Cox, J., Spitznagel, E. L., Bunch, K., Schorr, J., & Smith, E. M. (2002). Coping, functioning, and adjustment of rescue workers after the Oklahoma city bombing. *Journal of Traumatic Stress, 15*, 171–175.

Pfefferbaum, B., North, C. S., Doughty, D. E., Gurwitch, R. H., Fullerton, C. S., & Kyula, J. (2003). Posttraumatic stress and functional impairment in Kenyan children following the 1998 American Embassy bombing. *American Journal of Orthopsychiatry, 73*, 133–140.

Pfefferbaum B., Stuber, J., Fairbrother, G., & Galea, S. (2006). Panic in reaction to the September 11 attacks in adolescents. *Journal of Traumatic Stress, 19*, 217–228.

Phillips, D., Prince, S., & Schiebelhut, L. (2004). Elementary school children's responses 3 months after the September 11 terrorist attacks: A study in Washington, D.C. *American Journal of Orthopsychiatry, 74*, 509–528.

Ranstorp, M. (2009). Mapping terrorism studies after 9/11/2001. In R. Jackson, M. Bryn Smyth, and J. Gunning (Eds.), *Critical terrorism studies,*(pp. 13–33). London: Routledge Publishers.

Reissman, D. B., Whitney, E. A. S., Taylor, T. H., Hayslett, J. A., Dull, P. M., Arias, I., et al. (2004). One year health assessment of adult survivors of *Bacillus anthracis* infection. *Journal of the American Medical Association, 291*, 1994–1998.

Richman, J. A., Wislar, J. S., Flaherty, J. A., Fendrich, M., & Rospenda, K. M. (2004). Effects on alcohol use and anxiety of the September 11, 2001 attacks and chronic work stressors: A longitudinal cohort study. *American Journal of Public Health, 94*, 2010–2015.

Richman, J. A., Cloninger, L., & Rospenda, K. M. (2008). Macrolevel stressors, terrorism, and mental health outcomes: Broadening the stress paradigm. *American Journal of Public Health, 98*, 323–329.

Roberts, S. B., Flannelly, K. J., Weaver, A. J., & Figley, C. R. (2003). Compassion fatigue among chaplains, clergy, and other respondents after September 11th. *Journal of Nervous and Mental Disease, 191*, 756–758.

Rubin, G. J., Brewin, C. R., Greenberg, N., Hughes, J., Simpson, J., & Wessley, S. (2007). Enduring consequences of terrorism: 7-month follow-up survey of reactions to the bombings in London July 7, 2005. *British Journal of Psychiatry, 190*, 350–356.

Rubin, G. J., Brewin, C. R., Greenberg, N., Simpson, J., & Wessley, S. (2005).Psychological and behavioral reactions to the bombings in London on July 7, 2005: cross sectional survey of a representative sample of Londoners. *British Journal of Psychiatry*. Retrieved December 1, 2010 from *http://www.bmj.com/content/331/7517/606.abstract.*

Salib, E. (2003). Effect of September 11, 2001 on suicide and homicide in England and Wales. *British Journal of Psychiatry, 183*, 207–212.

Schlenger, W. E., Caddell, J. M., Ebert, L., Jordan, B. K., Rourke, K. M., Wilson, D., Thalji, L., Deniis, J. M., Fairbank, J. A., & Kulka, R. A. (2002). Psychological reactions to terrorist attacks: findings from the national study of Americans' reactions to September 11. *Journal of the American Medical Association, 288*, 581–588.

Schuster, M. A., Stein, B. D., Jaycox, L. H., Collins, R. L., Marshall, G. N., Elliott, M. N., et al. (2001). A national survey of stress reactions after the September 11, 2001 terrorist attacks. *New England Journal of Medicine, 345*, 1507–1512.

Seo, D. D., & Torabi, M. R. (2004). National study of emotional and perceptual changes since September 11. *American Journal of Health Education, 36*, 37–45.

Shalev, A. Y., & Freedman, S. (2005). PTSD following terrorist attacks: A prospective evaluation. *American Journal of Psychiatry, 162*, 1188–1191.

Silver, R. C., Holman, E. A., McIntosh, D. N., Poulin, M., & Gil-Rivas, V. (2002). Nationwide longitudinal study of psychological responses to September 11. *Journal of the American Medical Association, 288*, 1235–1244.

Stein, B. D., Elliot, M. N., Jaycox, L. H., Collins, R. L., Berry, S. H., Klein, D. J., & Schuster, M. A. (2004). A national longitudinal study of the psychological consequences of the September 11, 2001 terrorist attacks: Reactions, impairment, and help-seeking. *Psychiatry, 67*, 105–117.

Stuber, J., Galea, S., Pfefferbaum, B., Vandivere, S., Moore, K., & Fairbrother, G. (2005). Behavior problems in New York City's children after the September 11, 2001 terrorist attacks. *American Journal of Orthopsychiatry, 75*, 190–200.

Terr, L. C. (1991). Childhood traumas: An outline and overview. *American Journal of Psychiatry, 148*, 10–19.

Thabet, A. A., Abed, Y., & Vostanis, P. (2002). Emotional problems in Palestinian children living in a war zone: A cross-sectional study. *Lancet, 359*, 1801–1804.

Van Der Kolk, B. (1996). The body keeps score. Approaches to the psychobiology of post traumatic stress disorder. In B. Van Der Kolk, A. McFarlane, & L. Weisaeth (Eds.), *Traumatic stress: The effects of overwhelming experience on mind, body, and society.* New York: Guilford Press.

Van der Kolk, B. (1987). The separation cry and the trauma response: Developmental issues in the psychobiology of attachment and separation. In B. Van Der Kolk (Ed.), *Psychological trauma* (pp. 31–62). Washington, D.C.: American Psychiatric Press.

Vazquez, C., Perez-Sales, P., & Matt, G. (2007). Posttraumatic stress reactions following the March 11, 2004 terrorist attacks in a Madrid community sample: A cautionary note about the measurement of psychological trauma. In B. Trappler (Ed.), *Modern terrorism and psychological trauma* (pp. 61–87). New York: Gordian Knot Books/Richard Altschuler & Associates.

Verger, P., Dab, W., Lamping, D. L., Loze, J. Y., Descaseaux-Voinet, C., Abenhaim, L., & Rouillon, F. (2004). The psychological impact of terrorism: An epidemiologic study of posttraumatic stress disorder and associated factors in victims of the 1995–1996 bombings in France. *American Journal of Psychiatry, 161*, 1384–1389.

Vlahov, D., Galea, S., Ahern, J., Resnick, H., & Kilpatrick, D. (2004). Sustained increased consumption of cigarettes, alcohol, and marijuana among Manhattan residents after September 11, 2001. *American Journal of Public Health, 94*, 253–254.

3 Theoretical Paradigms for Understanding the Psychology of Fear

"Just as courage imperils life, fear protects it."
Leonardo da Vinci

On a very basic level, fear is adaptive. It is what keeps us alive in a fundamental, evolutionary sense and allows us to adapt and survive as a species. It is what stops us from stepping out into traffic on a busy highway, or walking in the direction of an 800-lb. moose and her calf in Maine while on a hiking trip with your best friend on a cold and rainy summer day. This actually happened to one of the authors (SJS) in 1995. As fear set in, SJS recalls that his sympathetic nervous system went from 0 to 100 m.p.h., and he sprinted off the Katahdin trail into the woods with his friends in tow, wondering whether the moose was still in chase. Fear is what gives you pause when confronted with a precipice over which several hundred feet separate you and the ocean below. It is the basic fear instinct that allows us to survive in the face of threats to our existence. These instincts have been hardwired into our brains and biological systems over time and generations to help us adapt to new environments and evolving threats.

In the aftermath of September 11, 2001, fear was widespread—as will be discussed in greater detail in Chapter 4. There was an almost constant reporting of threat information by the government in the days that followed, and people worried about when and where the next attack would occur. Members of our government were being flown to "secret locations" in bunkers outside of Washington, D.C., to ensure continuity of government were something catastrophic to occur.

Both authors of this volume experienced this fear firsthand, as SJS was working in downtown Boston and DA was living within a mile of the Twin Towers in New York City when the attacks occurred. Living only a couple of miles outside Boston, SJS recalls riding his bike home from work, starting in the financial district in downtown Boston and heading west, and riding through Copley Square—only to be stopped in his tracks by several thousand people who had amassed outside a hotel where one of the terrorists' handlers was believed to be holed up. Then came the anthrax attacks in the fall of 2001, and random searches on the subway to identify potential biological and chemical agents. Commuting to work by public transportation became more complicated, as people were subjected to random searches of their belongings, slowing down the process and flow of people. Even today the Massachusetts Bay Transportation Authority (MBTA) continues its public announcements over the PA speaker system, warning subway riders to "report anything suspicious" to MBTA personnel.

In New York City, a decade after 9/11/2001, random checkpoints where the police search people's personal belongings continue. There is an occasional sighting of heavily armored police officers with automatic weapons and bomb-sniffing dogs walking through subway cars and train stations. All of this is, of course, because New York City continues to be a primary target of terrorism—as evidenced at least in part by the Homeland Security Advisory threat level being elevated consistently since the 9/11/2001 attacks.

In January 2005, the national media reported that there was evidence to suggest that multiple Chinese and Iraqi nationals had crossed the border from Mexico into California and were on their way to Boston to detonate a nuclear device. The *Boston Globe* reported that the Federal Bureau of Investigation (FBI) had begun a massive manhunt for these individuals, and then-Governor Mitt Romney abruptly left commitments in Washington, D.C., to fly home to Boston to reassure the public. In 2006, multiple transatlantic British Airways flights were cancelled due to the threat of terrorism. These warnings have saturated our media; some have suggested they have caused the general public to become desensitized, while others believe they have perpetuated a general culture of fear (McDermott & Zimbardo, 2007).

At the time of writing this book, 10 years have passed since the 9/11/2001, and warnings from our government continue to be disseminated. For example, the headline news on Dec. 29, 2009, was almost exclusively focused on a Nigerian man who attempted to detonate a bomb while on a flight from Europe to Detroit, Michigan. Although vast bodies of research have suggested a general decline in rates of specific psychological disorders in the months that follow major terrorist incidents (summarized in Chapter 2), there is evidence to suggest that many people continue to experience a significant amount of fear as a result of terrorism. Both preliminary research and national polling data that support this claim are presented in Chapter 4. However, before moving into this research it is first important to present different frameworks for understanding fear as a dynamic process. The purpose of this chapter is to introduce and discuss a variety of important theoretical paradigms for understanding the nature and quality of terrorism fears.

THEORETICAL FRAMEWORKS FOR UNDERSTANDING TERRORISM FEARS
Selye's (1956) Theory of Stress

In his book *The Stress of Life*, Canadian-born Hans Selye (1956) was one of the first to develop a multi-stage model of stress. Basing his theories primarily on his own animal studies, Selye (1956) discussed how organisms evolve through a series of adaptation stages when exposed to external stressors. During the first stage (alarm), someone is first presented with a threatening stimulus and the body prepares itself for either meeting this threat or escaping it quickly. The sympathetic nervous system accelerates the release of epinephrine and norepinephrine from the adrenal glands, and blood flow is redirected from the digestive system to other parts of the body, including the brain and muscle groups, to meet and respond to this new threat. Blood pressure rises and various adrenal hormones are released into the bloodstream to prepare the body for battle and/or flight. Some have discussed this phase as the point at which a person prepares for "fight or flight"—that is, for meeting the threat directly or eluding it in a rapid way.

The difficulty with the alarm stage is that the body is not able to sustain this fight-or-flight response over a long period of time. During the second phase (resistance), the person acclimates somewhat to the threat and enters into a longer-term management approach. As such, the person continues to resist and/or manage the threat, although the body begins the process of again achieving equilibrium. People may continue to be very stressed during this period, and as a result their other defenses may begin to break down and they become more vulnerable to both physical (e.g., getting sick) and psychological (e.g., having less patience, increased irritability, mood lability, etc.) consequences.

During the final phase (exhaustion), chronic stress drains the person's coping faculties and makes him or her highly vulnerable to exhaustion and illness. The body is depleted of both physical and psychological energy and begins to shut down. During this stage, the person may also begin to experience chronic conditions such as hypertension and stress-induced headaches due to being physically and emotionally activated for such a long period.

Although Selye (1956) developed this model quite some time ago, there are clear and linear applications of this to various issues of terrorism and threat dissemination. More recently McDermott and Zimbardo (2007) discussed in parallel terms how the American color-coded terror alert system has appeared to move people through these stages in a highly maladaptive way. At least over the past 6 or 7 years since the inception of the warning system (which will be discussed in more detail in

Chapters 5 and 7), threats have been communicated in both vague and often paradoxical ways. People's initial reaction to these first warnings was alarm. For those more proximal to areas already affected by terrorism (e.g., New York, Washington, D.C.) or other areas associated with increased risk (e.g., major metropolitan areas, nuclear power plants), the impact was felt more intensely, and for some it exacerbated an already acute post-traumatic stress disorder (PTSD) process. Many people moved into the alarm stage and experienced the same kinds of fight-or-flight responses discussed above—where their bodies were thrown into overdrive in an attempt to survive survival.

McDermott and Zimbardo (2007) discussed how these threat warnings generated a slew of negative reactions in the general population, including fear, anger, disgust, depression, and so forth. Confusion also set in due to the inconsistencies of the general message: to be both vigilant and aware of these various "credible threats" on the one hand, and on the other hand to live life normally and go about our business as usual. This process happened over and over again as the threat levels were raised in response to these specific threats, and then lowered as these threats subsided. No one knew why these threats had passed, nor when the next would manifest. It was like an emotional yo-yo ride, up and down and then up again.

Some research suggests that communications that induce high levels of fear do little to change people's underlying belief systems when there is no *specific* information available on how to avoid some negative outcome. That being said, fear induction may be useful to communicate a message and change a belief system when there is a specific and clear-cut set of directions on how to neutralize a given threat. For example, Brehm, Kassin, and Fein (2005) found that campaigns to have people quit smoking were more effective when gruesome scenes of lung cancer procedures were presented as opposed to basic statistics and graphs. One of the major criticisms of the new terror alert system (levied by people such as McDermott and Zimbardo, 2007) is that these threat messages have been vague and contain no specific direction as to how people should respond.

Over time, these more immediate fear/panic reactions morph into more chronic responses (i.e., ongoing low mood, fear, sadness, anger) as a function of time passing and additional color-coded alerts being issued, with no change in outcome. This manifested in the United States as the debate over the terror alert system heated up significantly, with many people arguing that the system did more harm than good. Essentially, there developed a conflict between the perpetual state of threat that was being communicated to the public, and the public's ability to negotiate this threat from a practical, psychological, and physiological point of view. The resulting discord between the two was poignant and increased debate about the meaning and effectiveness of the alert system. We will discuss this further in Chapters 5 and 7.

Ultimately, it could be argued that people just got to a point where they were both exhausted by and completely numb to the threat warnings that were being issued. Some have likened this to the classic Aesop's fable *The Boy who Cried Wolf*, where people become conditioned to associate threat communications with no response or attack. McDermott and Zimbardo (2007) have also argued that cognitive dissonance plays a significant role here, where people are instructed both to live their lives normally and to be on the lookout for impending danger—two recommendations that appear to be highly discordant.

As Festinger (1957) has taught us, people strive for a sense of underlying cognitive consistency, where beliefs about a given issue are congruent overall. When a given set of beliefs becomes highly discordant with one another, such as in the case above—when people are warned about an extreme threat but are advised to live as if nothing is wrong or aberrant—a state of cognitive tension ensues. This is a primary example of cognitive dissonance. Most people are motivated to reduce this tension by modifying their attitudes and beliefs such that the underlying beliefs are consistent.

With respect to the issue of terrorism, one could argue that people have altered their beliefs over time in a way as to find these threat warnings less believable or likely. That is to say, there are likely some people who have begun to associate these vague threat warnings, which were void of any directions or instructions as to how to respond, with no attacks. This pattern follows a classic operant extinction model: when there are no resulting reinforcements of the original behavior or experience (i.e., fearing an attack will occur), the original set of beliefs and experiences extinguish over time. These two diametrically opposed forces cancel one another out, and the result is that the actual meaning of the threat communications changes. That is, the inherent message means something altogether different to people when they hear it.

Psychobiology and the Trauma Response

As noted throughout this volume, fear (as with any emotion) is a complex, evolutionarily rooted response to real or perceived environmental stimuli. Many researchers have focused on the underlying emotional and/or cognitive systems that are at play, while others (including some of those mentioned above) have tended to concentrate their efforts on the social and political consequences. While all of these domains are very important, it is also critical to understand that fear is biologically ingrained within us as a means of helping us adapt to our environment. Fear is hardwired within us to help us steer clear of danger and survive. However, as noted above, fear can sometimes morph over time in negative ways. This can also be understood in terms of our underlying biology, and the impact that repeated trauma can have on the fear response.

Known as a pioneer for his work in this area, van der Kolk (1987, 1996) conducted an extensive literature review on this area of research and found that people who have endured repeated traumatic events throughout their lives manifest lower levels of the neurotransmitter serotonin and excrete significantly lower levels of cortisol in their urine. He also found that those repeatedly traumatized had, on average, smaller hippocampal volume (a region of the brain known to be associated with the storage of memory). While initially people experience a surge in their sympathetic nervous system as they prepare to mount a fight-or-flight response, van der Kolk's work demonstrates that people's bodies cannot sustain this over time, and physiological changes begin to occur.

Van der Kolk (1987) also speaks to this issue on another level in terms of the neurobiological changes that can occur due to chronic trauma. These changes produce either overactivity or underactivity in various neurotransmitter systems in the brain, which in turn leads to a propensity for chronic disorders such as depression and anxiety. As a result, the ways in which people negotiate future traumatic experiences may be altered as a result of this shifting physiology. In Chapter 6, we will briefly discuss some neurobiological research related to coping with and resilience to stress and trauma.

With respect to the government's color-coded terror alert system, McDermott and Zimbardo (2007) argued that the system itself did more to generate fear and panic than the actual threat itself. From a psychobiological point of view, these repeated warnings about imminent threats likely affected people's underlying responses over time. Initial fear responses likely were rooted in people preparing themselves physiologically to meet some threat. Likewise, this lack of response and increased frustration represents, at least in part, the inability of people to maintain a fight-or-flight posture, and resulting physical fatigue.

Terror Management Theory

Terror management theory (TMT) (Pyszczynski et al., 2003) is another theoretical framework that has received considerable attention since the 9/11/2001 attacks, in part because of its unique name. TMT was originally developed by a group of friends while in graduate school. The story goes that while bowling, Pyszczynski and colleagues began to discuss existential issues such as mortality and meaning-making, and how people at large are motivated by primary drives to transcend death by forming lasting impressions of themselves in relationships and society. Hence, the "terror" as originally used in TMT was not specific to "terrorism" as it is used throughout this book, but rather had to do with people's basic terror (fear) about their own mortality. Since 9/11/2001, TMT has been used more and more as a means of providing a framework for understanding both how people experience and protect against their fears of dying in a terrorist attack, as well as how people come to transcend these fears in order to die while committing a terrorist attack (Pyszczynski et al., 2003).

Rooted in existential and social psychology, TMT focuses on the issue of people's awareness of their own mortality, and assumes that all people experience *varying* levels of terror as a function of multiple factors, including being aware of their impending death. Based on an exhaustive number of experimental studies conducted by the developers of TMT, there appear to be two very broad factors that account for this variability: (1) a sense of location within and connectedness to a broader community and culture and (2) a core belief that one is a meaningful part of and contributor to this larger reality. Put more eloquently, Pyszczynski and colleagues (2003, p. 16) note:

And the core implication of TMT is that to maintain psychological equanimity through-out their lives, people must sustain: 1) faith in a culturally derived worldview that imbues reality with order, stability, meaning, and permanence; and 2) belief that one is a significant contributor to this meaningful reality.

As people become more detached from this larger culture and/or believe they are less meaningfully connected to this reality, existential terror sets in—as a function of realizing that once death occurs, they are permanently gone. In contrast, as the above goals are achieved, TMT would posit that people move into a position where they transcend death, as pieces of them will live on even after their own departure from the physical world. According to Pyszczynski and colleagues (2003), it is this connection to something greater than one's self that allays the terror associated with mortality—by ensuring that their contribution to this reality, either material or otherwise, continues even in the face of death.

For example, Pyszczynski and colleagues (2003) would likely argue that writing this book is one means by which the two of us seek to contribute to some larger collective, bigger than ourselves, as a means of experiencing a sense of connection and contribution. In doing so, a part of us theoretically lives on after our deaths—and this is a way for us to have a piece of us survive even after we die. Another example often cited by people is the act of having children, and continuing our genetic line into the future. As we perform these kinds of acts within our lives, the tendency to fear death is minimized.

Following the 9/11/2001 attacks, Pyszczynski and colleagues (2003) published a book applying the tenets of TMT to issues of terrorism in general and the 9/11/2001 attacks specifically. In this book, they discuss how polls began to illustrate that people's fears over extinction spiked and that many viewed terrorism as a likely and immediate mechanism for dying. They cited one November 2001 Gallup poll showing that roughly half of those queried believed that they or someone they loved would die in a terrorist attack, and three quarters believed a terrorist attack was imminent. A similar 2003 poll in Washington, D.C., noted that half of residents feared they would die in a terrorist attack (Morin, 2003). Prior to the 2004 presidential elections, an Associated Press poll found that roughly two thirds of those sampled believed the country would be attacked before the elections and one third believed the political conventions in Boston and New York City would be a target.

Finally, a 2005 CNN/Gallup poll taken after the July 7, 2005, attacks in London reported that over half of the American public believed another attack in the United States was likely over the following weeks.

Pyszczynski and colleagues (2003) argued that from a TMT perspective these fears primed the imminence and immediacy of one's mortality, something that usually most people are not aware of as they go about their daily business. This was due in part to the difficulty escaping reminders of this fact. That is to say, one would only need to turn on the television news or pick up a newspaper in the months and years following the 9/11/2001 attacks to be reminded of this immediate threat to survival and the imminence of death. In contrast to the many research studies cited by Pyszczynski and colleagues (2003), where mortality was primed through methods including watching fatal car wrecks (e.g., Nelson et al. 1997) or more subtle reminders such as questions being included in some brief personality questionnaires (e.g., Ochsmann & Mathy, 1994), the constant and almost deafening drumbeat of threat information that followed 9/11/2001 was like someone screaming at you that you are only temporary and finite.

The impact of 9/11/2001, and the associated threat communications that followed, was that people became much more aware of their own sense of mortality. Pyszczynski and colleagues (2003) cited over 150 research articles that have supported these core TMT tenets and have generally shown that by inducing mortality salience, or the conscious awareness of the inevitability of death, people are more prone to protect and uphold cultural worldviews in the face of challenge (Rosenblatt, Greenberg, Solomon, Pyszczynski, & Lyon, 1989; Greenberg et al., 1995; Greenberg, Solomon, & Pyszczynski, 1997). The model assumes that when people are made aware of the potential for death, there is a greater need to adhere to and protect a sense of culture and belonging. Of note, Pyszczynski and colleagues (2003) argued that this is one primary reason there was such a widespread display of US flags and other illustrations of unity and patriotism following 9/11/2001. As Pyszczynski and colleagues (2003, p. 89) noted, "A variety of studies have shown that mortality salience generally increases identification with and pride in one's country, university, and gender."

Along these lines, one of us (SJS) recalls having conversations with friends and colleagues in Boston who were amazed at both the show of unity and random acts of kindness that were being displayed by people. Some remarked that driving in Boston had changed dramatically, from an environment where it was often a contentious and competitive race against fellow drivers to get where you were going to one where people were much more accommodating and allowed others to cut in lines. In essence, the "feeling" of Boston changed.

Similarly, DA vividly remembers the unity exhibited in New York City, and on the deserted streets south of 14th Street in Manhattan, in the aftermath of 9/11/2001. Although the police and army had closed down the area south of 14th Street for regular traffic and nonresidents, the restaurants and bars were still open, and they became gathering spots for everyone living in the area and a place to talk about the event. Everyone would talk to everyone, as everyone had one very significant and salient thing in common: the 9/11/2001 event. Not one person was *unaffected* by the event. The discussions would be broken up only when a vehicle, such as an ambulance, police car, fire truck, or army vehicle, would drive by, at which time everyone would stop talking and instead start applauding loudly to recognize the remarkable work being done by the numerous rescue workers at Ground Zero.

Although not TMT theorists *per se*, McCann and Pearlman (1992) also argued that much of the variability in the extent to which traumatic experience negatively affects individuals is accounted for by social connection (McNally, Bryant, & Ehlers, 2003) and self-esteem. Beck (1979) also stated that harmonious interpersonal relationships provide significant buffers against the development of cognitive distortions and subsequent mental disorders. In his work on trauma, van der Kolk (1987, p. 31) further argued this point, noting, "Emotional attachment to others is essential for survival in children as well as for a sense of existential meaning in adults."

In support of this, McNally and colleagues (2003) conducted a meta-analysis on this relationship and found multiple studies showing the negative relationship between social support and the development of PTSD. They went on to argue that promoting social support is a necessary component in promoting healthy recovery after a traumatic event. Ozer, Best, Lipsey, and Weiss (2003) also conducted a meta-analysis of these factors and reported 68 studies that identified social support as being a significant negative predictor of PTSD in the wake of a traumatic event.

Awareness of the inevitability of death has also been associated with derogating groups of people not considered part of the dominant culture, out of a desire to protect this critical source of meaning (McGregor et al., 1998). Pyszczynski and colleagues (2003, p. 77) argued that "mortality salience engenders negative attitudes, physical distancing, and physical aggression toward people who are different by virtue of subscribing to dissimilar cultural worldviews." The TMT model assumes that, in the aftermath of the 9/11/2001 attacks, much of the aggression towards those from different cultures occurred because these people appeared in stark contrast to members of the dominant culture, the latter of which was seen as critical in providing the ultimate source of security in a time of fear. At points, these victims of violence were seen as *more* similar to the perpetrators of 9/11/2001, causing greater polarization.

In support of this, Pyszczynski and colleagues (2003) cited a December 2001 *New York Times*/CBS News Poll showing that 80% of Americans supported the indefinite detention of people who were not U.S. citizens when there was a potential threat to national security. Likewise, 70% approved of the government monitoring conversations between suspected terrorists and their lawyers, and 64% *approved of the president being authorized to change the Constitution*. This illustrates how fears generated after 9/11/2001 drove people to go to greater lengths to protect culture, even at the expense of basic civil liberties.

Pyszczynski and colleagues (2003, p. 126) argued that "PTSD is the result of a general breakdown in the terror management system that leaves the person unable to cope with the fears to which the traumatic event has given rise." When people come face to face with something that challenges their core beliefs about their own personal safety and security, as well as that of the general community and society in which they live, pathological fear sets in and mortality salience is primed. This is what occurred following 9/11/2001—that is, fear permeated the population and resulted in both positive and negative consequences, which we will discuss further in the following chapters.

In a similar vein, Bonanno (2004) argued for years that three variables, which he called traits of "hardiness," serve to buffer people against severe traumatic response: a desire to attain purpose in life, a belief that one can manipulate one's environment, and a belief that one can change and evolve in healthy and adaptive ways after experiencing traumatic events. Hardy people, he argued, can better adapt to traumatic life events because they are more confident, connected to others for support, and able to cope with distress. As a result, traumatic events are experienced as less threatening.

Many TMT tenets follow more classic social psychological theories, including Lewin's (1939) field theory. Field theory posits that people will move towards goals with a positive valence within the social/cultural field that surrounds them, and will move away from goals or entities that have a negative valence and/or that threaten their goals. In the context of threatened violence and/or extermination, these positive valences include moving towards one's social group and amassing protection in numbers. Similarly, one could begin to understand how derogating out-groups or those seen as similar to the attackers is a manifestation of moving away from negative valences.

Others, including Victor Frankl (1992), have written about existential psychology, and the ultimate need for people to locate meaning within life as a means of transcending anxiety about death. Frankl argued that this meaning can be found even in dire circumstances, and it allows a person to make sense out of situations that are seemingly unbearable—and even traumatic. In his book *Man's Search for Meaning*, Frankl discussed personal examples of this while a prisoner in the Nazi concentration camps during the 1940s, and ways in which his relationships with other prisoners made the experience meaningful despite the atrocities going on around them.

A Cognitive-Behavioral Model of Psychopathology

Another theoretical model that is useful in terms of understanding the underlying mechanisms of terrorism fears is cognitive-behavioral theory (CBT; Beck, 1976, 1979). In essence, this theory focuses on how people construct their experience and derive meaning in the world (Beck, 1976, 1979, 1995). Similar to Piaget (1954),

Beck (1976, 1979) argued that all people are active participants in navigating experience. As this navigation process unfolds, people begin to develop ways of appraising their experience by developing cognitive schemas. These schemas are cognitive structures that form the basis for screening and interpreting incoming data. The navigation process involves a synthesis of both internal and external stimuli and manifests as a person's "stream of consciousness" (Beck, 1979, p. 8).

CBT is essentially a model for understanding how people develop specific kinds of thought patterns, or schema, that then result in different kinds of emotional experiences and behavioral trends. For example, people who are highly anxious in social situations may have underlying cognitive patterns that focus disproportionately on what it would mean to be embarrassed, say something silly, stand out in a crowd, and so on. They may even attach high likelihoods of this happening to various social experiences, which may then predispose them to very high levels of anxiety and stress when in particular social situations. As a function of these cognitive trends and resulting emotional experiences, people may then be more prone to making changes in their behaviors, including avoiding social situations or places where they believe these things are likely to be present.

When the way in which constructing this experience is significantly altered due to events that are inconsistent with existing cognitive structures, distortions in cognitive processing sometimes occur that affect emotional and behavioral experience. From a psychological perspective, the CBT model focuses on helping a patient become aware of and challenge and correct these cognitive distortions (Beck, 1979). According to Beck (1979, p. 3), the model is "based on an underlying rationale that an individual's affect and behavior are largely determined by the way in which he structures the world." Although emotions and behaviors are critical model components, maladaptive cognitive processes are conceptualized as being primary. According to Judith Beck (1995), the cognitive model centers on the distorted or dysfunctional thinking patterns that affect mood and behavior, and that underlie most psychological disorders. When the cognitive distortions are evaluated and modified in therapeutic settings, the characteristic mood and behaviors are also often changed.

Cognitive theory assumes that different psychological disorders are characterized by unique patterns of cognitive distortion. This idea has been termed the "cognitive content-specificity hypothesis" (Beck, 1976; Schniering & Rapee, 2004). The basic premise is that people who suffer from different emotional disorders are characterized by specific thought content. In the case of depression, themes of loss and failure are often primary. Young, Weinberger, and Beck (2001) argued that these maladaptive cognitive processes are reflected in a "cognitive triad": depressed individuals usually have a negative view of themselves, their environment, and the future. People who suffer from depression may distort information they receive from the environment, which serves to maintain the negative views they have about themselves, the world, and the future (Beck, 1979). Young and colleagues (2001) went on to say that these distortions represent deviations in the normal thinking processes typically used by people.

In anxiety-related disorders, cognitive processes often revolve around themes of threat and potential danger (Beck, 1976; Schniering & Rapee, 2004). Clark (1986) argued that the cognitive processes characterizing anxiety focus on future harm, threat, and uncertainty. As core schemas about safety and security are damaged by specific events (e.g., terrorism), the cognitive filter screening incoming information may potentially distort the interpretation process. Information is construed in all-or-nothing and catastrophic terms, where people are often overwhelmed by a sense of helplessness and inability to stop focusing on the threat (rumination). According to Cottraux (2004, p. 51), "Pathological worry is viewed to be shaped by cognitive distortions, which result from maladaptive schemas of danger." Ruminating on these perceived threats and dangers inhibits the ability to function in a normal way, leading to feelings of losing control.

As all people develop, cognitive processing evolves through a process of assimilation (incorporating new experience into existing schemas) and accommodation (modifying existing schemas to allow for the integration of new experience) as a result of new experience. In the case of terrorism violence, the impact of the traumatic event depends on the extent to which people's core assumptions, or schemas, about themselves and the world are disrupted and the extent to which people have come to distort new information as a result. These belief systems include schemas about whether the world is a safe place, as well as whether one is perceived as being in a constant state of threat or danger. Traumatic experience, such as the terrorism violence experienced by many on 9/11/2001 in New York City, March 11, 2004, in Madrid, and July 7, 2005, in London, significantly altered core schemas people have regarding their safety and security, and potential threat to them. According to the cognitive model, the effects for some people have included a significant reorganization of the cognitive structures that organize incoming information (Beck, 1979). This has subsequently led to increased distortion of new, incoming data.

The effects of traumatic experiences associated with terrorism may either be in perpetuating negative schemas people already have (e.g., I am not safe, I lack trust in the world) or disrupting positive schemas that people have (e.g., I am safe, I am in control). According to McCann and Pearlman (1992), developers of the constructivist self-development theory of trauma, "This process is psychologically painful and has a profound effect on the individual's identity, as well as his or her emotional and interpersonal life" (p. 190). These new cognitive distortions reinforce the cycle of painful emotional experience and modification of behavior, which in turn serve to perpetuate the underlying cognitive distortions.

Najavits, Gotthardt, Weiss, and Epstein (2004) argue that the construction of lists of cognitive distortions can be helpful in isolating themes to be addressed in treatment. Lists of cognitive distortion have been developed for depression (Burns, 1980; Beck, Steer, & Brown, 1996), PTSD (Briere, 1997, 2001), and anxiety disorders

(Beck, Epstein, & Brown, 1988), among others. Although there has been widespread application of these lists in clinical settings, Najavits and colleagues (2004) point out that very little has been done in the way of empirically testing these models (cognitive distortions), as very few measures of cognitive distortions have been developed.

In their literature search of "cognitive distortions" across social sciences journals, only 195 entries appeared, and few involved psychometric testing of scales designed to assess distortions. In a literature search conducted for this study, similar results were found. To address this issue, Najavits and colleagues (2004) developed and psychometrically tested the Cognitive Distortions Scale to measure distortions associated with comorbid PTSD and substance use disorder. Distortions were derived by "listening closely to patients' language and experience while treating them as part of outcome trials to test Seeking Safety" (Najavits et al., 2004, p. 160). According to the authors, assessing these distortions allows the therapist to target specific thought processes in treatment.

A Cognitive-Behavioral Model of the Psychological Impact of Terrorism

CBT provides a useful framework for thinking about how people are affected by the ongoing threat of terrorism, and ways in which thought, emotion, and behavior patterns change over time in the face of this threat. Figure 3.1 illustrates a basic, four-pronged CBT model of this pattern and presents a basic example of how people may vary over time in terms of their beliefs and behaviors as a function of fearing the terrorism threat.

As noted in different ways throughout this chapter, fear is conceptualized here as involving a complex interaction between the individual and environment, where different markers in the latter may prime or enhance vulnerabilities in the former

Cognitive
Catastrophic thought process; perseverating thoughts of disaster and catastrophe like 9/11 developing into schema around tragedy and cataclysm

Behavioral
High avoidance behaviors, lashing out against those perceived as responsible, altering daily life activities

Emotional
Profound anxiety, fear of dying, pretraumatic stress, concerns for loved ones, hyperarousal, numbness.

Physiological
Increase heart and respiration rate, perspiring, adrenaline release, headaches, shaking, dizziness

FIGURE 3.1. A CBT model of the psychological impact of terrorism: I.

to manifest a feeling of terror. As is the case with many types of violence, experiencing a terrorist attack (i.e., immediately witnessing an attack and/or through repeated exposure via electronic and other media) fundamentally alters beliefs about security and safety. In the wake of 9/11/2001, people were on very high alert that more terrorist attacks were imminent, and were constantly scanning their environment for cues to confirm this may be occurring. People saw their government officials being flown to secret bunkers, and Cold War protocols focused on continuity of government being resurrected. While not evidence for an attack *per se*, this type of posturing by the government and media provided people with immediate data that there was a significant risk, thus fundamentally altering how people understood the general safety of themselves and their family.

Although the attacks themselves were discrete events, the months and years that followed saw a steady stream of threat reporting. High-profile and well-respected academics (e.g., Allison, 2004) began to suggest there was a 50% probability that a nuclear device would be detonated on U.S. soil in the next decade, and others in the government stated that the United States has already had situations arise where they believed this threat was imminent (Tenet, 2007). Both Allison (2004) and Tenet (2007) independently discussed a scenario shortly after the 9/11/2001 attacks where there was reason to believe someone had smuggled a nuclear weapon into New York City, which subsequently led to a massive search of the city for the weapon. Although the intelligence turned out to be false, the inherent message was one of immediate threat. Others have also written about the impending threat of weapons of mass destruction being used on the general population (Williams, 2004, 2005).

As has been documented repeatedly in a variety of large-scale research studies, the impact of this threat was most severe in the areas directly affected (Galea et al., 2002). People's general schemas and thought patterns related to the dangers they and their loved ones faced accommodated over time from a position of security ("My family and I are generally safe from any immediate threats to our safety") to one of imminent threat ("My family and I are at high risk"). Part of the reason this occurred was because of the quality of the threat. That is, most threatening situations are temporary and situational (e.g., being mugged, running from a moose in the woods, your house catching fire), and there is typically a definitive end to the experience. Further, most of these sorts of experiences are clear in terms of cues suggesting either the immediacy or end to the threat. In contrast, the threat of terrorism post-9/11/2001 was neither. That is, it has been ongoing with no clear/definitive end, and no data with which to evaluate this threat prospectively. The result was a complete lack of control for an indefinite period of time.

As a consequence of these new and/or reorganized cognitive schemas, emotional consequences manifest, including profound anxiety and/or sadness, increased emotional arousal, fear, and potentially emotional numbing. As has been evidenced in the literature, many people will develop full-blown anxiety and mood disorders, including PTSD, generalized anxiety disorder, panic disorder, acute stress disorder, and major depressive disorder, while others will simply experience an intense and heightened sense of fear and dread about the future. In a post-9/11/2001 environment, government warnings and dire claims by those in academia have perpetuated these fears and have made it difficult for people to attend to anything else.

As these intense schemas and emotional experiences appear, it is hypothesized that many will began to modify their behaviors in significant ways (one primary rung in the CBT model). Behavioral modifications include avoiding public places, mass transit systems, and areas rich with high-profile targets (e.g., New York City, Washington, D.C.). Modifications may also include changes in social and occupational activities: fearful and/or depressed people are more likely to become reclusive as a consequence of fear and/or lack of motivation. Behavioral responses also include lashing out in anger against those perceived as being similar to those who perpetrated the terrorist acts, including against those of Middle Eastern, Arabic, and/or Islamic backgrounds. This was seen with some frequency around the country in the wake of the 9/11/2001 attacks, and is also explained well within the context of TMT in terms of how people cling to their in-groups and at points derogate members of the out-group. As new data from various sources are entered into the cognitive-behavioral model (e.g., new terrorist attacks, new government warnings, new claims by academics), the cycle accelerates and perpetuates itself (Fig. 3.2).

For example, a man in New York City, so profoundly affected by the 9/11/2001 attacks, may begin to selectively monitor all news broadcasts relating to his safety and security in such a way as to confirm evidence of how unsafe he is, paying no attention to news to the contrary (such as the 2004 FBI report of a reduction in violent crime). When the Madrid and London terrorist attacks occurred, these events would significantly reinforce his beliefs about his lack of safety (cognitive prong), which would perpetuate his extremely fearful emotional response (emotional prong), need to modify his behavior (such as avoiding public places or transportation—behavioral prong), and distorted way of organizing his experience (back to the cognitive prong). As these events unfold, he tends to always think the worst is going to happen. Cognitive distortions, such as catastrophizing and overgeneralization (Beck, 1979, p. 261), are the ways in which this process manifests as psychopathology.

Cognitive Distortions

According to Beck (1976, 1979), systematic errors in the ways in which people construct experience lead to and maintain various forms of psychopathology, including anxiety and depression. These distortions are maintained even in the face of contradictory data. Cognitive distortions essentially shape the lens through which the world is viewed and experience is interpreted in people who manifest psychopathology. Beck (1995) categorized these distortions for purposes of helping

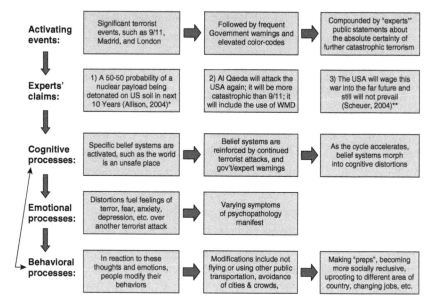

Activating events:	Significant terrorist events, such as 9/11, Madrid, and London	Followed by frequent Government warnings and elevated color-codes	Compounded by "experts'" public statements about the absolute certainty of further catastrophic terrorism
Experts' claims:	1) A 50-50 probability of a nuclear payload being detonated on US soil in next 10 Years (Allison, 2004)*	2) Al Qaeda will attack the USA again; it will be more catastrophic than 9/11; it will include the use of WMD	3) The USA will wage this war into the far future and still will not prevail (Scheuer, 2004)**
Cognitive processes:	Specific belief systems are activated, such as the world is an unsafe place	Belief systems are reinforced by continued terrorist attacks, and gov't/expert warnings	As the cycle accelerates, belief systems morph into cognitive distortions
Emotional processes:	Distortions fuel feelings of terror, fear, anxiety, depression, etc. over another terrorist attack	Varying symptoms of psychopathology manifest	
Behavioral processes:	In reaction to these thoughts and emotions, people modify their behaviors	Modifications include not flying or using other public transportation, avoidance of cities & crowds,	Making "preps", becoming more socially reclusive, uprooting to different area of country, changing jobs, etc.

FIGURE 3.2 A CBT model of the psychological impact of terrorism: II.

people identify, understand, and begin to work with their own faulty thinking patterns. The goal of treatment would be to challenge these distortions by seeking evidence to the contrary, a process of empirical testing and experimenting. Based on the literature, among those distortions that are hypothesized to be primary with most anxiety disorders (Brown, Antony, & Barlow, 1992) and anticipatory fear, or Zimbardo's (2003a, 2003b) notion of a "*pre*-traumatic stress syndrome," are catastrophizing, helplessness, and rumination.

Catastrophic worrying (**catastrophizing**) is the notion that the worst possible outcome will occur despite a complex array of information that is either inconsistent or not compatible with this belief (Beck, 1979, 1995; Young, Weinberger, & Beck, 2001). For example, someone who fears public speaking may have catastrophic thoughts around how he or she will be perceived and treated in the context of a public presentation. With respect to the issue of terrorism, catastrophizing has to do with the ingrained and patterned belief that the threat of terrorism will be enormous and debilitating over time and will likely never abate. These people would assign very high probabilities to future terrorist attacks and overall destruction and would also believe it is highly likely that they or someone they love will be a victim of terrorism.

Much of what has been studied about **helplessness** has typically centered around mood disorders such as depression. For example, Abramson, Seligman, and Teasdale (1974) developed the learned hopelessness model of depression, following on the work of Beck (1976), and discussed two basic processes at work in those who manifest depression: (1) a negative-outcome expectancy and (2) a helplessness expectancy (Abramson, Metalsky, & Alloy, 1989). The first of these processes essentially mirrors that of catastrophizing, or the sense that despite whatever attempts are made to propagate positive outcomes in one's life, the future will be bleak and replete with bad experiences. However, they argued that the second construct is also central to disorders like depression, where one's sense of agency and ability to affect different circumstances in life in positive ways diminishes and disappears altogether.

In terms of the ongoing threat of terrorism, because there is no end in sight and no ability to enhance protection or security, many people have come to feel a general lack of agency in terms of being able to affect these circumstances. As a result, they feel more vulnerable and defenseless in light of this threat, with no control or ability to take steps to reduce this overall sense of impotence. In essence, they become completely impotent and powerless.

Whereas catastrophizing has to do with magnifying a threat and helplessness relates to the impact of worrying about one's circumstances, **rumination** has to do with the degree to which someone engages in these negative patterns (Nolen-Hoeksema, Morrow, & Fredrickson, 1993). In other words, while catastrophizing may be the music itself and helplessness the way it makes you feel, rumination is the volume on the stereo that allows you to dial it up or down as a central component of your ongoing thought process. Rumination is the degree to which people think about and mull over things in their lives, and becomes maladaptive when the magnitude is inconsistent with the actual experience. For example, if a person thinks about that terrible presentation at school or work over and over again and becomes consumed in thinking it may occur again, the process may become increasingly debilitating in terms of negotiating similar experiences in the future.

In her pioneering work in this area, Nolen-Hoeksema (1987, 1991) suggested that how people manifest disorders like depression, both in terms of severity/intensity and frequency, is directly associated with how they respond to their general mood states. For example, those who ruminate on or perseverate about their level of sadness and anhedonia (lack of feeling pleasure) display a pattern of exacerbating their mood states further and amplifying their underlying depression or negative affect. This is in contrast to those who, despite feeling lousy and sad, have the ability to redirect themselves to other things going on in their lives—much of which may be inconsistent with negative mood and may also be uplifting.

Nolen-Hoeksema and colleagues (1993) argued that people who engage in rumination "hyper-focus" on their negative mood states and the detrimental effects of their symptoms. This differs from people who spend time and effort focusing on their symptoms and functioning, but do so from the standpoint of solving their problems and trying to improve their mood. Those who ruminate spend a lot of time focusing on their negative affect but do very little to change this dynamic. Nolen-Hoeksema and colleagues (1993) argued that rumination contributes to negative affect in three basic ways: (1) by negatively influencing and coloring how people think about and affectively mark their experiences; (2) by negatively affecting people's ability to think cogently and focus attention, which may also have deleterious effects; and (3) by inhibiting people's ability to negotiate more complex problems as they arise in life, which may compound their difficulties over time.

An Empirical Model of Catastrophizing

According to the literature, chronic pathological worrying is a primary feature underlying many anxiety disorders (Brown, Antony, & Barlow, 1992; Startup & Davey, 2001), especially generalized anxiety disorder (GAD), and depression (Garnefski, Teerds, Kraaij, Legerstee, & Kommer, 2004). According to Startup and Davey (2001), pathological worrying presents in a number of ways, including the priority that threat perceptions are given in cognitive processing (i.e., rumination), where the processing of threatening information is primary. It can also manifest as a tendency to interpret most stimuli in a threatening way, and a tendency to persistently think about the worst possible outcomes related to the topic of worry. This process involves a perpetual proclivity to ask "what if" instead of allowing the appraisal process to come to a close (Startup & Davey, 2001). With terrorism, this iterative process may involve a series of "what if" questions having to do with whether one's family or self will die in the next terrorist attack, or whether there is a good chance a nuclear, biological, or chemical weapon would be used.

Despite the large body of research in this area, Najavits and colleagues (2004) argued that little has been done to develop and empirically test instruments assessing cognitive distortions such as catastrophizing. This is relevant here as a means of providing some background for the rationale behind developing the Terrorism Catastrophizing Scale (TCS), which is presented in Chapter 4 (Sinclair & LoCicero, 2007, 2010; Sinclair, 2010). A review of the literature revealed that there have been some efforts to develop measures of catastrophizing, although most of these measures relate to specific constructs, such as pain, stress, insomnia, and anxiety associated with music performance, precluding use in other settings (Rosenstiel & Keefe, 1983; Sullivan, Bishop, & Pivik, 1995; Harvey & Greenall, 2003; Zinn, 2004). Also, the underlying theoretical models for catastrophizing, specifically which processes are being measured, have not always been consistent. This has much to do with the ongoing debate about how terms such as "catastrophizing" are defined, and lack of consensus as to how to measure these constructs adequately.

In their work on emotion regulation, Garnefski, Kraaij, and Spinhoven (2001) developed the Cognitive Emotion Regulation Questionnaire (CERQ), which measures nine coping strategies that people engage in following adverse life events. In developing their measure, Garnefski reported that they used a rational approach to the development of items and scales and drew upon many other existing instruments, including the Coping Orientations to Problems Experienced (COPE) (Carver, Scheier, & Weintraub, 1989), the Coping Inventory for Stressful Situations (CISS; Endler & Parker, 1990), and the Ways of Coping Questionnaire (Folkman & Lazarus, 1988). Two of the scales included in the CERQ are catastrophizing and rumination, although these constructs were not identified in existing measures and were based on the model constructed by Sullivan and colleagues (1995) and the rumination model by Nolen-Hoeksema, Morrow, and Fredrickson (1993).

Perhaps the most recent and widely used measure of catastrophizing was developed by Sullivan, Bishop, and Pivik (1995). It measures the degree to which people exhibit catastrophic worries about their level of pain. Sullivan and colleagues (1995, p. 524) noted that while there not been any consensus on how to define the term, it entails an "exaggerated negative orientation toward a noxious stimuli." Others have suggested that the term "catastrophizing" relates to magnifying and worrying about specific life events (Chavez & Brown, 1978, 1987), as well as manifesting an inordinate amount of focus and attention on negative life events (Spanos, Radtke-Bodorik, & Ferguson, 1978). Following on this, Rosenstiel and Keefe (1983) put forth the argument that catastrophic worrying is fueled by an underlying propensity to experience helplessness and a general inability to cope in the face of existing stressors.

Sullivan and colleagues (1995) were the first to develop a measurement model of catastrophizing that took into account the inherent complexity and multidimensional quality of the underlying latent trait. In doing so, they evaluated whether these constructs were distinct or components of the same overarching process using a variety of factor analytic and other psychometric approaches. Results indicated the latter, where rumination, helplessness, and magnification were all seen as interrelated constructs reflecting some higher dimension of catastrophizing.

Ultimately, the model of catastrophizing developed by Sullivan and colleagues (1995) involved the derivation of three interrelated and correlated sub-components: rumination, magnification, and helplessness. A principal components analysis (PCA) revealed that rumination accounted for 41% of the total item variance, magnification for 10%, and helplessness for 8%. Osman and colleagues (1997, 2000) replicated these PCA findings, although the variance explained by each factor was somewhat larger, and also tested model fit for several different factor solutions using confirmatory factor analysis (CFA). They found that the data best fit the three-factor solution for catastrophizing presented by Sullivan and colleagues (1995). Based on an extensive literature review, this is the only known empirically derived model of catastrophizing rooted in cognitive theory that has been tested with favorable results.

From a CBT perspective, these results are important in the sense that they provide new dimensions into how people think about and catastrophize the terrorism threat. This model also illustrates how people become caught in a cycle where negative thought patterns contribute to elevated fear and increased avoidance patterns, and vice versa, and also how there is a blurry line between catastrophic worrying that is pathological in quality versus worry that is reality-based and adaptive. Despite the research that suggests both immediate spikes in rates of psychological disorders and subsequent decline over the subsequent 6 to 12 months, there are also data (presented in detail in Chapter 4) to suggest that fear lingers in the general population and has lasting effects in terms of how people live their lives. While not classified as clinically significant in a psychopathological sense, fear for some people does affect their life in meaningful ways. Further attention is given to this issue in Chapter 4.

Relative Risk Appraisal

Perhaps one of the most relevant lines of research to be applied to the issue of terrorism and fear specifically in the aftermath of 9/11/2001 is what Marshall and colleagues (2007, p. 307) term "relative risk appraisal." This line of research appropriately follows that of cognitive theory in terms of how one's thought process patterns over time as a function of the interaction between one's experience and interpretations/beliefs about those experiences. Essentially, the work that has been done in this area illustrates the complex interplay between the person, environment, and past experience—all of which influence perceptions of risk or threat about any given situation or event. Marshall and colleagues (2007) provided a nice summary of this research over the past few decades, and specifically how one's perception of risk "is a global judgment, not a rational calculation." These judgments are based on implicit affective and cognitive processes, and not explicit reasoning or problem-solving, where past experiences provide a metric from which to evaluate subsequent situations.

Everyone manifests these underlying patterns of thinking and feeling, where past experiences shape the interpretations of new ones. Within the CBT framework, these underlying cognitions and interpretations are automatic and affect our negotiation of new experiences. Where these cognitive patterns become inconsistent with the surrounding environment, there may be evidence for cognitive distortions (as discussed previously). Often these distortions revolve around likelihood or probability estimation. For example, within the context of war and engaging in combat, a sense of hyper-vigilance and high estimation of threat is adaptive—it enhances one's ability to survive in a threat environment. However, in a different environment where this threat does not exist—such as when these soldiers return home in the absence of threat—these underlying cognitive patterns and threat estimation become maladaptive. In fact, many people suffering from disorders such as PTSD manifest hallmark symptoms such as being hyper-vigilant and physiologically aroused, avoiding situations perceived as being threatening, and experiencing a significant amount of intrusive ideation about past threats.

Slovic and Peters (2006) discussed "dual-process" models of decision-making as entailing two global and parallel systems: the first includes automatic, intuitive, and implicit factors involved in perceiving reality and the second involves more explicit, reasoning, and analytical systems. With respect to the former, Slovic and Peters (2006) argued that complex affective systems rooted evolutionarily play a central role in terms of how people negotiate more ambiguous and uncertain situations, particularly those seen as threatening. As Slovic and Peters (2006, p. 322) aptly pointed out:

Strong visceral emotions such as fear and anger sometimes play a role in risk as feelings. These two emotions appear to have opposite effects—fear amplifies risk estimates, and anger attenuates them (Lerner, Gonzalez, Small, & Fischhoff, 2003; Lerner & Keltner, 2000).

Marshall and colleagues (2007) discussed how all events are perceived in complex ways and range along multiple continuums—including from probable to improbable. In situations where there is both a high level of perceived threat and a greater sense of being unpredictable, risk estimates increase. This may explain why, following the events of 9/11/2001, the constant reporting of threat by the media and government fueled within the general population a higher estimated likelihood or probability of something happening and stoked a sense of fear as the primary affective process. This interaction of factors led people to fear something more as a function of the unpredictability (and therefore elevated probability of it occurring again) and sense of dread associated with it. As Marshall and colleagues (2007, p. 309) noted:

In contrast, we propose that the 9/11/2001 attacks signaled a perceived new threat— that foreign terrorists had penetrated the US environment and could cause death and destruction—as danger that was also poorly understood by the public and was therefore unpredictable.

Lerner and colleagues (2003) framed these risk appraisal dynamics within the context of appraisal tendency theory, where there is assumed to be a reciprocal and interacting relationship between emotions and cognitive appraisals. They pointed out that while specific emotions affect subsequent decision-making and cognitive appraisal in the moment, they also form a pattern over time to create a new lens through which to perceive new experiences. One of the central components of this process is the issue of perceived control and the degree to which one believes one can affect a particular situation. Based on any given dynamic where there is greater or lesser perceived control, underlying emotions such as fear or anger may be triggered—influencing subsequent appraisals and response.

As Lerner and colleagues (2003) noted, a sense of underlying fear elicits a greater perceived lack of control and uncertainty, which in turn fuels an underlying sense of fear and dread. In contrast, anger has been associated with a greater sense of control and certainty, which has been shown to affect risk judgments differently. They went on to argue (p. 144):

Consistent with appraisal tendency theory, laboratory studies have found that anger triggered in one situation evokes more optimistic risk estimates and risk-seeking choices in unrelated situations. Fear does the opposite, evoking pessimistic estimates and risk-averse choices (Lerner & Keltner, 2000, 2001). Appraisals of certainty and control moderate and (in the case of control) mediate these effects (Lerner & Keltner, 2001, p. 144).

In a ground-breaking study conducted following the 9/11/2001 attacks, Lerner and colleagues (2003) experimentally induced three different emotional states—anger, sadness, and fear—and then had people rate estimates of risk and their amenability to different approaches to public policy. As hypothesized, the authors found that inducing anger led to more optimistic interpretations about the future, whereas inducing fear led to greater pessimism. Those induced to experience anger further reported a greater tendency for retribution, whereas those induced with fear favored approaches more directed at precaution and conciliation. These results illustrate in a powerful way the vastly different effects that varied emotional states, and fear specifically, have on risk perception and subsequent negotiations.

Evolutionary Theory and Other Models of Conflict

Yet another theoretical paradigm that is useful to consider when thinking about terrorism and fear is evolutionary psychology. As Liddle, Bush, and Shackelford (2011) pointed out in a recent issue of the journal *Behavioral Sciences of Terrorism and Political Aggression*, three conditions are required for an organism to evolve. The first is variation in the characteristics of the organism, some of which would be expected to evolve and others not. These differences are determined by our DNA and facilitate or impede our negotiation of any given environment. The second condition is heritability, or the notion that these characteristics are passed down to new generations. Finally, the third condition is varying likelihoods of survival across species as a function of the first two conditions.

Natural selection, a principle originally identified by Charles Darwin (1859) in his book *On the Origin of Species*, refers to the notion that variations in a given set of traits for any species depend on the environment in which this and other species live. Where certain traits are more adaptive in helping a given species survive in a specific environment, these organisms are more likely to survive long enough to procreate and pass these traits down to the next generation of organisms—ensuring the overall survival of the species. Negotiating the environment for most species involves securing basic necessities, including sustenance, water, shelter, and safety, being able to fend off one's enemies, and adequate ability to procreate. As a function of achieving these and other necessities, a given species is able to pass down specific traits to subsequent generations, which then makes these characteristics more common within the population.

In many circumstances, species compete for common resources. For example, the first author remembers living in South Florida during the 1980s and 1990s and hearing about the plight of the manatees—who were being run over by boats in waterways frequented by humans. Slowly, competition between the two species (human and manatee) led to the near extinction of the latter. Similarly, in Massachusetts the Asian longhorn beetle was recently introduced into the forests and is now threatening the existence of many varieties of hardwood trees in the state, again illustrating how different species compete for resources within a given environment.

A key assumption underlying evolutionary psychology is that humans are not born as blank slates, and are instead pre-programmed to negotiate immediate survival needs, including finding food and water, as well as a mate to pass down one's genetic material. On one level, the events of 9/11/2001 primed an underlying, inherent need for survival, where fear served as the motivating force for protection and security. In the aftermath of these events, the constant threat reporting and perceived likelihood of additional attacks elicited within people a more poignant drive to subsist in the face of potential extinction. This parallels the tenets of TMT in terms of how one's sense of mortality drives one to seek greater security and a higher probability of survival.

On another level, these dynamics reflect how two groups of people (within-species) may compete for certain resources and use tactics such as fear or "terror-ism" to affect the behavior of their perceived enemy. Some, including Osama bin Laden in his 1996 declaration of war against the United States, have argued that one of the primary reasons the United States and the West in general has been targeted for terrorism is because of the latter's ongoing presence in the Middle East, and Saudi Arabia specifically, and the negative perception of U.S. treatment of people within these countries. Although hotly debated on both sides, a dynamic arises where one group of people perceive themselves as being targeted and in some cases killed, which threatens the existence of that group. They respond by attacking the other group (the United States), which elicits a similar response—that is, feeling as though there is an immediate threat to survival. This results in further attacks in the name of survival, and a complex back-and-forth between two groups of people vying for many of the same basic necessities—that is, safety, survival, and subsistence.

Fear is a central component in this dynamic. On the one hand, it is elicited within the species that is attacked and primes a need for response to ensure survival. In essence, it becomes the fuel running the engine that is violence. On the other hand, it is used as a tactic to affect change within the perceived attacker. That is to say, in most definitions of terrorism, the purpose is to instill "terror" or fear as a means of changing some dynamic that is perceived as threatening. Some have argued that ter-rorism is used to alter some political reality, while others believe it is religiously motivated. Others propose that terrorism is a form of aggression that is undertaken for revenge, anger, vengeance, a response to being humiliated, and so on.

Regardless of the specific dynamic, however, the pattern is the same—that is, acts of terrorism are being committed because of some perceived wrong and/or threat to another's way of living. Fear then becomes a weapon, as a means of challenging another group that is perceived as threatening one's way of life, and ensuring the sur-vival of one's own group. The result is the survival of one's immediate way of life and culture, and ensuring that these factors are passed down to subsequent generations.

One classic example of this was the robber's cave experiment conducted by Sherif and colleagues (1961), where boys at a summer camp were divided into two groups—the "Eagles" and the "Rattlers." Conditions were then manipulated to induce competition between the groups, which led to enhanced in-group coherence and derogation of and hostility towards out-groups. Within this dynamic, two groups of people get to a place where they see the other as a threat (literal in many cases, figurative in others) to their existence. These dynamics give rise to negative emotions including fear and hostility, which at a basic level revolve around the survival of the individual and immediate group.

The "Troubles" in Northern Ireland over the past several decades also seem to mirror many of these dynamics, where two main factions of people (Catholic Nationalists and Protestant Unionists), divided along religious lines, have engaged in a protracted conflict with complex political, ideological, and spiritual undertones for years (McAloney, 2010; Blackbourn, 2011). On the one side, the Nationalists have been motivated to reunite Northern Ireland with the rest of Ireland, while the Unionists have fought for the country to remain part of the United Kingdom. During the 1970s, 1980s, and early 1990s, this conflict became particularly violent, as each group saw the other as a mortal threat to a particular way of life. Although the year 1998 saw the Good Friday Agreement, where most paramilitary groups ceased engaging in acts of violence, these groups continue to be divided.

In their research, Sherif and colleagues (1961) found that one of the only mechanisms to reduce this conflict, fear, and hostility was the introduction of a superordinate goal, where both groups were forced into a dynamic of cooperation. In one case, the camp truck became disabled and both groups were forced to pull the truck up a hill. Aaronson (1978) also demonstrated this phenomenon in his work on "jigsaw classrooms," where a diverse group of students was broken up into sections and each student was required to learn a specific topic and teach it to the other students. Results showed that children in these types of contexts were less likely to be prejudiced and more likely to have intact self-esteem.

In the current political reality, one can see how these dynamics have manifested in different ways. For example, one could argue that the overarching goal of peace and eliminating conflict and violence led to the Good Friday Agreement in Northern Ireland in 1998, and a different sort of effort to work towards a compromise solution to the conflict. The agreement, which was signed by most of the Northern Ireland political factions, required that all parties moving forward would engage only in peaceful and democratic process to resolve future conflicts.

Although the United States and Russia were embedded in a long period of discord (the Cold War), more recently they have engaged in mutual acts of cooperation to address overarching threats that affect both nations—including terrorism. As of August 2010, the news included joint U.S.–Russian military operations over the Pacific Ocean, where both nations were engaging in a mock response to a hijacked airplane. Although one could argue that there remains a certain level of discord between these nations, this type of mutuality and cooperation has surely altered the political and psychological landscape between them.

SUMMARY AND CONCLUSIONS

The purpose of this chapter was to present a variety of theoretical frameworks for better understanding the concept of fear as it relates to terrorism. Selye's (1956) model of stress mirrors much of what we have learned more recently about the biological/physiological effects of continued stress over time (e.g., van der Kolk, 1987, 1996) and the negative toll this takes on the person. Whereas a person confronted with something threatening initially displays the fight-or-flight response, the ongoing threat of imminent terrorism has likely contributed to a more general fatigue and exhaustion in the general population, and particularly in those who live in the areas directly affected by terrorism. This is due in part to the physiological depletion of resources, as well as the impact this has on a person's ability to focus attention and concentrate—which may then make it tough to pay attention and concentrate fully on government terror alerts as they are issued. Over time, this may morph into a general sense of apathy, where a combination of "alert fatigue" and repeatedly being warned of something that does not occur contributes to increased ennui.

Both terror management and evolutionary psychology theories nicely illustrate the complex social and existential dynamics that underlie fear, and the factors that ameliorate these fears. For example, social connection and self-efficacy could be understood as ways of both transcending the fear of mortality and increasing the chances that one would survive and be able to pass down crucial genetic material to the next generation. That is, both are very important existential and evolutionary constructs, and in different ways speak to the ability of the person to maintain survival.

Cognitive-behavioral and risk appraisal theories are important in terms of understanding the micro-processes that people engage in when evaluating threat in the environment. Those who perceive more threat in the environment (perhaps when there are data to the contrary) and manifest more of a heightened fear response are likely to engage more in specific underlying cognitive patterns, including magnification, rumination, and learned helplessness. Within the context of terrorism, fear is fueled by a tendency to explode the threat within one's mind, to spend a significant amount of time thinking about this threat over time, and thus to experience a heightened sense of vulnerability and impotence as a consequence.

These automatic processes underlie what Slovic and Peters (2006) termed "affect heuristics," which then affect how people make estimations of future risk. Lerner, Gonzalez, Small, and Fischhoff (2003) and Slovic and Peters (2006) went on to note that whereas fear amplifies the general perception of risk, anger reduces this tendency. Some have asserted that this is due, at least in part, to the issue of perceived control and the sense that one can exert systematic influence on one's environment when operating from a position of anger—as opposed to fear, when there may be a greater sense of lack of control.

As fear is primed, there is a natural tendency to adhere closely to one's social niche as a means of protection and survival of the group. Research has also shown that people who feel threatened in this way are more prone to derogating those perceived as "out-group" members, especially those seen as a direct threat to the survival of the group. This manifested in many ways following the 9/11/2001 attacks, where people perceived as being similar to the terrorists (in terms of race/ethnicity, or other factors such as language or apparel) were targeted by other people in the community. These sorts of negative social dynamics have also been experimentally induced to illustrate how greater perceived hostility and conflict between two groups leads to increased divisiveness and competition. Fear is a central part of this process, where concerns about the safety and security of the in-group fuel hostility and resentment toward the out-group.

In contrast, there has also been considerable research to suggest that much of this conflict (and fear) is reduced by implementing a super-ordinate goal towards which both groups can orient themselves (as opposed to one another). For instance, following decades of heightened fear and hostility towards one another, the United States and Russia have engaged in collaborative exercises over the past decade, including joint military drills aimed at responding to terrorism threats. While the two nations may not be totally allied at the moment, one could argue that this change in dynamics and insertion of a mutual goal (an effective response to terrorism) led to a decrease in direct conflict and a slight increase in cooperative behaviors. The situation in Northern Ireland is another example: in the late 1990s both sides of the conflict appeared to be motivated by an overarching goal (to reduce violence in the community and restore peace), which led to a fundamental change in the quality of their relationship. Moving forward, it will be important to continue to understand how negative emotions such as fear have the potential to be divisive, and how fostering collaboration and cooperative enterprise may serve to reduce fear and conflict in general.

REFERENCES

Aronson, E., Blaney, N., Stephin, C., Sikes, J., & Snapp, M. (1978). *The jigsaw classroom.* Beverly Hills, CA: Sage Publishing Company.

Abramson, L. Y., Metalsky, G. I., & Alloy, L. B. (1989). Hopelessness depression: A theory-based subtype of depression. *Psychological Review, 96*, 358–372.

Abramson, L. Y., Seligman, M. E. P., & Teasdale, J. D. (1974). Learned helplessness in humans: Critique and reformulation. *Journal of Abnormal Psychology, 87*, 49–74.

Allison, G. (2004). *Nuclear terrorism: The ultimate preventable catastrophe.* New York: Times Books.

Beck, A. T. (1976). *Cognitive therapy and the emotional disorders.* New York: Basic Books.

Beck, A. T. (1979). *Cognitive therapy of depression.* New York: The Guilford Press.

Beck, J. S. (1995). *Cognitive therapy: Basics and beyond.* New York: Guilford.

Beck, A. T., Epstein, N., & Brown, G. (1988). An inventory for measuring clinical anxiety: psychometric properties. *Journal of Consulting and Clinical Psychology, 56,* 893–897.

Beck, A. T., Steer, R. A., & Brown, G. K. (1996). *Beck Depression Inventory-Second Edition.* San Antonio: The Psychological Corporation & Harcourt Brace & Company.

Blackbourn, J. (2011). The evolving definition of terrorism in UK law. *Behavioral Sciences of Terrorism and Political Aggression, 3,* 131–149.

Bonanno, G. A. (2004). Loss, trauma, and human resilience. *American Psychologist, 59,* 20–28.

Brehm, S. S., Kassin, S., & Fein, S. (2005). *Social psychology* (6th ed.). Boston: Houghton Mifflin.

Briere, J. (1997). *Psychological assessment of adult posttraumatic states.* Washington, D.C.: American Psychological Association.

Briere, J. (2001). *Cognitive Distortions Scale.* Los Angeles: Psychological Assessment Resources.

Brown, T. A., Antony, M. M., & Barlow, D. H. (1992). Psychometric properties of the Penn State Worry Questionnaire in a clinical anxiety disorders sample. *Behaviour Research & Therapy, 30,* 33–77.

Burns, D. (1980). *Feeling good: The new mood therapy.* New York: William Morrow.

Carver, C. S., Scheier, M. F., & Weintraub, J. K. (1989). Assessing coping strategies: A theoretically based approach. *Journal of Personality and Social Psychology, 56,* 267–283.

Chavez, J. F., & Brown, J. M. (1978). *Self generated strategies for the control of pain and stress.* Paper presented at the 86th Annual Conference of the American Psychological Association, Toronto, Ontario.

Chavez, J. F., & Brown, J. M. (1987). Spontaneous cognitive strategies for the control of clinical pain and stress. *Journal of Behavioral Medicine, 10,* 263–276.

Clark, M. M. (1986). Personal therapy; A review of empirical research. *Professional Psychology: Research and Practice, 17,* 541–543.

Cottraux, J. (2004). Recent developments in the research on generalized anxiety disorder. *Current Opinion in Psychiatry, 17,* 49–52.

Darwin, C. (1859). *On the origin of species.* London: John Murray.

Endler, N. S., & Parker, J. D. (1990). Multidimensional assessment of coping: A critical evaluation. *Journal of Personality and Social Psychology, 58,* 844–854.

Festinger, L. (1957). *A theory of cognitive dissonance.* Evanston, IL: Row, Peterson.

Folkman, S., & Lazarus, R. S. (1988). Coping as a mediator of emotion. *Journal of Personality and Social Psychology, 54,* 466–475.

Frankl, V. (1992). *Man's search for meaning.* Boston: Beacon Press.

Galea, S., Resnick, H., Ahern, J., Gold, J., Bucuvalas, M., Kilpatrick, D., et al. (2002). Posttraumatic stress disorder in Manhattan, New York City, after the September 11th terrorist attacks. *Journal of Urban Health, 79,* 340–353.

Garnefski, N., Kraaij, V., & Spinhoven, P. (2001). Negative life events, cognitive emotion regulation and emotional problems. *Personality and Individual Differences, 30,* 1311–1327.

Garnefski, N., Teerds, J., Kraaij, V., Legerstee, J., & van den Kommer, T. (2004). Cognitive emotion regulation strategies and depressive symptoms: Differences between males and females. *Personality and Individual Differences, 36,* 267–276.

Greenberg, J., Simon, L., Harmon-Jones, E., Solomon, S., Pyszczynski, T., & Lyon, D. (1995). Testing alternative explanations for mortality salience effects: Terror management, value accessibility, or worrisome thoughts? *European Journal of Social Psychology, 25,* 417–433.

Greenberg, J., Solomon, S., & Pyszczynski, T. (1997). Terror management theory of self esteem and cultural worldviews: Empirical assessments and conceptual refinements. In M. Zanna (Ed.), *Advances in experimental social psychology* (Vol. 29, pp. 61–139). Orlando, FL: Academic Press.

Harvey, A. G., & Greenall, E. (2003). Catastrophic worry in primary insomnia. *Journal of Behavior Therapy and Experimental Psychiatry, 34,* 11–23.

Lerner, J. S., Gonzalez, R. M., Small, D. A., & Fischhoff, B. (2003). Effects of fear and anger on perceived risks of terrorism: A national field experiment. *Psychological Science, 14,* 144–150.

Lerner, J. S., & Keltner, D. (2000). Beyond valence: Toward a model of emotion-specific influences on judgment and choice. *Cognition and Emotion, 14,* 473–493.

Lerner, J. S., & Keltner, D. (2001). Fear, anger, and risk. *Journal of Personality and Social Psychology, 81,* 146–159.

Lewin, K., Lippitt, R., & White, R. K. (1939). Patterns of aggressive behavior in experimentally created social climates. *Journal of Social Psychology, 10,* 271–299.

Liddle, J. R., Bush, L. S., & Shackelford, T. (2011). An introduction to evolutionary psychology and its application to suicide terrorism. *Behavioral Sciences of Terrorism and Political Aggression, 3,* 176–197.

Marshall, R. D., Bryant, R. A., Amsel, L., Suh, E. J., Cook, J. M., & Neria, Y. (2007). The psychology of ongoing threat: Relative risk appraisal, the September 11 attacks, and terrorism-related fears. *American Psychologist, 62,* 304–316.

McAloney, J. (2010). Life after prison: The experiences of prison officers serving during the Troubles in Northern Ireland. *Behavioral Sciences of Terrorism and Political Aggression, 3, 20–34.*

McCann, I. L., & Pearlman, L. A. (1992). Constructivist self development theory: A theoretical framework for assessing and treating traumatized college students. *Journal of American College Health, 40,* 189–196.

McDermott, R., & Zimbardo, P. G. (2007). The psychological consequences of terrorist alerts. In B. Bongar, L. Brown, Beutler, L., J. Breckenridge, & P. Zimbardo (Eds.), *The psychology of terrorism* (pp. 357–370). Oxford: Oxford University Press.

McGregor, H., Lieberman, J. D., Greenberg, J., Solomon, S., Arndt, J., Simon, L., et al. (1998). Terror management theory and aggression: Evidence that mortality salience motivates aggression against worldview-threatening others. *Journal of Personality and Social Psychology, 74,* 590–605.

McNally, R. J., Bryant, R. A., & Ehlers, A. (2003). Does early psychological intervention promote recovery from posttraumatic stress? *Psychological Science in the Public Interest, 4,* 45–79.

Morin, R. (2003). *Most in area are edgy, getting ready.* Retrieved Dec. 31, 2004, from www.washingtonpost.com.

Najavits, L. M., Gotthardt, S., Weiss, R. D., & Epstein, M. (2004). Cognitive distortions in the dual diagnosis of PTSD and substance use disorder. *Cognitive Therapy and Research, 28,* 159–172.

Nelson, L. J., Moore, D. L., Olivetti, J., & Scott, T. (1997). General and personal mortality salience and nationalistic bias. *Personality and Social Psychology Bulletin, 23,* 884–892.

Nolen-Hoeksema, S. (1991). Responses to depression and their effects on the duration of depressive episodes. *Journal of Abnormal Psychology, 100,* 569–582.

Nolen-Hoeksema, S. (1987). Sex differences in unipolar depression: Evidence and theory. *Psychological Bulletin, 101,* 259–282.

Nolen-Hoeksema, S., Morrow, J., & Fredrickson, B. L. (1993). Response style and the duration of episodes of depressed mood. *Journal of Abnormal Psychology, 102,* 20–28.

Ochsmann, R., & Mathy, M. (1994). *Depreciating of and distancing from foreigners: Effects of mortality salience.* Unpublished manuscript, University of Mainz, Mainz, Germany.

Osman, A., Barrios, F. X., Gutierrez, P.M., Kopper, B.A., Merrifield, T., & Grittman, L. (2000). The Pain Catastrophizing Scale: Further psychometric evaluation with adult samples. *Journal of Behavioral Medicine, 23,* 351–365.

Osman, A., Barrios, F. X., Kopper, B. A., Hauptmann, W., Jones, J., & O'Neill, E. (1997). Factor structure, reliability, and validity of the Pain Catastrophizing Scale. *Journal of Behavioral Medicine, 20,* 589–605.

Ozer, E. J., Best, S. R., Lipsey, T. L., & Weiss, D. S. (2003). Predictors of posttraumatic stress disorder and symptoms in adults: A meta-analysis. *Psychological Bulletin, 129,* 52–73.

Piaget, J. (1954). *The construction of reality.* New York: Basic Books.

Pyszczynski, T., Solomon, S., & Greenberg, J. (2003). *In the wake of 9/11: The psychology of terror.* Washington, D.C.: American Psychological Association.

Rosenblatt, A., Greenberg, J., Solomon, S., Pyszczynski, T., & Lyon, D. (1989). Evidence for terror management theory: I. The effects of mortality salience on reactions to those who violate or uphold cultural values. *Journal of Personality and Social Psychology, 57,* 681–690.

Rosenstiel, A. K., & Keefe, F. J. (1983). The use of coping strategies in chronic low back pain patients: Relationship to patient characteristics and current adjustment. *Pain, 17,* 33–44.

Scheuer, M. (2004). *Imperial hubris.* Washington, D.C.: Brassey's, Inc.

Schniering, C. A., & Rapee, R. M. (2004). The relationship between automatic thoughts and negative emotions in children and adolescents: A test of the cognitive content-specificity hypothesis. *Journal of Abnormal Psychology, 113,* 464–470.

Selye, H. (1956). *The stress of life.* New York: McGraw Hill.

Sherif, M., & Hovland, C. I. (1961). *Social judgment: Assimilation and contrast effects in communication and attitude change.* New Haven: Yale University Press.

Sinclair, S. J., & LoCicero, A. (2007). Anticipatory fear and catastrophizing about terrorism: Development, validation, and psychometric testing of the Terrorism Catastrophizing Scale (TCS). *Traumatology, 13,* 75–90.

Sinclair, S. J. (2010). Fears of terrorism and future threat: Theoretical and empirical considerations. In D. Antonius, A. D., Brown, T. Walters, M. Ramirez, & S. J. Sinclair (Eds.), *Interdisciplinary analyses of terrorism and aggression,* (pp. 101–115). Cambridge, England: Cambridge Scholars Publishing.

Sinclair, S. J., & LoCicero, A. (2010). The Terrorism Catastrophizing Scale (TCS): Assessing the ongoing psychological impact of terrorism. In L. Baer & M. Blais (Eds.), *Handbook of clinical rating scales and assessment in psychiatry and mental health* (pp. 278–285). Boston: Humana Press.

Slovic, P., & Peters, E. (2006). Risk perception and affect. *Current Directions in Psychological Science, 15,* 322–325.

Spanos, N. P., Radtke-Bodorik, H. L., Jones, B., & Horner, D. (1978). The effects of hypnotic susceptibility suggestions for analgesia in the reduction of reported pain. *Journal of Abnormal Psychology, 88,* 282–292.

Startup, H. M., & Davey, C. L. (2001). Mood as input and catastrophic worrying. *Journal of Abnormal Psychology, 110,* 83–96.

Sullivan, M. J. L., Bishop, S. R., & Pivik, J. (1995). The Pain Catastrophizing Scale: Development and validation. *Psychological Assessment, 7,* 524–532.

Tenet, G. (2007). *At the center of the storm: My years at the CIA.* New York: Harper Collins Publishers.

Van der Kolk, B. (1996). The body keeps score. Approaches to the psychobiology of post traumatic stress disorder. In B. van der Kolk, A. McFarlane, & L. Weisaeth (Eds.), *Traumatic stress: The effects of overwhelming experience on mind, body, and society.* New York: Guilford Press.

Van der Kolk, B. (1987). The separation cry and the trauma response: Developmental issues in the psychobiology of attachment and separation. In B. van der Kolk (Ed.), *Psychological trauma* (pp. 31–62). Washington, D.C.: American Psychiatric Press.

Williams, P. L. (2005). *Al Qaeda connection: International terrorism, organized crime, and the coming apocalypse.* New York: Prometheus Books.

Williams, P. L. (2004). *Osama's revenge: The next 9/11: What the media and the government haven't told you.* New York: Prometheus Books.

Young, J. E., Weinberger, A. D., & Beck, A. T. (2001). Cognitive therapy for depression. In D. H. Barlow (Ed.), *Clinical handbook of psychological disorders: A step-by-step treatment manual* (3rd ed.). New York: The Guilford Press.

Zimbardo, P. (2003a). *Overcoming terror.* Retrieved February 2004 from http://www.brucekluger.com/PT/PT-OvercomingTerror-JulAug2003.html

Zimbardo, P. (2003b). *The political psychology of terrorist alarms.* Retrieved February 2004 from http://www.zimbardo.com/downloads/2002%20Political%20Psychology%20of%20Terrorist%20Alarms.pdf

Zinn, M. (2004). Development of a self-report inventory to assess cognitive dysfunction in musicians. *Dissertation Abstracts International: Section B: The Sciences and Engineering, 65*(4-B), 2004, 2122.

4 Terrorism and Fear
New Models for Understanding the Impact of Political Violence

"If you are distressed by anything external, the pain is not due to the thing itself, but to your estimate of it; and this you have the power to revoke at any moment."
Marcus Aurelius

The central thesis of this book is that despite declines in discrete psychological disorders in the 6 to 12 months following the terrorist attacks of September 11, 2001, a substantial amount of fear has remained in the general population. Following on this, we will argue here that these fears affect people's lives in meaningful ways, and because they are not part of the established models for assessing mental health (i.e., the American Psychiatric Association's *Diagnostic and Statistical Manual of Mental Disorders* [DSM-IV]; APA, 2000), the impact of these fears may go more unnoticed. The purpose of this chapter is to begin to unpack the complexity underlying these fears, provide evidence for its existence and impact, discuss its inconsistency with existing mental health frameworks, and present new models for measuring and addressing fears of terrorism in people.

A CHANGE IN ZEITGEIST FOLLOWING 9/11/2001

It is not difficult to argue that the events of 9/11/2001 led to a paradigm shift in terms of how people think about themselves in the world. As we will discuss in further detail below, beliefs about safety and security, as well as the perception of risk in one's life, was fundamentally altered on this day. While Chapter 3 provided an array of theoretical frameworks for thinking about terrorism fears, we will argue here that the very concept of fear does not fit nicely within existing paradigms of mental health. The implications of this are significant and reflect an underlying vulnerability within the population that is not being evaluated or addressed adequately.

The term "terrorism" has become common in our diction, and some have argued it is used with great frequency without any real or specific definition (Rapin, 2009). Some have also argued that even though the attacks of 9/11/2001 are what set this process in motion, people's underlying "terrors" have been stoked in an ongoing way by popular media, as well as the government, as a means of achieving some other ends (e.g., better ratings, winning an election, etc.). All of these points are still hotly debated within our society, and while people vary considerably in terms of where they fall within this spectrum of opinion, we believe everyone can agree that there has been an underlying shift in terms of how people think about and understand issues of safety and security. For example, Burnham (2007) demonstrated a clear shift in terms of what U.S. children feared following the 9/11/2001 attacks, with terrorism emerging as a frontrunner, even though overall fears remained stable pre- and post-9/11/2001.

Close to a year after the 9/11/2001 attacks, North and Pfefferbaum (2002) published an editorial in the esteemed *Journal of the American Medical Association* in which they discussed models for understanding the mental health impact of terrorist incidents. They highlighted many of the methodological and contextual challenges of studying the psychological impact of terrorism and the importance of achieving both adequate timing and appropriate sampling targets. They were quick to point out that not all people exposed to a terrorist attack wind up with diagnosable psychological disorders, even though they experienced considerable amounts of emotional distress. As North and Pfefferbaum (2002, p. 634) specifically noted:

"While normalization of psychological effects of disasters can be reassuring for the majority of survivors, it is important to recognize the significant distress of those whose emotional upset does not reach proportions that would qualify for a diagnosis of PTSD. The emotional distress that falls clearly below the diagnostic threshold for PTSD (subdiagnostic stress) that is prevalent among individuals exposed to catastrophic events deserves different mental health interventions from the customary psychiatric treatment for the minority who develop a diagnosable disorder."

Marshall and colleagues (2007) provided an excellent discussion of this phenomenon and wrote at length about how the psychological effects of terrorism do not map well onto existing mental health frameworks like the DSM (APA, 2000). In particular, they argue that traditional models of PTSD have used "bull's eye" frameworks to describe the inherent relationship between the degree of exposure and subsequent psychological impact. Those who are most proximal to a traumatic event have historically manifested more severe symptoms of psychological distress.

However, as the distance increases between the individual and the traumatic stimulus, the psychological impact has been shown to be decrease—with all other things being equal.

In contrast to these traditional models, Marshall and colleagues (2007) posited that large-scale acts of terrorism, like 9/11/2001, led to extraordinary levels of distress across people in the general population, in addition to those directly exposed. They discussed many of the studies that were reviewed in Chapter 2 and talked about how psychological distress spiked in people across the United States, not just those in the areas directly affected. Marshall and colleagues (2007, p. 304) noted, "In other words, indirect exposure to the 9/11 attacks appears to have been responsible for causing clinically significant levels of PTSD symptoms in the general US population, with an unknown long-term impact on mental health and functioning, public health, the economy, and society."

At the core of this debate is the issue of direct exposure. According to the DSM-IV-TR (APA, 2000), multiple clusters of psychological symptoms must be present for a diagnosis of PTSD to be made. These include re-experiencing the event in some ongoing way (such as through dreams or intrusive thoughts); ongoing avoidance behaviors, or efforts aimed at eluding reminders of the traumatic event; and elevated arousal or stress. However, Criterion A requires that someone "experienced, witnessed, or was confronted with an event or events that involved actual or threatened death or serious injury, or a threat to the physical integrity of self or others" (APA, 2000, p. 218).

As Marshall and colleagues (2007) pointed out, there has been considerable debate in the academic community about what constitutes direct exposure meeting Criterion A, and whether those living in the general population could in fact qualify. North and Pfefferbaum (2002) suggested that many in the scientific community interpret these criteria literally—where simply viewing these events on television would not satisfy this requirement. However, Marshall and colleagues (2007) argued that being able to witness these events via different technological media (e.g., by watching these images on television or the Internet, seeing images in the newspaper, etc.) has generated an *indirect* exposure effect and contributed to a preponderance of distress in the general population.

One of the major qualitative differences in recent years, and particularly following the 9/11/2001 attacks, is the role that the media has played in terms of exposure. Both Marshall and colleagues (2007) and North and Pfefferbaum (2002) argued that the constant stream of terrorism reporting following 9/11/2001 and people bearing witness over and over again to the planes flying into the buildings helps explain why so many people *not* directly exposed to the terrorist attacks met symptom criteria for PTSD following the attacks. Some have even discussed this process as a "vicarious traumatization," where via different media outlets people were indirectly exposed and perceived themselves as being at risk in the same way as if they had been directly confronted with the experience. As North and Pfefferbaum

(2002, p. 635) noted, "The implications of how to rate indirect exposure through media viewing are enormous. Classification of individuals exposed to the events of September 11 through the media as PTSD cases could potentially identify vastly increased numbers in the New York City area and nationally."

In contrast to the position held by Marshall and colleagues (2007), North and Pfefferbaum (2002) went on to argue that even though the magnitude and intensity of psychological distress following the 9/11/2001 attacks was significant for those indirectly exposed, "these responses are distinct from PTSD." On the other side of the argument, Marshall and colleagues (2007) argued that factors like diffuse media exposure have contributed to similar constellations of symptoms (and PTSD specifically) in populations directly and indirectly affected.

However, these are debates centered around discrete psychological (diagnostic) constructs, and most academics (including North and Pfefferbaum, and Marshall and colleagues) have consistently agreed upon the significant and widespread levels of distress in the general population irrespective of specific psychological disorders. North and Pfefferbaum (2002) discussed at length how the larger community and nation were affected following the Oklahoma City attacks, as well as after the 9/11/2001 strike. Similarly, Marshall and colleagues (2007, p. 305) discussed how, in addition to research that has focused on more classic models of psychopathology, "the presence of persistent fears in the general population of being personally harmed in future terrorist attacks is a poorly understood phenomenon that may represent a vulnerability in the general population."

Drawing on the concept of "relative risk appraisal" outlined in greater detail in Chapter 3, Marshall and colleagues (2007) discussed the issue of proximity to a given threat as being only one component in a large matrix of factors that predispose someone to fear. With respect to the issue of terrorism specifically, they went on to discuss other factors, including the ongoing and unpredictable quality of the threat, as well as the perceived high-impact nature of it. These factors are then propagated by a media system that disseminated threat information in a constant stream following the 9/11/2001 attacks, and a government system that constantly warned of new and impending attacks—both of which heightened the perceived probability, unpredictability, and never-ending risk of further terrorist attacks in the general population.

This combination (and unique interaction) of factors creates a threat dynamic that is distinct from other threatening events, such as natural disasters—which are more finite and predictable (at least in the sense that many storms and other natural disasters can be forecasted with better precision than a terrorist attack, and include definitive start and end points). For example, in the context of Hurricane Katrina in 2005, where it could be argued that the media also had a significant presence, most in the region were not acutely worried that another hurricane was imminent and could appear without warning. Further, unlike events such as Hurricane Katrina or a tornado, where there is some forecasting in terms of the destruction that might result, the terrorist threat was much more unpredictable in this respect. That is to say, at least within the United States the national debate on terrorism exploded following 9/11/2001 to include discussions about the likelihood of nuclear and other chemical/biological weapons being used. The magnitude and scope of what was "likely" grew exponentially overnight, and this contributed to stoking fears in an already nervous public—in part because of the magnitude and unpredictability, and chronic (never-ending) nature of the threat.

In addition to relatively consistent research findings about rates of discrete psychological disorders in the general population, similar research has reported on the preponderance of fear and distress as distinct from specific forms of psychopathology. Following the logic of both Marshall and colleagues (2007) and North and Pfefferbaum (2002), those who do *not* meet full criteria for disorders such as PTSD but who *do* report ongoing fear and distress represent a unique group of people not accounted for by existing emergency mental health systems. The following section documents some of these research findings.

EVIDENCE OF FEAR IN THE GENERAL U.S. POPULATION FOLLOWING TERRORISM

In the wake of the 9/11/2001 events, research has begun to report on people's fears of terrorism as separate from the link between terrorism and identifiable psychiatric conditions. Much of this research was designed to evaluate for specific forms of psychopathology, but went on to report that fear and distress in the general population remained prevalent even when people did not meet full criteria for DSM-defined conditions. This research began to manifest in both empirical social science research as well as in many of the national polling studies that were done following 9/11/2001. These studies are discussed briefly below.

Empirical Research

Since the 9/11/2001 attacks a steady stream of research has reported both on the immediate psychological effects of the attacks themselves, as well as the degree to which people have been fearful and distressed moving forward. For example, Boscarino, Figley, and Adams (2003) sampled roughly 1,000 people living in the New York City area approximately 1 year following the 9/11/2001 attacks and found that almost half of the respondents reported being "very concerned" about another major terrorist attack. As has been replicated by other studies, those living in lower Manhattan were more likely to report ongoing fears about another attack, as were women and African-American and Hispanic individuals. Despite these elevated fears, the researchers noted that only 6% of the sample reported having made any preparations in case an attack did occur. This may reflect some degree of avoidance and/or attempts to not think about or address this threat in any sort of concrete manner, which is perhaps consistent with an underlying PTSD-type constellation of symptoms.

Following on Marshall and colleagues' (2007) concept of relative risk appraisal, Boscarino and colleagues (2003) also reported that roughly 43% of participants worried about a terrorist attack using nuclear weapons and 50% were concerned about the use of biological weapons, despite the low likelihood (statistically) of such an event occurring. A follow-up study by these same researchers involved a survey of New York residents 2 years after the 9/11/2001 attacks (Boscarino, Adams, Figley, Galea, & Foa, 2006). While roughly the same percentage (45%) of people remained very concerned about another terrorist attack, the percentage of people who reported making preparations for future attacks had more than doubled, to roughly 15%. It is unclear whether this change reflects differences in the samples themselves or variations in the environment. For example, between these two time points (1 and 2 years following the 9/11/2001 attacks) the government website www.ready.gov (as well other information-based websites) was launched; it facilitates disaster planning and coordination on the part of general citizens. This may, at least in part, account for the greater percentage of people reporting some degree of preparedness.

Boscarino and colleagues (2006) went on to report that the percentages of those fearing nuclear (41%) and biological (45%) terrorism remained relatively consistent 2 years after the attacks. Further, they found that slightly fewer people would wait for instructions from public health or police officials at 2 years following the attacks (43%) as compared to the year earlier (47%), and slightly more people reported they would leave the area without feedback from officials (34% vs. 30%). From a public health and response standpoint, these findings are striking and would indicate greater potential difficulties for those responding to the actual disaster because one third of the population would be expected to operate without direction from response teams. These findings also emphasize the importance of effective risk communication to the public (something addressed more in Chapter 5) as a way to reduce fears by promoting a sense of self-protection and locus of control. As Boscarino and colleagues (2006, p. 511) noted, "It has also been suggested that effective risk communications can have the effect of not only reducing fear but also promoting self-protecting behaviors, building trust, and preventing the spread of misinformation."

Silver and colleagues (2002) conducted a longitudinal survey of a large sample of Americans representative of the general population and reported that the percentage manifesting symptoms of 9/11/2001-related post-traumatic stress was 17% at 2 months following the attacks and 5.8% at 6 months. In stark contrast to these findings, however, they went on to report that roughly 65% manifested fears (at least "sometimes") of further acts of terrorism at 2 months, and approximately 60% reported fears that a family member would be harmed. At the 6-month follow-up these fears decreased to roughly 38% and 41%, respectively, although they continued to affect a significant cross-section of people. These findings further highlight the discrepancy between people who meet criteria for specific psychological disorders versus those who do not but remain in a state of fear.

In perhaps the first national study on the psychological effects of 9/11/2001 to be published following the attacks, Schuster and colleagues (2001) queried a large nationally representative sample of people in the United States 3 to 5 days following the attacks about a number of different reactions. They found that 36% believed that terrorism was a very or somewhat serious threat to their region of the country, and that 44% of people worried that terrorism would get worse over the following 5 years. These reactions were positively correlated with television viewing, contributing to the notion that repeatedly viewing images of disaster may lead to vicarious traumatization.

In a multi-wave epidemiological study, Richman, Cloninger, and Rospenda (2008) found that a considerable percentage (23%) of people from the Midwest United States remained fearful in 2003 of another terrorist attack occurring in the future, and that these fears were significantly predictive of escapist motives for drinking alcohol over time. They also noted that approximately 30% reported being more pessimistic about world peace, and 28% had less faith that their government could protect them. Similar to the thesis presented in this volume, they discussed these results in terms of how existing mental health frameworks pay too much attention to individual-level stressors (e.g., the death of a loved one, immediate exposure to something traumatic, etc.) and not enough attention to larger, macro-level stressors (e.g., a large-scale terrorist attack) in terms of how they affect the person. As Richman and colleagues (2008, p. 326) noted, "Thus, our data suggest that political terrorism is a macro-level stressor of major public health importance."

Eisenberg and colleagues (2009) recently published a study in the *American Journal of Public Health* that extended the above findings by also demonstrating that those typically identified as "vulnerable" in terms of manifesting negative mental health outcomes in the context of disaster were more prone to worry about terrorism, to perceive a greater threat of terrorism, and to exhibit avoidance behaviors as result. In their random sample of Los Angeles residents, they found that African-Americans, Latinos, Chinese Americans, Korean Americans, non-U.S. citizens, and disabled persons manifested greater fears and were more likely to avoid different experiences because of these worries.

The prevalence of fear, as distinct from discrete psychological disorders, in the general population has also been reported in a number of international research studies. For example, Rubin and colleagues (2005, 2007) surveyed a large sample of people in London 1 to 2 weeks following the July 2005 attacks in London, and then again 7 months later (in 2006). Both global distress reactions and specific risk perceptions about the ongoing threat were assessed. As can be seen in Figure 4.1, although there was a general decline in distress and perceived risk between these two time points, a sizeable portion of the sample continued to report considerable worries even at 7 months following the attacks. While there was a precipitous drop in the

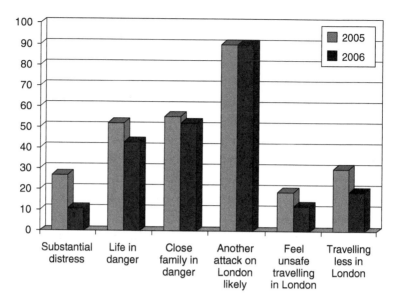

FIGURE 4.1 Percentage of those living in London reporting fears across various domains (Rubin et al., 2007).

percentage of people experiencing "substantial distress" from 2005 (27%) to 2006 (11%), many continued to believe that their lives (52% vs. 43%, respectively) and those of their loved ones (55% vs. 52%, respectively) were in danger from terrorism. Perhaps most striking, the vast majority of people queried believed that another attack in London was likely in the "near future" (90% at both time points).

In a compelling analysis of risk factors for persistent distress, Rubin and colleagues (2007) discussed how specific worry about relatives or friends being the victims of a terrorist attack is a significant predictor of chronic distress over time. Further, and pursuant to the issue of effective communication following a terrorist attack, these researchers reported that not being able to contact others by cellular telephone and uncertainty about the well-being of loved ones predicted persistent levels of emotional distress. This need for connection and fluid communication in the context of disaster follows much of what we know to be true about psychological disorders in general, as well as the tenets of terror management theory (TMT) specifically—where social cohesion and connectedness have been shown to ameliorate the negative effects of stress and anxiety.

Conejero and Etxebarria (2007) evaluated the emotional response of Spanish citizens following the March 11, 2004, terrorist attacks in Madrid and found that immediately following the attacks there were elevated rates of negative emotions in the population, including sadness, anger, guilt, contempt, and fear, among others. While these rates generally declined over time, they remained significant at 2 months following the attacks. These researchers also found that most people overestimated these negative emotions in other people, especially fear. In other words, most people rated other's fear reactions as being higher than their own. Finally, as would be expected, fear was the single best predictor of subsequent avoidance behaviors in the general population immediately following the Madrid attack.

In Israel, there has been considerable work documenting how rates of worry and anticipatory anxiety spike following terrorist attacks, and how many in the general population have begun contacting emergency hotlines because of these prospective fears as opposed to reacting to past events (Somer, Tamir, Maguen, & Litz, 2005). Despite relatively lower estimated rates of disorders such at PTSD (see Bleich, Gelkopf, & Solomon, 2003), Somer and colleagues (2005) cited a number of studies showing that over half of the population exhibited elevated rates of fears and anxieties about future terrorism, and that these fears contributed to other difficulties, such as with sleeping, breathing, and avoidance behaviors.

Polling Research

Polling research by various sampling agencies has also yielded compelling evidence to suggest that people remain fearful of terrorism in the general population. Pyszczynski and colleagues (2003) provided a nice summary of these early results, citing a November 2001 Gallup Poll showing that 40% of Americans worried that they or a family member would be the target of terrorism, and 74% were fearful that an attack was probable in the near future. These fears have also been shown to affect how people think about public policy. For example, Toner and Elder (2001) reported a *New York Times*/CBS News poll in December 2001 showing that roughly four fifths of the population favored detaining potential terror suspects for indefinite periods of time, and approximately two thirds thought the government should be allowed to monitor discussions between suspects and their lawyers. Perhaps most significant, they reported that two thirds of people polled supported granting the president powers to change the U.S. Constitution as a means of ensuring safety.

Figure 4.2 summarizes data from an ongoing *USA Today*/Gallup poll. The figure reports the percentage of people living in the United States between 2001 and 2006 who believed it was "very" or "somewhat" likely that the United States would be attacked in the next couple of weeks. These data are available in raw form at http://www.pollingreport.com/terror.htm. A number of interesting trends can be seen in this graph. First, despite some variability over time, the perception that future terrorist attacks are imminent remains elevated over time. Second, these perceptions appear to vary according to world events. For example, despite some decline over the first year, the perception that an attack was likely at the first anniversary of 9/11/2001 remained at roughly two thirds. Rates declined by July 2003 but then rose again in July 2004 in the context of the US presidential elections (and news reports that the elections would be targets of terrorism) and the Madrid bombings in March. This poll also provides a nice contrast between risk perception in the United States before and after the July 2005 London bombings and demonstrates that international terrorism appears to have some association with risk perception in the

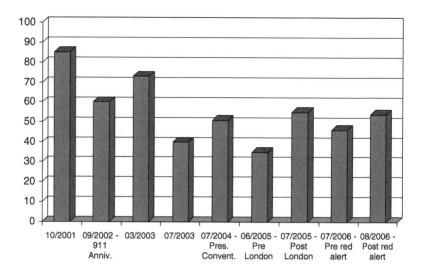

FIGURE 4.2 Percentage reporting it is "very/somewhat likely" the United States will be attacked in the next couple weeks (2001 to 2006).
Source: USA Today/Gallup Poll (See http://www.pollingreport.com/terror.htm)

United States. Finally, the poll also illustrates some elevation in perceived risk following the brief (and only) raising of the American color-coded terror alert system to "Red: Severe" for all flights leaving the United Kingdom to the United States.

Figure 4.3 summarizes the same statistics between the years 2007 and 2010. In contrast to the first 5 years following 9/11/2001, the graph illustrates that people were generally consistent in terms of their perception of threat between 2007 and 2010: 30% to 40% reported the perceived likelihood of imminent terrorism. This is also consistent with a CNN report in 2008 showing that only 35% of Americans

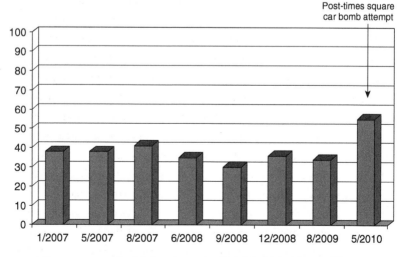

FIGURE 4.3 Percentage reporting it is "very/somewhat likely" the United States will be attacked in the next couple weeks (2007 to 2010).
Source: CNN/Opinion Research Corporation Poll (See http://www.pollingreport.com/terror.htm)

believed a terrorist attack in the United States was likely over the next few weeks (Silverleib, 2008). Silverleib (2008) argued that the CNN poll reflected the fact that terrorism fears within the United States were declining as time increased from 9/11/2001. However, these results are significant for two reasons. First, despite some degree of decline, the presence of fear remained substantial in the general population, continuing to affect at least one out of three people. Second, and perhaps more significant, the graph demonstrates that these fears are sensitive to even foiled attacks, as evidenced by the spike (almost doubling) in fears following the attempted attack on New York City's Time Square in May 2010. Thus, one could argue that the CNN headline "Poll: Terrorism Fears are Fading" (Silverleib, 2008) is misleading to an extent and ignores the impact of specific events that ignite people's fears and insecurities. Perhaps a more accurate assessment would be that people's fears of terrorism appear to be highly influenced by contextual factors that either heighten (such as with an attempted act of terrorism) or ameliorate (such as with extended periods of time without evidence of terrorism) people's worries and concerns.

These patterns do not appear to be consistent across attempted terrorist attacks, which raises further questions about the dynamics that underlie people's fears. For example, Saad (2010) reported that the American public's fears about being victimized by terrorism remained unchanged following an attempt by a Nigerian man to detonate a bomb on a Northwest flight on Christmas Day 2009. As Saad (2010) pointed out, Gallup polls showed that prior to the attack, 39% of Americans reported being "very" or "somewhat" worried that they or a family member would be the victim of terrorism, compared to 42% following the attack in January 2010. This discrepancy in trends may reflect the difference between perceiving that an attack is likely somewhere within the United States (a higher overall perceived probability), as was assessed in the former poll, as opposed to fearing that one is personally vulnerable to an attack (which may be perceived as slightly less likely), which was evaluated in the latter poll. Regardless of these differences, all of these polls demonstrate that many people continue to manifest an ongoing fear about terrorism into the future. As will be discussed further below, these fears have consequences.

FACTORS CONTRIBUTING TO FEAR

It is easy to see, in the months and years following 9/11/2001, how this new zeitgeist of fear has taken root. One need only review the headlines of the day to see this. For example, a December 2008 story in *Newsweek* titled "1900 Days and Counting" consisted of an interview with Sen. Bob Graham, who was at the time co-chairman of a Congressionally appointed bipartisan commission (Isikoff & Hosenball, 2008). Senator Graham stated in this interview that the commission had been developed to assess the risk of weapons of mass destruction being used in a large US city, and the members had interviewed a sizeable international sample of scientists and other academics with expertise in this area. The commission concluded that the probability stood at better than 50%. This is consistent with Professor Graham Allison's (2004, p. 15) assessment in his book *Nuclear Terrorism*, where he noted "... a nuclear terrorist attack on America in the decade ahead is more likely than not."

Some have suggested that terrorism fears have been stoked for political advantage. Although it is unclear whether this was his intention, a *Politico* headline earlier in 2008 read "Giuliani Warns of 'New 9/11/2001' if Dems Win" (Simon, 2007). In this article, former Mayor Giuliani was quoted by Roger Simon (2007) of *Politico* as saying, "The Democrats do not understand the full nature and scope of the terrorist war against us. . . If we are on defense [with a Democratic President], we will have more losses and it will go on longer." Simon (2007) went on to report that after he was more direct with his questioning, Giuliani stated that the United States would be safer with a Republican leader.

A *Washington Post* article in 2008 detailed the contentious debate between then-President George W. Bush and Congress over the authority to wiretap foreigners without approval from US courts (Wolf, 2008). The article detailed how Democratic members of Congress accused the President of using fear to implement more aggressive security policies. Wolf (2008) quoted Bush as responding, "Because Congress failed to act, it will be harder for our government to keep you safe from a terrorist attack."

A number of well-respected academic and government officials have contributed to stoking these fears, as they have presented their assessments of the threat dynamic we face. For example, Harvard Professor Graham Allison (2004) outlined the myriad of ways terrorists could acquire and use a nuclear weapon, and even went so far as to provide an interactive website map where people could enter their ZIP code and plot the different impact/fallout zones of a nuclear weapon detonation (http://www.nuclearterror.org/blastmaps.html). As noted above, he stated that the chances were better than not that a nuclear weapon will be detonated in the coming decade. This is consistent with the statement by former Governor and Chair of the 9/11/2001 Commission Thomas Kean (2005) on the television program *Meet the Press* (May 29, 2005). He cited the same probability, although a slightly narrower time frame.

It appears as though the U.S. government has been faced with this scenario before. Both Allison (2004) and former CIA Director George Tenet (2007) discussed a situation in October 2001, shortly after the 9/11/2001 attacks, where there was intelligence to suggest that a nuclear weapon had already been smuggled into New York City. As a result, government teams were dispatched to search the city for the weapon, although they subsequently came to learn that the intelligence was faulty. As Tenet reported in his 2004 testimony to the US Senate, another "catastrophic" attack on the United States was the objective towards which terrorist groups such as Al Qaeda were working.

Former Senators Gary Hart and Warren Rudman (2002, p. 9) reported shortly after 9/11/2001 that terrorist groups were working towards future attacks that would result in greater damage and loss of life, and that the United States remained "dangerously unprepared." Shortly thereafter, former Secretary of Homeland Security Tom Ridge reported to the press in 2004 that the upcoming political conventions and presidential election would provide multiple symbolic targets for terrorists (Mintz, 2004). Following on this, former Attorney General John Ashcroft and FBI Director Robert Mueller reported in May 2004 that preparations for another terrorist attack were 90% complete, and they would likely occur during the summer.

Former CIA official and Chief of the agency's "Bin Laden Unit," Michael Scheuer (2004), provided a nice discussion of the complicated threat posed by groups such as Al Qaeda in his book *Imperial Hubris*. In it he wrote about how Osama bin Laden sought approval from a cleric in Saudi Arabia to use nuclear weapons against the United States, as justice for what he reported to be 4 million Muslims murdered by Americans in recent history. Scheuer argued that bin Laden went about this as a result of the criticism that was levied against him following the 9/11/2001 attacks, which were not religiously sanctioned in an appropriate manner.

These are only a smattering of the statements and headlines that have been circulated since 9/11/2001. Regardless of how true these statements are, or the context they were made in, these and other headlines illustrate the new cultural dynamic we live in, where the threat of future terrorism remains a primary topic for the media and government officials. While people will surely continue to debate these questions well into the future, the fact that these debates even take place demonstrates that our world has changed in fundamental ways. Issues of security and the terrorism threat have become prominent topics in public discourse, and we argue here that they continue to stoke people's fears in an ongoing and unending way.

PRE-TRAUMATIC STRESS SYNDROME

As noted in greater detail in Chapter 2, most people reporting psychological symptoms consistent with various forms of mood and anxiety disorders return to pre-event levels of functioning. This is evidenced by multiple studies showing that anxiety and depression symptoms return to baseline after spiking immediately after the attacks (Silver et al., 2002; DeLisi et al., 2003). Despite this, the effects of the 9/11/2001 attacks continue to manifest and affect people in different ways as a function of the new threat dynamic that has been created—where academics and government officials alike report on the likelihood of a similar event occurring again. While researchers have noted these declines with respect to the 9/11/2001 attacks as a discrete event, there are very few data assessing the extent to which people are affected by living within this new post-9/11/2001 environment.

One factor that has contributed to this new dynamic has been the implementation of the American color-coded terror alert system. The alert system contains five categories: Green (Low), Blue (Guarded), Yellow (Elevated), Orange (High), and Red (Severe) (the differences between the levels are discussed in Chapter 5). Since its inception, the alert level has stayed primarily on the middle (Yellow) category, although it has been elevated to Orange for specific locales (e.g., New York City) and transit sectors (e.g., air transportation) for the past several years. Although this color-coded alert system was initially developed to help inform the public about the current threat dynamic faced by the country, it soon came under intense criticism.

For example, Stanford Professor and former President of the American Psychological Association Philip Zimbardo reported that the system did more to terrorize the population than terrorism itself (Zimbardo, 2003a, 2003b). He went on to explain that the system failed to provide adequate information as to how to ensure protection and left people feeling intense fear and total lack of control. He also pointed out the interesting dynamic where people were instructed to be vigilant to possible threat around them—on the subway, on an airplane, and so forth—but also to live their lives normally. The resulting phenomenon was one of cognitive dissonance, where the discord in the messages being conveyed left people feeling unsettled. Zimbardo talked about how over time these negative emotions can morph into a more chronic state of fear and anxiety, which has the potential to negatively affect one's mental health. He referred to this phenomenon as a *"pre*-traumatic stress" syndrome, where instead of experiencing psychological distress focused on a past event, the fear is anticipatory in quality and focused on something that has not occurred yet but is expected to happen imminently.

Until recently, there has been no research evaluating the effects of the terror alert system on people's psychological health and well-being. Kramer, Brown, Spielman, Giosan, and Rothrock (2003) were able to assess the psychological symptoms of New York City disaster workers over time; while their study was not originally designed to evaluate the effects of the terror alert system, its longitudinal design allowed them to assess changes in psychological symptoms at different points corresponding to alterations in the alert system. As hypothesized, results suggested a trend in terms of the association between psychological distress and fluctuations in the alert status. These data supported the argument made by Zimbardo (2003a, 2003b) and others (McDermott & Zimbardo, 2007) that the terror alert system has contributed to elevating people's fears above and beyond terrorism itself by repeatedly presenting people with an immediate threat and allowing them no control over mitigating this threat.

More recently, Sinclair and LoCicero (2006) sought to empirically evaluate the issue of anticipatory anxiety, or *pre*-traumatic stress, and found that people were still very much affected by terrorism even 3 years following the 9/11/2001 attacks. In their small study of university undergraduates who were surveyed in 2004, 100% of participants reported that the United States was at least somewhat vulnerable to another attack, 26% reported they personally feared dying in another terrorist attack, and 24% reported they had no control at all in protecting themselves.

Only 6.8% reported that terrorism did not scare them at all, and 20% reported that terrorism was not a threat to them personally. When terror alerts were issued by the government, 61% reported they altered their daily activities at least somewhat, and 82% reported it scared them. Clearly, there is still a psychological effect of living in this new era of terrorism threat.

The second portion of the study examined whether social functioning and health status, acting either as "buffer" or "vulnerability" variables, would predict fears of terrorism after accounting for other covariates. The results supported social functioning and mental health as being significant predictors of terrorism fears, where better social functioning and mental health were associated with less terrorism fear, after accounting for other known covariates. This is supported by the research on trauma, which identifies social functioning and "hardiness" (Bonanno, 2004) as being a significant buffer against the manifestation of psychopathology following traumatic life events (McCann & Pearlman, 1992; Pyszczynski et al., 2003; Ozer et al., 2003). This study presented some of the first evidence for the relationship between social functioning and health status, and fears of new catastrophic terrorism.

THE TERRORISM CATASTROPHIZING SCALE: A MEASUREMENT MODEL FOR ASSESSING TERRORISM FEARS

Recognizing that fear and worry about future terrorism exists in the general population in a meaningful way, separate from more traditional models of mental health, *and* the fact that there has been no method for evaluating these fears or the impact they have on people's lives, Sinclair and LoCicero (2007) developed the Terrorism Catastrophizing Scale (TCS) to contribute to this area of science. As Ruzek, Maguen, and Litz (2006, p. 260) recently argued, "Although some interventions exist to help individuals cope with the aftermath of trauma and terrorism, there is scarce information about how people deal with the ongoing and potential threat of terrorism, especially in communities at risk." Because there is no outcomes research evaluating treatment following terrorist attacks, they made recommendations for interventions that were extrapolated from the existing literature on disaster mental health. Although there is some utility in this approach, Flynn (2004, p. 164) aptly noted that "research is not nearly as extensive and complete as it needs to be and we are far too dependent on extrapolation from other types of traumatic events."

Conceptual Basis of Catastrophizing

As discussed in great detail in Chapter 3, Beck's (1976, 1979) cognitive model assumes that catastrophizing is one specific cognitive style that underlies anticipatory anxiety. With respect to the issue of terrorism, it is the notion that some people engage in a perseverative and amplified thought process about the threat of terrorism. For many, these fears and anxieties affect the ability to function, as was evidenced by Kramer and colleagues (2003) and Sinclair and LoCicero (2006, 2007). Although PTSD rates and other discrete psychological disorders specific to the 9/11/2001 attacks have returned to baseline rates overall, a general fear of future attacks remains elevated, as is evidenced by many of the research studies and polls discussed above. This fear is qualitatively different from PTSD, as it is experienced in anticipation of a future traumatic event. Fremont (2004, p. 381) also discussed this phenomenon, saying, "The unpredictable, indefinite threat of terrorist events, the profound effect on adults and communities, and the effect of extensive terrorist-related media coverage exacerbates underlying anxieties and contributes to a continuous state of stress and anxiety."

Since 9/11/2001 the vast majority of empirical research has focused on understanding the psychological effects of those attacks as a discrete event. There has been less analysis of the effects of anticipating and fearing new terrorism, and how people manage terrorism-related anxiety in a post-9/11/2001 world. Many have recently recognized the lack of assessment and treatment-based research specific to assessment following terrorist attacks, and have been calling for new screening and treatment methodologies that are terrorism-specific, as opposed to the existing models that are extrapolated from disaster mental health, including natural and unintentional human disasters (Flynn, 2004; Bongar, 2006; Ruzek et al., 2006). The TCS was developed as an effort to begin this process of understanding.

TMT would assume that after 9/11/2001 people became very aware of their own mortality (Pyszczynski et al., 2003). As a result of 9/11/2001, people became more and more focused on terrorism as a potential cause of their impending mortality. Those who found great connection with and derived meaning from their culture, and who thought of themselves as significant contributors to this culture, were assumed to have a significant buffer against this existential anxiety. Pyszczynski and colleagues (2003) argued that this was why so many people flew American flags outside their homes or on their cars, were willing to donate blood, traveled to Ground Zero in Manhattan to help out in whatever way they could, and subverted their own needs for the good of the larger culture. In contrast, the TMT model assumes that those without social and cultural connections and with an inherent lack of self-worth were at greater risk for experiencing these anxieties. TMT provides a useful model for understanding the experience of terrorism from a macro view, and raises both social/cultural connections and self-worth as being critical factors in the negotiation of anxiety and fear (Pyszczynski et al., 2003).

On an individual level, Beck's (1976, 1979) cognitive model of psychopathology would assume that those who construct experience in specific ways, using various cognitive distortions as a lens through which to view the world, are more vulnerable to manifesting psychopathology. As has already been noted (Beck, Weissman, Lester, & Trexler, 1974; Beck, Brown, Steer, Eidelson, & Riskind, 1987; Brown et al.,

1992; Beck, 1995; Startup & Davey, 2001; Cottraux, 2004), one of the primary distortions underlying most anxiety disorders is catastrophizing. According to Clark (1986), catastrophizing is a cognitive process focused on misinterpreting future harm, threat, and uncertainty. Because core belief systems, or schemas, about safety are altered by specific acts of terrorism, the cognitive filter screening incoming information distorts the interpretation process of new information. New information is processed in catastrophic terms, and people are often over-whelmed by a sense of helplessness and inability to stop focusing on the threat (rumination). Based on this model, it would be expected that individuals who spend a lot of time thinking and worrying about future terrorism would be more likely to experience psychopathology, including anxiety and other mood disorders such as depression. However, there is no standard measure of catastrophizing related to the experience of terrorism.

In developing their measure of catastrophizing, specifically as it pertains to the experience of pain and stress (the Pain Catastrophizing Scale), Sullivan and colleagues (1995) noted that there is a general lack of consensus for how to define catastrophizing (Najavits, Gotthardt, Weiss, & Epstein, 2004). However, existing research has focused on three interrelated concepts in their definitions: magni-fication, rumination, and helplessness. Sullivan and colleagues (1995) and others (Osman et al., 1997, 2000) have tested this model repeatedly and in different settings, and have provided strong empirical support for it. The TCS is rooted in Beck's cognitive model of psychopathology and uses the three-factor model derived by Sullivan and colleagues (1995) as a general conceptual framework, which includes the Magnification, Rumination, and Helplessness subscales.

Magnification is a cognitive pattern whereby people tend to amplify the risk of something in their mind, often to an extent that is inconsistent with the actual threat posed. With respect to terrorism, it is the notion that the threat of terrorist violence only gets worse over time and is perceived as a highly probable event. **Rumination** is the extent to which people perseverate or focus their thinking on the threat posed by terrorism. In the extreme case, one cannot think about much else and terrorism occupies a significant amount of one's thought process. Finally, **helplessness** has to do with the perception that despite any efforts that are made, one really has no sense of control over this threat and is vulnerable to it in an ongoing way.

Development of the TCS

The TCS was developed in a multi-stage process in which items for each of these three constructs were developed and refined through initial psychometric testing. From the original pool of 21 items, 13 items were retained for scaling based on con-firmatory factor analysis (CFA) and a comprehensive evaluation of scaling assump-tions (Campbell & Fiske, 1959; Nunnally & Bernstein, 1994; Ware et al., 1997). Normative data from the general U.S. population were then collected in 2006 for

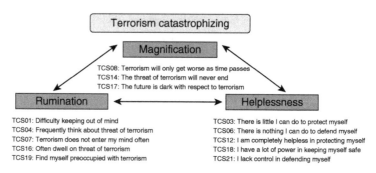

FIGURE 4.4 The Terrorism Catastrophizing Scale ($k = 13$).

the final version of the scale. The Rumination and Helplessness subscales each contain five items, while the Magnification subscale contains three items. Each of these individual subscales is scored and then aggregated into an overarching Catastrophizing score.

Figure 4.4 presents the measurement model for the 13-item TCS, and specifically how the items map onto their respective constructs. The full TCS is given in Figure 4.5. More information about the TCS, including greater detail about its

Currently, how much do you agree or disagree with the following statements? *Please mark one box on each line*				
	Strongly agree	**Agree**	**Uncertain**	**Disagree**	**Strongly disagree**
1. I have difficulty keeping the threat of terrorism out of my mind.	☐1	☐2	☐3	☐4	☐5
2. There is little I can do to protect myself from terrorism.	☐1	☐2	☐3	☐4	☐5
3. I frequently think about the threat of future terrorism.	☐1	☐2	☐3	☐4	☐5
4. There is nothing I can do to defend myself from future terrorist attacks.	☐1	☐2	☐3	☐4	☐5
5. The threat of terrorism does not enter my mind that often.	☐1	☐2	☐3	☐4	☐5
6. I worry that terrorism will only get worse as time passes.	☐1	☐2	☐3	☐4	☐5
7. I think that I am completely helpless in protecting myself from future terrorism.	☐1	☐2	☐3	☐4	☐5
8. I worry that the threat of terrorism will never end.	☐1	☐2	☐3	☐4	☐5
9. I often dwell on the threat of future terrorism.	☐1	☐2	☐3	☐4	☐5
10. I believe the future is dark with respect to the threat of terrorism.	☐1	☐2	☐3	☐4	☐5
11. I have a lot of power in keeping myself safe from terrorism.	☐1	☐2	☐3	☐4	☐5
12. I frequently find myself preoccupied with thinking about terrorism.	☐1	☐2	☐3	☐4	☐5
13. I lack control in defending myself and my loved ones against terrorism.	☐1	☐2	☐3	☐4	☐5

FIGURE 4.5 The Terrorism Catastrophizing Scale (TCS).

development and scoring methodology, is available elsewhere (LoCicero, Brown, & Sinclair, 2009; Sinclair, 2010; Sinclair & LoCicero, 2007, 2010a, 2010b).

One major advantage of the TCS is its scoring methodology: all subscales are scored to have a mean of 50 and a standard deviation of 10 in the general population. As a result, meaningful comparisons can be made in terms of how a person's score compares to that of the population, as well as how someone's scores vary across each of the subscales. For example, someone with a TCS score of 60 falls one standard deviation above the population average and is in the 84th percentile. This means that this person is reporting fear (as operationalized by the TCS) at or above 84% of other people in the United States. One can also evaluate the specific sub-dimensions of catastrophizing to see how a specific person is affected by the threat of terrorism. For example, someone may tend to explode the threat in his or her mind (magnification) and feel helpless as a result (helplessness), but may exhibit little tendency to think about the threat (rumination) and may in fact show more of a tendency to avoid reminders of this altogether. In contrast, another person may be flooded with thoughts about terrorism (rumination) and may tend to magnify the threat of terrorism and experience helplessness as a result.

Another important assumption underlying the construct, particularly as it relates to hypothesis testing using inferential statistics, is that of normality, the notion that scores are evenly distributed in the general population. As shown in Figure 4.6, this assumption was met, with the majority of people falling within the average range (scores of 40 to 60), and fewer people falling within the "tails" of the distribution (i.e., less than 40 or greater than 60). Another important aspect of this graph is the notion that very few people experience *no* fears about terrorism in the population.

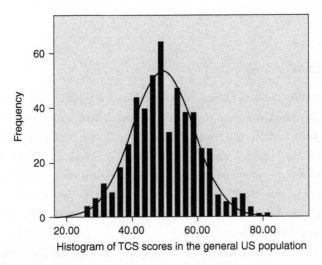

FIGURE 4.6 Distribution of Terrorism Catastrophizing Scale scores in the general U.S. population.

Using the TCS

One of the major lessons learned from the 9/11/2001 events was that there was a general lack of understanding of how to assess people at risk and respond to them in a helpful manner. One primary purpose of the TCS was to develop a measurement model for evaluating these fears, which is linked to existing psychological treatments such as cognitive-behavioral therapy (CBT). For example, the TCS would have been an ideal instrument to assess anticipatory anxiety in the recent study conducted by Somer, Tamir, Maguen, and Litz (2005) that compared phone-based CBT and treatment as usual for a sample of Israeli citizens who were experiencing anticipatory fears about future terrorist attacks and who called into an Israeli crisis hotline. Results from the study indicated that CBT was significantly better in ameliorating the negative effects of anticipating terrorism compared to treatment as usual. The development of a tool such as the TCS would allow researchers and practitioners to quickly assess the extent to which people are affected by terrorism and to streamline treatment approaches to focus on specific underlying psychological processes. For example, someone high in magnification but low in helplessness might benefit more from a cognitive restructuring approach to modify existing beliefs about threat. In contrast, someone low in magnification but high in helplessness might respond better to behavior modification with a goal of achieving a greater degree of (perceived) control.

The tool also provides a sort of ruler for measuring the impact of terrorist attacks; this would be useful for assessing the magnitude of change from a normative standard. As Bongar (2006, p. 6) pointed out, "At present the psychological science needed to provide proper and effective treatment for victims of horrendous events such as September 11 . . . simply does not exist." The TCS is proposed here as a model for evaluating people's fears following terrorist attacks, which subsequently can be used to inform individual treatment and more global policy decision-making.

Implications

The TCS contributes to the literature in several key ways. First, it is the first known, theoretically rooted, empirically validated, and psychometrically sound measure of terrorism fears to date. As a result, and in contrast to the bulk of the literature to date, which has evaluated discrete psychological disorders specific to individual attacks, this new measurement system allows for the assessment of ongoing, general fears of terrorist violence. The resulting measure allows for systematic evaluation of fears in any population, and for meaningful comparisons (both within-person and across groups) to be made as a result.

A second implication of this research is the preponderance of fear in the population, despite claims made by academics that psychological distress in the general population has subsided to pre-attack levels. For example, Sinclair and LoCicero (2007) reported that only 9.8%, 6.0%, 2.4%, and 0.2% scored at the floor (i.e., reflecting absolutely no fears) for the Rumination, Magnification, Helplessness, and Overall Catastrophizing scales, respectively. These results are consistent with the social science and polling research discussed above, which also reported the prevalence of these fears, separate from the psychological and public health research that has suggested this return to normal.

Third, and following on the tenets of TMT, this research by Sinclair and LoCicero (2007) demonstrated that factors including self-efficacy and social connectedness were significant buffers against fear, and helped people maintain psychological equanimity in the context of threat. This follows much of what we know about the trauma literature at large, which has indicated that people who have access to more social supports and see themselves as hardy individuals are less likely to succumb to negative mental health outcomes. This in part likely relates to the issue of control, and the ability of people to affect their environments in meaningful ways. It stands to reason that those who see themselves as lacking control and social supports are more at risk for experiencing fear.

Fourth, and following the model of CBT, this research demonstrated that those more likely to engage in catastrophic thinking about the ongoing terrorist threat were more at risk for developing symptoms of depression, anxiety, and physiological stress. Similarly, and likely related to an underlying PTSD process, people more affected by terrorism fears were more likely to change their behaviors as a means of achieving a greater sense of control and safety (e.g., avoiding public places, not using public transportation, etc.). These findings may also explain in part the findings by Boscarino and colleagues (2003), who noted that very few people made preparations for a terrorist attack—perhaps as another manifestation of avoidance.

Finally, from the standpoint of psychological and public health intervention, this research illustrates the need for people to be assessed differently and for these assessment methodologies to be directly linked to mental health treatment models. Walser and colleagues (2004) outlined how CBT would be an intervention of choice following a terrorist attack. They borrowed from Ehlers and Clark's model (2003, p. 59) and focused on:

"1) identifying and testing problematic beliefs about the long-term effects of trauma and personal symptoms experienced post-trauma; 2) organize and complete the trauma memory in order to integrate it into one's life; and 3) overcome the avoidance, safety behaviors, and ruminations that prevent memory elaboration, exacerbate symptoms, and interfere with reappraisals of beliefs."

As noted above, Somer and colleagues (2005) published one of the first known quasi-experimental studies evaluating CBT for people experiencing anticipatory fears about future terrorism in Israel. CBT was implemented as a treatment of choice because of its widespread application in treating anxiety and mood disorders (Beck, 1979; Brown et al., 1992; Startup & Davey, 2001; Garnefski et al., 2001). They assessed whether brief phone-based CBT interventions helped reduce people's fears more than treatment-as-usual models, and as hypothesized the CBT treatments were found to be superior. This study is significant because it also highlights the fact that people are presenting to mental health professionals because of fear and anticipatory anxiety about impending terrorism. However, the research lacked a specific measurement system for fear and instead relied on existing instruments designed to assess symptoms of PTSD.

Given its documented success in treating anxiety and mood symptoms (Brown et al., 1992; Startup & Davey, 2001; Garnefski et al., 2001) as well as terrorism fears specifically (Somer et al., 2005), the TCS would be an ideal tool for these kinds of studies. First, it would provide a measurement system that is directly associated with the treatment, as well as a specific method for measuring treatment outcomes. Second, it allows mental health professionals to identify and understand the degree to which people catastrophize about terrorism in general, but also how they are affected in sub-domains such as rumination, magnification, and helplessness. Interventions could then be tailored to the individual based on impact within and across domains.

THE IMPACT OF TERRORISM FEARS

As discussed above, there is clear evidence from both social science and polling research to suggest that terrorism fears in the general population were significant in the months and years following 9/11/2001. In many of these studies, rates of people experiencing these fears far surpassed those meeting criteria for specific forms of psychological disorders, and many in the academic community have questioned whether these fears reflected unique psychological sequelae not currently accounted for by existing mental health models (North & Pfefferbaum, 2002; Marshall et al., 2007). Only recently has research begun to emerge documenting the impact these fears have on people's lives. This section details some of this emerging research.

As part of the process that led to the development of the TCS, one of the authors (SJS) conducted a large-scale survey of the general U.S. population in 2006 and collected a variety of clinical and demographic information separate from the TCS. Several key findings emerged from this research. First, fear (as measured by the TCS) was found to be a significant predictor of symptoms of anxiety, depression, and general physiological stress after accounting for other demographic and clinical variables. This would suggest that people who experience high levels of fear following a terrorist attack will be more vulnerable to developing specific forms of psychopathology, including mood and anxiety disorders.

Second, and consistent with TMT (Pyszczynski et al., 2003), Sinclair and LoCicero (2007, 2010a, 2010c) found that people who had low self-esteem and who lacked meaningful social connection were more at risk for catastrophizing about terrorism. These results are consistent with the TMT literature, as well as the literature on trauma more globally, which has repeatedly found that factors such as social belonging and "hardiness" (Bonanno, 2004) have served as buffers to anxiety and negative mental health outcomes.

Finally, and perhaps more significant, results indicated that people who express more fears were more likely to alter their lives in significant ways. For example, people reporting elevated fears were more likely to avoid public places such as malls or restaurants; traveling by public transportation (i.e., airplanes, trains, subways); working or living in populated areas; and socializing with others perceived as dissimilar to one's cultural group. Figure 4.7 presents adjusted TCS scores (controlling for demographic and other clinical correlates; see Sinclair & LoCicero, 2007, 2010a, 2010c) across groups of people who reported changing their behaviors within these domains versus those who reported no change.

The results reported by Sinclair and LoCicero (2007) are consistent with those of Eisenberg and colleagues (2009). Eisenberg and colleagues extended these findings by demonstrating that certain demographic groups within the population will be more vulnerable to terrorism fears and will be more likely to exhibit avoidance behaviors as a result of these fears. These groups included a variety of different ethnic minority groups, people who are disabled or who suffer from a mental illness, and those who are not U.S. citizens but who are living in the United States. Overall, this research is consistent with the broader study of the psychological effects of terrorism, where many of these same groups were also seen to be vulnerable to

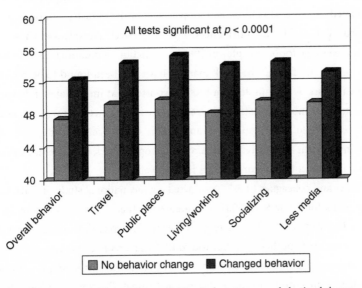

FIGURE 4.7 Adjusted mean Terrorism Catastrophizing Scale scores across behavioral change groups.

specific forms of psychopathology (e.g., PTSD) following terrorist attacks. From a public health standpoint, they illustrate the fact that some groups may require additional support following terrorist incidents.

Terrorism fears have been shown to affect the political spectrum as well. As noted above, Toner and Elder (2001) reported that in a December 2001 *New York Times/CBS News* poll, roughly two thirds of those queried said they were in favor of granting the US President additional powers to change the constitution to keep the nation safe, and the same amount also thought the government should be allowed to monitor conversations between suspects and their lawyers. Approximately 80% also supported the indefinite detention of terror suspects.

This pattern reflects the tendency of people to place more trust in their governments to keep them safe from future violence following large-scale terrorist attacks (Chanley, 2002; Chanley, Rudolph, & Rahn 2000; Sinclair & LoCicero, 2010b). For example, Chanley and colleagues (2000) noted prior to the attacks that overall trust in government had declined markedly, but that 9/11/2001 had primed people's fears to such an extent that trust in government "rose to a level not seen since the mid-1960s" (Chanley, 2002, p. 469). Sinclair and LoCicero (2010b) sought to empirically test this phenomenon and demonstrated that fears of terrorism and the impact of changes in the government's color-coded alert system were found to be significant predictors of trust in government for protection. The authors explained these findings within the context of both attachment theory and evolutionary psychology, where people are motivated to seek a sense of security from an authority figure when in the presence of significant threat.

Fears of terrorism following a terrorist attack have also been shown to affect the economy. For example, in the years following 9/11/2001, airlines suffered billions of dollars in losses and were forced to lay off tens of thousands of employees. Congress was forced to pass a $15 billion bailout package for the industry, although it can be debated whether this had much effect. Two airlines (US Airways and United) were also forced to file for bankruptcy in 2002 as a function of plummeting revenues and more people not flying. The stock markets have also been found to be sensitive to terrorism fears. For example, Lim (2004) reported that immediately following the location of a bomb beneath the train tracks in Paris in 2004, the Dow Jones Industrial Average declined by 80 points. Granted, this event occurred after the Madrid bombings, which also likely played a role in people's fears, but it demonstrated the economic impact that terrorism fears have as well.

Lerner and colleagues (2003) conducted a large, national study of Americans in the months following 9/11/2001 to evaluate whether different emotions (fear vs. anger) had different effects in terms of people's perceptions of risk and policy preferences. As hypothesized, they found that fear predicted greater perceived risk than anger, and was associated with greater preferences for taking precautionary, conciliatory measures to reduce the external threat. Findings also indicated that people exhibited greater optimism in the context of increased anger, and greater pessimism in the context of fear. One of the explanations for these patterns is that, unlike fear, anger may lead people to experience a greater locus of control over their environment. In contrast, increased fear was associated with less perceived control.

CONCLUSIONS

A central thesis of this volume is that although rates of various forms of psychopathology have normalized following large-scale acts of terrorism, anticipatory fear and distress over further acts of terrorism have remained in the population. The degree to which it has remained and the impact it has on people has varied as a function of the different methods employed to evaluate this phenomenon. Regardless, this pattern has been replicated in numerous empirical research and polling studies, both within the United States and abroad.

Only recently have people begun to understand the impact of these fears on people's lives, in part through the development of specific measurement models to evaluate fear explicitly—as distinct from discrete forms of psychiatric illness. Overall, these data indicate that people continue to report ongoing anticipatory fear and distress associated with the terrorism threat, even if they do not meet full criteria for a psychiatric diagnosis. These studies also suggest that as a function of fear, people will become more likely to alter their behaviors and routines, as well as beliefs about political issues and trust in the government, among other things. This pattern of findings supports the argument made by Marshall and colleagues (2007, p. 305), who noted that "the presence of persistent fears in the general population of being personally harmed in future terrorist attacks is a poorly understood phenomenon that may represent a vulnerability in the general population."

In some of the international conferences we have attended since 9/11/2001, we have become more familiar with the debate over using terms such as "terrorism"— mainly because of the pejorative quality often attached to it. We have also recently heard arguments that the term itself is inaccurate in terms of describing the phenomenon. In particular, we have heard the perspective that "terror" is too strong a word to use to describe what is probably more accurately mild fear or anxiety, as well as the fact that using such terms ignores the reality that only a small cross-section of people in the population have been shown to manifest negative psychological effects over time. The argument is that most people are not "terrorized," so the terms have no meaning or relevance.

As many before us have pointed out, both defining the term "terrorism" on the one hand and efforts to generate another more accurate term on the other hand have proved challenging, with little consensus to date. Although we do hold a position within these debates, the purpose of this volume is not to discuss the meaning of "terrorism" but rather to demonstrate that people are fearful of terrorism and that these fears have consequences. In doing so, we would like to take the opportunity to present a different perspective on some of the arguments made by Rapin (2009), who summarized some of the same literature presented in this volume and reached different conclusions.

First, and perhaps most significant, in his review of the literature on the psychological effects of various terrorist attacks in the past decade, Rapin (2009, p. 171) ultimately makes the argument that "the attacks turned out to produce no objectively verifiable major public health crisis." However, as Marshall and colleagues (2007) noted, it is critical to remember that many of the statistics presented both by Rapin (2009) and in this volume represent rates of PTSD and other forms of psychological distress *specific* to events such as 9/11/2001, and in many cases they match or even exceed *lifetime* prevalence rates presented in the DSM-IV-TR (APA, 2000). That is to say, contrary to Rapin's (2009) argument that the psychological impact of various terrorist attacks was not "proportional to the intensity of the attacks," much of the research reviewed in this volume would suggest otherwise.

Following on this point, Rapin (2009) appeared to conflate symptoms of psychopathology with the more general experience of fear and stress, and appeared to make the point that based on the former it could be argued that the psychological impact of terrorism has been more limited than expected. However, as Marshall and colleagues (2007) argued, additional studies have documented the significant experience of fear in the population even after accounting for discrete forms of psychopathology—much of which is also summarized above. For example, Rapin (2009) neglected to cite or discuss two of the largest research studies following the 9/11/2001 attacks, which evaluated the issue of fear specifically and how people have been affected in areas such as New York City. By excluding this research and focusing on conventional models of psychopathology almost exclusively, Rapin (2009) presented a one-sided picture of the data. As Marshall and colleagues (2007) and others (e.g., North & Pfefferbaum, 2002) have noted in this regard, recent acts of terrorism do not map well onto existing mental health paradigms, and further development is needed to fully appreciate the psychological impact of terrorism. Thus, it seems somewhat premature of Rapin (2009) to suggest that terrorism has not led to the "objectively verifiable" crisis that was expected.

Rapin (2009) went on to discuss work by Schmid and Jongman (2005), who postulated that the psychological fallout from terrorism is not what is relevant, but rather that the intention of the person committing the act is what delineates whether it is an act of terrorism. That is to say, they argued that the intention of instilling fear for some other purpose is what determines whether the violent act (or threat of violence) is terrorism. Rapin (2009, p. 172) provided the example of hostage-taking as being an act of terrorism without the inherent objective of instilling fear, saying, "The aim of the hostage taker is neither to terrify their victims nor to intimidate the general population." Rapin (2009) argued that the objective of the hostage-takers is rather to place themselves in a position of strength to negotiate their demands, whatever they may be. There are two flaws with respect to this argument.

First, how does he know this to be true at all, and true of all hostage-takers? Does this not exemplify the same problem of trying to apply a blanket definition to a phenomenon that is laden with nuances, as with "terrorism"? Second, one could counter Rapin's (2009) argument and say that the means by which hostage-takers place themselves in a position of advantage from which to negotiate their demands is through the fear they instill in those with whom they are negotiating. The pressure placed on those in authority who are the focus of negotiations for the hostage-taker is rooted in the distress and perhaps even fear that a hostage will be harmed or killed in the process. To make the statement, as Rapin (2009, p. 172) did, that "authorities are not frightened by the situation" assumes both that Rapin knows what the authorities are feeling and that fear is never a part of this experience and is simply nonsensical. In essence, he made the same mistake that many do within the context of the terrorism debate: he attempted to provide some broad definition to a phenomenon that is inherently complex and nuanced.

In his analysis, Rapin (2009) also called into question whether terms such as "fear," "distress," "stress," and terror are synonymous. He also raised the issue that in some studies the terms "feeling upset" contain a different emotional valence from terms used in other research (e.g., "feeling *very* upset"). Finally, Rapin (2009) pointed out that in some of the studies that have evaluated fear and distress levels in the population, there has been a disconnect between the magnitude of fear and/or distress reported and the "excessively alarming picture presented." Rapin (2009) pointed out that in some of this research only minor levels of fear/distress are reported along the Likert scales that were used, and this is seemingly inconsistent with the conclusions drawn from this research.

All of these points are quite valid, and in fact we agree that these reflect some of the complexities that exist in terms of how we evaluate and understand fear in the population—as a function of terrorism. We also agree that there needs to be an ongoing discussion about how we define and characterize terms such as "terrorism," as well as the psychological sequelae that ensue, for purposes of informing and refining research methodology and response paradigms into the future. That being said, there are problems with this line of argument.

First, if fear and distress exists in minor form or major form, does it not still exist? And, if it exists, is there not reason to believe that these fears have consequences, as has been found in preliminary research (Sinclair & LoCicero, 2007)? We understand the basic premise that Rapin (2009) was trying to make, specifically that even mild fears are being characterized as underlying "terror" (and how this may be misleading), but would argue that these fears are significant in many ways—as was detailed above. Second, and perhaps more significant, this argument relies on averages reported across different studies and fails to acknowledge that some within the population distribution reside within the tails (the outliers) and experience these fears in more intense, severe terms. Because the average of those sampled reported only minor fears, does this preclude the fact that others are affected more acutely?

Finally, and related to this last point, Rapin (2009) seems to imply that because the psychological effects of terrorism are "inconsistent" across groups exposed to terrorist violence (due in part to differing methodologies, as Rapin pointed out), the fact that most did not manifest a clear-cut experience of "terror" would indicate that the term does not adequately apply. Bleich and colleagues (2003) recently came under some criticism for inadequately defining "terrorism" in their study of Israelis who were affected by terrorism, and concluded: "Unfortunately, terrorism is usually a legitimate cause for some, and a curse for others. This does not make it less dreadful for those who live with its consequences and clearly does not make it an unscientific subject of study." Following on this comment, we would respectfully submit in light of Rapin's (2009) argument that even though many people are not affected by terrorism in an acute, severe way, there are people who do experience a sense of fear and terror as a result. Thus, to redefine the category of violence in a way that is less emotionally valenced would mean to mischaracterize these people's experiences. Thus, while we agree with Rapin (2009) that there continues to be a need to debate these terms and their larger meaning, terrorism is terrifying for some people even if not for all people.

REFERENCES

Allison, G. (2004). *Nuclear terrorism: The ultimate preventable catastrophe.* New York: Times Books.

American Psychiatric Association. (2000). *Diagnostic and statistical manual of mental disorders- Fourth edition-Text revision.* Washington, D.C.: American Psychiatric Association.

Associated Press (2008). Panel: Biological attack likely by 2013. Retrieved Dec. 2, 2008, from http://msnbc.com.

Beck, A. T. (1976). *Cognitive therapy and the emotional disorders.* New York: Basic Books.

Beck, A. T. (1979). *Cognitive therapy of depression.* New York: The Guilford Press.

Beck, J. S. (1995). *Cognitive therapy: Basics and beyond.* New York: Guilford.

Beck, A. T., Brown, G., Steer, R. A., Eidelson, J. I., & Riskind, J. H. (1987). Differentiating anxiety and depression: A test of the cognitive-content specificity hypothesis. *Journal of Abnormal Psychology, 96,* 179–183.

Beck, A. T., Weissman, A., Lester, D., & Trexler, L. (1974). The measurement of pessimism: The hopelessness scale. *Journal of Consulting and Clinical Psychology, 42,* 861–865.

Bleich, A., Gelkopf, M., & Solomon, Z. (2003). Exposure to terrorism, stress-related mental health symptoms, and coping behaviors among a nationally representative sample in Israel. *Journal of the American Medical Association, 290,* 667–670.

Bonanno, G. A. (2004). Loss, trauma, and human resilience. *American Psychologist, 59,* 20–28.

Bongar, B. (2006). The psychology of terrorism: Describing the need and describing the goals. In B. Bongar, L. Brown, Beutler, L., J. Breckenridge, & P. Zimbardo (Eds.), *The psychology of terrorism* (pp. 3–12). Oxford: Oxford University Press.

Boscarino, J. A., Adams, R. E., Figley, C. R., Galea, S., & Foa, E. B. (2006). Fear of terrorism and preparedness in New York City 2 years after the attacks: Implications for disaster planning and research. *Journal of Public Health Management Practice, 12,* 505–513.

Boscarino, J. A., Figley, C. R., & Adams, R. E. (2003). Fears of terrorism in New York after the September 11 attacks: Implications for emergency mental health and preparedness. *International Journal of Emergency Mental Health, 5*, 199–209.

Brown, T. A., Antony, M. M., & Barlow, D. H. (1992). Psychometric properties of the Penn State Worry Questionnaire in a clinical anxiety disorders sample. *Behaviour Research & Therapy, 30*, 33–77.

Burnham, J. (2007). Children's fears: A pre 9/11/2001 and post 9/11/2001 comparison using the American Fear Schedule Survey for Children. *Journal of Counseling and Development, 85*, 461–466.

Campbell, D. T., & Fiske, D. W. (1959). Convergent and discriminant validation by the multitrait-multimethod matrix. *Psychological Bulletin, 56*, 81–105.

Chanley, V. A. (2002). Trust in the government in the aftermath of 9/11/2001: Determinants and consequences. *Political Psychology, 23*, 469–483.

Chanley, V. A., Rudolph, T. J., & Rahn, W. M. (2000). The origins and consequences of public trust in government: A time series analysis. *Public Opinion Quarterly, 64*, 239–256.

Clark, M. M. (1986). Personal therapy; A review of empirical research. *Professional Psychology: Research and Practice, 17*, 541–543.

Conejero, S., & Etxebarria, I. (2007). The impact of the Madrid bombings on personal emotions, emotional atmosphere and emotional climate. *Journal of Social Issues, 63*, 273–287.

Cottraux, J. (2004). Recent developments in the research on generalized anxiety disorder. *Current Opinion in Psychiatry, 17*, 49–52.

DeLisi, L. E., Maurizio, A., Yost, M., Papparozzi, C. F., Fulchino, C., Katz, C. L., et al. (2003). A survey of New Yorkers after the September 11, 2001 terrorist attacks. *American Journal of Psychiatry, 160*, 780–782.

Ehlers, A., & Clark, D. M. (2003). Early psychological interventions for adult survivors of trauma: A review. *Biological Psychiatry, 53*, 817–826.

Eisenberg, D. P., Glik, D., Ong, M., Zhou, Q., Tseng, C., Long, A., Fielding, J., & Asch, S. (2009). Terrorism-related fear and avoidance behavior in a multiethnic urban population. *American Journal of Public Health, 99*, 168–174.

Flynn, B. (2004). Commentary on "A national longitudinal study of the psychological consequences of the September 11, 2001 terrorist attacks: Reactions, impairment, and help-seeking. Can we influence the trajectory of psychological consequences to terrorism?" *Psychiatry, 67*, 164–166.

Fremont, W. P. (2004). Childhood reactions to terrorism-induced trauma: A review of the past 10 years. *Journal of the American Academy of Child and Adolescent Psychiatry, 43*, 381–392.

Garnefski, N., Kraaij, V., & Spinhoven, P. (2001). Negative life events, cognitive emotion regulation and emotional problems. *Personality and Individual Differences, 30*, 1311–1327.

Hart, G., & Rudman, B. (2002). *America still unprepared—America still in danger.* Retrieved Nov. 8, 2002, from http://www.cfr.org/publication.php?id=5099.

Isikoff, M., & Hosenball, M. (2008). 1900 days and counting. Retrieved Dec. 3, 2008, from http://www.newsweek.com/2008/12/01/1900-days-and-counting.html.

Kean, T. (2005). Transcript from *Meet The Press,* May 29, 2005. Retrieved June 22, 2004, from www.msnbc.com.

Kramer, M. E., Brown, A. D., Spielman, L., Giosan, C., & Rothrock, M. (2003). Psychological reactions to the national terror alert system. *The ID, 1*, 67–70.

Lerner, J. S., Gonzalez, R. M., Small, D. A., & Fischhoff, B. (2003). Effects of fear and anger on perceived risks of terrorism: A national field experiment. *Psychological Science, 14*, 144–150.

Lim, P. J. (2004). *Scared street: Terrorism fears spook the stock market.* Retrieved Dec. 2, 2008, from http://www.usnews.com.

LoCicero, A., Brown, A. J., & Sinclair, S. J. (2009). Fear across America in a post-9/11/2001 world. In M. J. Morgan (Volume and Series Ed.), *The impact of 9/11/2001 on psychology and education: The day that changed everything?*(pp. 97–113). New York: Palgrave MacMillan.

Marshall, R. D., Bryant, R. A., Amsel, L., Suh, E. J., Cook, J. M., & Neria, Y. (2007). The psychology of ongoing threat: Relative risk appraisal, the September 11 attacks, and terrorism-related fears. *American Psychologist, 62,* 304–316.

McCann, I. L., & Pearlman, L.A. (1992). Constructivist self development theory: A theoretical framework for assessing and treating traumatized college students. *Journal of American College Health, 40,* 189–196.

McDermott, R., & Zimbardo, P. G. (2007). The psychological consequences of terrorist alerts. In B. Bongar, L. Brown, L. Beutler, J. Breckenridge, & P. Zimbardo (Eds.), *The psychology of terrorism* (pp. 357–370). Oxford: Oxford University Press.

Mintz, J. (2004). *Precautions raised for preelection terrorism.* Retrieved April 20, 2004, from http://www.washingtonpost.com.

Najavits, L. M., Gotthardt, S., Weiss, R. D., & Epstein, M. (2004). Cognitive distortions in the dual diagnosis of PTSD and substance use disorder. *Cognitive Therapy and Research, 28,* 159–172.

North, C. S., & Pfefferbaum, B. (2002). Research on the mental health effects of terrorism. *Journal of the American Medical Association, 288,* 633–636.

Nunnally, J. C., & Bernstein, I. H. (1994). *Psychometric theory* (3rd ed.). New York: McGraw-Hill.

Osman, A., Barrios, F. X., Gutierrez, P. M., Kopper, B. A., Merrifield, T., & Grittman, L. (2000). The Pain Catastrophizing Scale: Further psychometric evaluation with adult samples. *Journal of Behavioral Medicine, 23,* 351–365.

Osman, A., Barrios, F. X., Kopper, B. A., Hauptmann, W. Jones, J., & O'Neill, E. (1997). Factor structure, reliability, and validity of the pain catastrophizing scale. *Journal of Behavioral Medicine, 20,* 589–605.

Ozer, E. J., Best, S. R., Lipsey, T. L., & Weiss, D. S. (2003). Predictors of posttraumatic stress disorder and symptoms in adults: A meta-analysis. *Psychological Bulletin, 129,* 52–73.

Polling Report. (2005). *War on terrorism polling reports.* Retrieved July 12, 2010, from www.pollingreport.com/terror.htm

Pyszczynski, T., Solomon, S., & Greenberg, J. (2003). *In the wake of 9/11/2001: The psychology of terror.* Washington, D.C.: American Psychological Association.

Rapin, A. J. (2009). Does terrorism create terror? *Critical Studies in Terrorism, 2,* 165–179.

Richman, J. A., Cloninger, L., & Rospenda, K. M. (2008). Macrolevel stressors, terrorism, and mental health outcomes: Broadening the stress paradigm. *American Journal of Public Health, 98,* 323–329.

Rubin, G. J., Brewin, C. R., Greenberg, N., Hughes, J., Simpson, J., & Wessley, S. (2007). Enduring consequences of terrorism: 7-month follow-up survey of reactions to the bombings in London July 7, 2005. *British Journal of Psychiatry, 190,* 350–356.

Rubin, G. J., Brewin, C. R., Greenberg, N., Simpson, J., & Wessley, S. (2005).Psychological and behavioural reactions to the bombings in London on July 7, 2005: cross sectional survey of a representative sample of Londoners. *British Journal of Psychiatry.* Retrieved Dec. 1, 2010, from http://www.bmj.com/content/331/7517/606.abstract.

Ruzek, J. I., Maguen, S., & Litz, B. T. (2006). Evidenced based interventions for survivors of terrorism. In B. Bongar, L. Brown, Beutler, L., J. Breckenridge, & P. Zimbardo (Eds.), *The psychology of terrorism* (pp. 3–12). Oxford: Oxford University Press.

Saad, L. (2010). U.S. fears of terrorism steady after foiled Christmas attack. Retrieved Aug. 5, 2010, from http://www.gallup.com/poll/125051/u.s.-fear-terrorism-steady-after-foiled-christmas-attack.aspx.

Scheuer, M. (2004). *Imperial hubris.* Washington, D.C.: Brassey's, Inc.

Schuster, M. A., Stein, B. D., Jaycox, L. H., Collins, R. L., Marshall, G. N., Elliott, M. N., et al. (2001). A national survey of stress reactions after the September 11, 2001 terrorist attacks. *New England Journal of Medicine, 345*, 1507–1512.

Silver, R. C., Holman, E. A., McIntosh, D. N., Poulin, M., & Gil-Rivas, V. (2002). Nationwide longitudinal study of psychological responses to September 11. *Journal of the American Medical Association, 288*, 1235–1244.

Silverleib, A. (2008). *Poll: Terrorism fears are fading.* Retrieved Dec. 2, 2008, from http://cnn.site.printthis.clickability.com.

Simon, R. (2007). Giuliani warns of "new 9/11/2001" if Dems win. Retrieved Nov. 11, 2008, from http://www.politico.com/news/stories/0407/3684.html.

Sinclair, S. J. (2010). Fears of terrorism and future threat: Theoretical and empirical considerations. In D. Antonius, A. D. Brown, T. Walters, M. Ramirez, & S. J. Sinclair (Eds.), *Interdisciplinary analyses of terrorism and aggression* (pp. 101–115). Cambridge, England: Cambridge Scholars Publishing.

Sinclair, S. J., & LoCicero, A. (2006). Development and psychometric testing of the Perceptions of Terrorism Questionnaire Short-Form (PTQ-SF). *New School Psychology Bulletin, 4*, 7–43.

Sinclair, S. J., & LoCicero, A. (2007). Anticipatory fear and catastrophizing about terrorism: Development, validation, and psychometric testing of the Terrorism Catastrophizing Scale (TCS). *Traumatology, 13*, 75–90.

Sinclair, S. J., & LoCicero, A. (2010a). Do fears of terrorism predict trust in government? *Journal of Aggression, Conflict and Peace Research, 2*, 57–68.

Sinclair, S. J., & LoCicero, A. (2010b). The Terrorism Catastrophizing Scale (TCS): Assessing the ongoing psychological impact of terrorism. In L. Baer & M. Blais (Eds.), *Handbook of clinical rating scales and assessment in psychiatry and mental health* (pp. 278–285). Boston: Humana Press.

Somer, E., Tamir, E., Maguen, S., & Litz, B. T. (2005). Brief cognitive behavioral phone-based intervention targeting anxiety about the threat of an attack: A pilot study. *Behaviour Research and Therapy, 43*, 669–679.

Startup, H. M., & Davey, C. L. (2001). Mood as input and catastrophic worrying. *Journal of Abnormal Psychology, 110*, 83–96.

Sullivan, M. J. L., Bishop, S. R., & Pivik, J. (1995). The Pain Catastrophizing Scale: Development and validation. *Psychological Assessment, 7*, 524–532.

Tenet, G. (2004). *The worldwide threat 2004: Challenges in a changing global context.* Retrieved March 10, 2004, from http://www.cia.gov.

Tenet, G. (2007). *At the center of the storm: My years at the CIA.* New York: Harper Collins Publishers.

Toner, R., & Elder, J. (Dec. 1, 2001). Public is wary but supportive on rights curbs. *New York: Times,* p. 1.

Walser, R. D., Ruzek, J. I., Naugle, A. E., Padesky, C., Ronell, D. M., & Ruggiero, K. (2004). Disaster and terrorism: Cognitive-behavioral interventions. *Prehospital and Disaster Medicine, 19*, 54–63.

Ware, J. E., Harris, W. J., Gandek, B. L., Rogers, B. W., & Reese, P. R. (1997). *MAP-R Multitrait/Multi-item analysis program—revised.* Boston, MA: The Health Assessment Lab.

Wolf, J. (2008). Democrats accuse Bush of fanning terrorism fears. Retrieved Dec. 2, 2008, from http://www.washingtonpost.com/wp-dyn/content/article/2008/02/16/AR2008021601830.html.

Zimbardo, P. (2003a). *Overcoming terror.* Retrieved February 2004 from http://www.brucekluger.com/PT/PT-OvercomingTerror-JulAug2003.html

Zimbardo, P. (2003b). *The political psychology of terrorist alarms.* Retrieved February 2004 from http://www.zimbardo.com/downloads/2002%20Political%20Psychology%20of%20Terrorist%20Alarms.pdf

5 Communicating Warning
The Art and Science of Threat Dissemination

"Today, the dangers extend beyond states alone to transnational security threats that respect no borders. These are threats that can arise from any part of the globe and spread anywhere, including to our own shores."
President Barack Obama (2008)

Life in New York City or Boston—or for that matter anywhere in the world—in the aftermath of September 11, 2001, was a time of constant reminders of the threat of terrorism. Not only did people in New York, Washington, D.C., and Pennsylvania experience terrorism firsthand, but most Americans and people worldwide were faced with constant media coverage about the event and the potential threats of new terrorist attacks that loomed in the near future. For many people, the world had become an unsafe place and terrorism came to the fore as the most significant threat to society.

This national and international sense of foreboding was exacerbated for many Americans and people worldwide when the anthrax attacks started 1 week following the 9/11/2001 attacks (United States Department of Justice, 2010a, 2010b). Letters laced with anthrax spores targeted numerous people in the media, as well as Senators Tom Daschle and Patrick Leahy, in this *bio*terrorist attack. In the end, the anthrax letter attacks killed 5 people and sickened 17. Perhaps even more significant, this act of bioterrorism instilled fear in many using the postal systems in both the United States and worldwide, as well as anyone handling letters. It also highlighted the many vulnerabilities that are manifest in defending against acts of terrorism.

Shortly after the anthrax attacks, Americans were once again reminded of the threat of terrorism when the "shoe bomb plot" was uncovered in December 2001. Flying from France to the United States, English-born Richard Reid, a self-admitted member of Al Qaeda, attempted to detonate explosives hidden in his shoes onboard a commercial aircraft. Fortunately, he was subdued by fellow passengers and airline personnel, although the event itself served as a reminder of the threat faced by many people.

Extensive media coverage after a large crisis event, such as the 9/11/2001 attacks, is of course to be expected in today's media-driven society. In fact, information-seeking behavior is common among the general public during crises; citizens use this information to restore some sense of normality in their life (Lachlan, Spence, & Seeger, 2009). This puts a tremendous pressure on those who construct and convey messages and warning signals about potential terrorist threats. By definition, these communications by government officials and other media sources are threatening, and depending on how they are crafted and disseminated, they may serve to instill fear (either by design or inadvertently) and disrupt normal behavior and daily life. As we will discuss in depth in this chapter, threat communication can be used to instill a sense of optimism and control on the one hand, and pessimism and fear on the other hand, depending on how the message is developed and conveyed.

Any dissemination of terrorism threat information must be based on thorough risk assessment. As stated by Willis (2006) in written testimony to the House Financial Services Committee, Subcommittee on Oversight and Investigations, and the House Homeland Security Committee, Subcommittee on Intelligence, Information Sharing, and Terrorism Risk Assessment, risk assessment should be analytic, deliberative, and practical. He further explained that to determine terrorism risk, the analytic process needs to address the threat, vulnerability, and consequence; the deliberative process should include transparency in reporting values and judgments and comprehensive discussion about outcomes; and the practical process refers to tenable data collection and management requirements that do not rely on only a single perspective or tool.

As part of obtaining more reliable information about risk and terrorist threat, government officials have approached people in academia to develop empirical and theoretical paradigms to help predict and respond to large-scale terrorist attacks (Antonius & Sinclair, 2009). The research in this area has increased substantially in the past 9 years, and today novel scientific information is being disseminated daily by a myriad of academic institutions and organizations, both nationally and internationally and across different academic disciplines. This theoretical and empirical work is critical for improving our understanding of the underlying mechanisms of terrorism and political aggression, as knowledge about how terrorism affects the public and governments may have a significant impact on current government policies.

In this chapter, we will describe and critically discuss the system created for communicating warnings of terrorist threats in the United States: the U.S. Department of Homeland Security Advisory System. We will also provide a brief description of a few other national terrorism alert systems, those of United Kingdom and France in particular. Further, we will discuss the effectiveness of a national alert system as it relate to the issue of terrorism threat, including the potential benefits of such a system and the negative consequences of threat messages and the impact they may have on the public. We will explore whether there are better alternatives to national terrorism alert systems, and whether it is time to eliminate the current terrorism threat alert system in the United States. Within this framework, we will also discuss scientific evidence from risk appraisal theorists showing the divergent influences threat messages may have, depending on the content of the messages, and how this may affect the public in different ways.

THE U.S. DEPARTMENT OF HOMELAND SECURITY ADVISORY SYSTEM

In the aftermath of 9/11/2001, the American government developed the Homeland Security Advisory System (officially established on March 12, 2002) in an attempt to provide a system that would inform the government, local authorities, and the general public about the current risk of terrorism (United States Department of Homeland Security, 2008). One of the primary purposes for the development of this alert system was to create a common language about national threat that all entities (including the government and the public) would understand. The goal was also to develop and install an alert system that would facilitate decision-making for individuals living and working across a wide array of public and private sectors.

The Homeland Security Advisory System provides warnings in the form of threat conditions, which are based on existing information about the risk of a terrorist event. For each threat condition, the federal departments and agencies have a set of protective measures they are ready to implement. There are five threat conditions based on level of risk, each identified by a color: (1) low level of threat = green; (2) guarded level of threat = blue; (3) elevated level of threat = yellow; (4) high level of threat = orange; and (5) severe level of risk = red (Fig. 5.1).

As one might expect, these threat conditions likely have significant effects on all aspects of society, and we will discuss this in more detail later in this chapter. The important responsibility for evaluating, deciding, and assigning level of threat resides with the U.S. Attorney General and the Assistant to the President for Homeland Security. However, before a decision is made and a corresponding threat level assigned, these officials also seek advice from other parties who are selected because they are considered experts in the field or because they have special knowledge immediately relevant to the potential threat. The assignment of threat level is primarily based on qualitative measures, and various factors are evaluated, including the degree to which the threat information is credible; the extent to which the threat information is corroborated; how specific and/or imminent the threat is; and

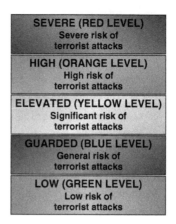

FIGURE 5.1 The U.S. Department of Homeland Security Advisory System. (Adapted from Department of Homeland Security, 2008.)

how grave the potential consequences of the threat are (United States Department of Homeland Security, 2008).

Initially, these threat levels were assigned to the entire nation, but this was modified such that a threat condition could be set for a limited geographical area or a particular industrial sector. For example, after the general threat level went down to an elevated (Yellow) level after 9/11/2001, New York City's threat level continued to be higher due to the assessed risk for future attacks in this specific region. At the time of writing this book, the national threat level is elevated (Yellow), while the threat level for all domestic and international flights is high (Orange; United States Department of Homeland Security, 2010). The US Department of Homeland Security reviews the threat levels periodically to ensure the appropriateness of the assigned threat condition.

The Threat Conditions

As mentioned above, each threat level is associated with the implementation of particular protective measures that are put into operation by the federal departments and agencies. The individual departments and agencies are responsible for developing their own set of appropriate measures, such that in the event of a terrorist attack they are prepared for a quick, effective, and suitable response. The specific protective measures are outlined annually in written reports that the federal departments and agencies are required to submit for evaluation to the President of the United States.

The low (Green) threat condition is assigned when there generally is a low risk of a terrorist attack occurring. At this level, the federal departments and agencies are mainly refining and organizing their protective measures plans and making sure that personnel and institutions are prepared for potential terrorist attacks. In their

"Citizen Guidance on the Homeland Security Advisory System" (United States Department of Homeland Security, 2009), the U.S. Department of Homeland Security suggests that during low risk levels, citizens should develop an emergency plan, be informed about shelters, and consider completing first aid/CPR courses should an incident occur.

At the guarded (Blue) level there is no clear risk of terrorism, but there is an insignificant general threat of an attack. Following on the requirement of the low risk level, the federal departments and agencies check, review, and update emergency responses and command locations. They also provide the public with information that will help individuals make the appropriate choices in the event of an attack. The "Citizen Guidance" (United States Department of Homeland Security, 2009) recommends that individuals store disaster supplies and be alert to any suspicious activity.

A significant risk of terrorism is present if the threat level is at the elevated (Yellow) condition. At this level, it is recommended that the federal departments and agencies increase surveillance of key locations, coordinate and prepare emergency plans with nearby jurisdictions, and re-evaluate their protective measures while also implementing new contingency and emergency response plans. Citizens are recommended to ensure that their emergency plans and emergency kits are up to date and that they have alternate routes to and from work, school, and other places they frequent.

At the high (Orange) condition there is an increased risk for a terrorist event. The protective measures at this level include close collaboration between federal, state, and local law enforcement agencies, as well as, if appropriate, the United States National Guard and the U.S. armed forces. Moreover, these agencies should be ready to quickly execute contingency procedures should disaster occur. The public is recommended to exercise extra precautions at public events and to consider alternate venues or events. The "Citizen Guidance" (United States Department of Homeland Security, 2009) advises individuals to be careful when traveling, to expect delays and baggage searches, and to expect certain restrictions at public buildings.

The severe (Red) level of threat is assigned only if there is a severe risk of a terrorist attack. At this level of threat, the protective measures call for increasing personnel who can address emergency needs and assigning them to the potentially critical areas. The federal departments and agencies will increase monitoring of the transportation systems and will be prepared to redirect or constrain these systems if necessary, as well as to close down public and government facilities that might be at risk. Citizens are recommended to stay tuned to radio and TV announcements and to be prepared for contingency procedures, including evacuation (United States Department of Homeland Security, 2009). Citizens are also warned to expect traffic delays and restrictions when traveling, and they are asked to provide volunteer services for which they are qualified.

OTHER ALERT SYSTEMS FOR TERRORISM THREATS

The U.S. Homeland Security Advisory System is not the only alert system that has been developed to assess the international threat of terrorism; other countries have also established terrorism alert systems. The United Kingdom Home Office has its own alert system for terrorism threats. Similar to that of the United States, the United Kingdom's system is also divided into five alert levels based on the significance of a threat and the possibility that an attack may occur: low, moderate, substantial, severe, and critical threat (United Kingdom Home Office, 2010).

France also uses a color-coded scheme similar to that of the United States to alert its citizens and government agencies about terrorism threats (de l'administration Française, 2010). Their system, "Vigipirate," has four levels: yellow indicates a low and imprecise risk, orange signifies a moderate or plausible risk, red denotes a probable risk, and scarlet represents a certain and imminent threat.

EFFECTIVENESS OF A TERRORISM THREAT ALERT SYSTEM

How effective is a terrorism threat alert system such as the Homeland Security Advisory System? Does it serve the purpose for which it was created, to warn the government and the public about potential terrorist threats? Do the advantages of having an alert system outweigh the disadvantages? These are important questions when considering and evaluating a terrorism alert system. The intentions behind the development of a terrorism alert system are undoubtedly positive. Clearly, the aim is to prevent future disasters and/or to be prepared in the best possible way should a terrorist attack take place. However, some critics have argued that a terrorist alert system may also serve the unfortunate and unwarranted purpose of actually eliciting or increasing terrorism fears and anxieties in the general public (Pena, 2002; McDermott & Zimbardo, 2007).

For example, Kramer and colleagues (Kramer, Brown, Spielman, Giosan, & Rothrock, 2003) conducted a study on the psychological reactions to the Homeland Security Advisory System in the aftermath of 9/11/2001 and found that increases in the national alert level from elevated to high were related to reports of increased physiological arousal, anxiety, and depression in a small sample of New York City disaster-relief workers. The authors pointed out that this was an interesting if not peculiar result when taking into account that the terror threat level was continuously high (and not elevated) in New York City during the time of the study. Therefore, one may not have expected any change in psychological reactions. The results, however, did indicate that changes in the national threat level may have a local effect. In this case the increased national threat appeared to be alarming to the disaster-relief workers, even though the actual threat in New York City remained the same.

This study by Kramer and colleagues (2003) suggested that, at the very least, there may be an association between elevated terrorism threat levels, as communicated by our government through this alert system, and negative psychological reactions such as fear and anxiety in certain groups of the population. This raises the question of whether some subgroups of the general population are more vulnerable to the effects of a national terrorism alert system. That is, are there subgroups of the population who are affected in more significant ways by ongoing threat of terrorism, and who may be more deeply influenced by a national terrorism alert system?

Eisenman, Glik, Ong, Zhou, Tseng, and other colleagues (2009) examined this question in a large sample of 2,317 people in the Los Angeles area. The authors were interested in examining whether vulnerable groups such as people with mental illness, people with disabilities, non-White racial/ethnic groups, and immigrants would be more susceptible to threats of terrorism and would subsequently avoid activities because of terrorism fears. They explored the fear of terrorism based on the participants' responses to questions about the current level of the Homeland Security Advisory System. The results showed that certain groups within the population—those who are mentally ill, those who are disabled, African Americans, Latinos, Chinese Americans, Korean Americans, and non-U.S. citizens—were more likely to perceive higher terrorism risk levels (severe or high levels, even though the actual level was only elevated) compared to the subjects of White ethnicity. In other words, these specific populations overestimated the actual threat of terrorism, perhaps making them more vulnerable to this ongoing threat and susceptible to fear. Adding further support to this contention, additional analyses demonstrated that these populations reported more worry about terrorist attacks and higher rates of avoidance behaviors due to terrorism concerns.

The study by Eisenman and colleagues (2009) is important because it demonstrates the potential negative effects a national terrorism alert system may have in certain "vulnerable" populations. Other research has shown that prolonged levels of worry, avoidance, and fear or symptoms of anxiety may lead to more chronic medical conditions (Wells, Golding, & Burnam, 1989), cardiac events (Strik, Denollet, Lousberg, & Honig, 2003), and/or substance abuse (Grant, Stinson, Dawson, Chou, Dufour, et al., 2004), just to name a few of the potential problems associated with this kind of response.

Boscarino, Adams, Figley, Galea, and Foa (2006) examined the relationship between perceived threats of terrorism and terrorist fears and preparedness in 1,681 individuals in New York City 2 years after 9/11/2001. Although the authors did not specifically explore the effects of the national terrorism alert system, the study findings revealed that almost half of the study participants continued to be very concerned about future attacks. However, and despite the high number of people who were concerned, only 14.8% had made specific preparations for future attacks. This might be surprising in the context of the national alert system being on high alert in New York City at the time of the study (as pointed out in the 2003 Kramer et al. study), and given the protective measures that are recommended when the alert system is on the high condition. However, 14.8% was actually an improvement from the 5.4% found in an earlier study done 1 year post-9/11/2001 by the same authors (Boscarino, Adams, & Figley, 2004).

Boscarino and colleagues (2006) found that terrorism fears were particularly high in Hispanics and in those who had less education, reported more negative life events within the past 12 months (e.g., divorce, death of spouse, problems at work), met criteria for post-traumatic stress disorder, had a fear of death, and were among the people who (in a hypothetical scenario) would flee a disaster area after a weapons of mass destruction attack even though they were recommended to do otherwise. Prior exposure to traumatic events, including 9/11/2001, was a predictor of *better* preparedness, however: these people reported having made plans for future disasters.

These findings are generally in support of the results reported by Eisenman and colleagues (2009) and suggest that some subgroups of the population are more vulnerable to the stress of dealing with terrorist threats and terrorist fears. More importantly, the Eisenman and colleagues (2009) and Boscarino and colleagues (2006) studies may have implications for the development of national terrorism alert systems and response procedures. That is, should an attack take place, it would be important to know that specific groups of people may require more substantial and different kinds of support and assistance during both actual terrorist attacks and periods of heightened threat.

There is preliminary scientific evidence to support the notion that job environment and/or one's occupation may influence the reaction to terrorism threat. In another study of the psychological impact of the Homeland Security Advisory System, Omer, Barnett, Castellano, Wierzba, Hiremath, Balicer, and Everly (2007) found that elevated alert status was not associated with increased stress in law enforcement personnel. This may suggest that certain groups of people, perhaps those who have a profession in which they are more prone to stressful situations, are better (psychologically speaking) equipped to handle potential crisis situations such as a terrorist attack or period of heightened terrorism threat. Although it is unclear from this study, it may be that the combination of training for stressful events and experiencing high levels of daily stress makes those working in law enforcement better psychologically prepared to cope with the threats of terrorism.

In a study from the United Kingdom, Kearon, Mythen and Walklate (2007) examined the public reaction to an advice booklet sent out by the United Kingdom government to 25 million households. The booklet provided information about what to do in preparation for major emergencies such as terrorist attacks. Even though the booklet was meant to convey information about what to do in general emergency situations, the authors found that the public became "firmly fixed on the sections of the booklet that discussed chemical, biological, and radiological attacks." Although the majority of the participants found the booklet informative, only about half found it helpful, with 86% finding that the booklet provided commonsense advice. Only 19% found that the government's strategy for communicating terrorist threat was effective.

ELIMINATING THE NATIONAL TERRORISM ALERT SYSTEM: ARE THERE BETTER ALTERNATIVES?

In a review of the Homeland Security Advisory System, Aguirre (2004) argued that the five-color alert system is inadequate to communicate the actual threat of potential terrorist attacks. Aguirre pointed out the lack of appropriate methodology to determine what the most useful warning messages are, as well as the system's ineffectiveness in communicating useful information to the media, local and state emergency agencies and politicians, and the general public. Aguirre also argued that the protective measures outlined by the Department of Homeland Security are too vague and unspecific, and thus have limited implications for how agencies and citizens are to react and respond in the case of an actual terrorist threat. Aguirre argued that instead of serving its intended purpose, the Homeland Security Advisory System functions more as a mitigation tool that is used by the government to discourage terrorist attacks by informing terrorist groups that the United States is prepared for any type of attacks (Aguirre, 2004).

Whether Aguirre's critique of the Homeland Security Advisory System is warranted and accurate is a matter of debate. However, an important question is whether there are better ways of informing the government and the public of potential threats. Several scholars (Perry & Lindell, 2003; Aguirre, 2004) have suggested that policy and government officials should look at warning and response systems to natural disasters (e.g., earthquakes, floods, avalanches, and volcanic eruptions) and technological disasters (e.g., oil spills, nuclear reactor accidents, and transportation accidents). The psychological impact of such disasters, as well as more general threats to public safety (e.g., crime and war), has been widely studied. For example, it is well known that some threats are more fear-inducing than others (Slovic, Fischhoff, & Lichtenstein, 1980). It is also known that fear is a common and expected emotional response during a disaster (Perry & Lindell, 2003). Despite experiencing fear, the majority of people affected by a disaster, regardless of the type of disaster, respond constructively and rationally (Goltz, Russell, & Bourque, 1992; Johnson, Feinberg, & Johnston, 1994); and crime rates have actually been found to decline in some cases after a disaster (Tierney, Lindell, & Perry, 2001).

The fact that most people do respond in a rational and controlled manner may be part of the problem faced by the Homeland Security Advisory System (Perry & Lindell, 2003). This alert system was developed after the U.S. government and the President of the United States came under enormous pressure following 9/11/2001. There was a public outcry that "something" had to be done immediately to prevent acts of terrorism. Government officials grew concerned about citizen panic and irrational behavior, and thus the alert system was created, in part, to avoid such counterproductive reactions (Perry & Lindell, 2003). However, as we pointed out above, it is atypical for humans to respond to major disasters with panic and irrational behavior. Instead, many people seem to prefer to engage in pro-social behavior in the immediate time after a terrorist attack (Perry & Lindell, 2003) and help those who are psychologically or physically injured. Thus, part of the reason the alert system was created may be based on false premises.

As discussed in Chapter 3, terror management theory (TMT) provides a nice discussion for why this might be the case and highlights the motivation of people to seek the company of those around them as a means of managing their fears of death or annihilation (Pyszczynski, Solomon, & Greenberg, 2003). As Pyszczynski and colleagues discussed in their book *In the Wake of 9/11/2001*, this explains why there was a strong showing of patriotism and fellowship following the 9/11/2001 attacks.

Some academics (Pena, 2002; Aguirre, 2004) have argued for the elimination of the Homeland Security Advisory System. Instead, they have proposed better education of the public about terrorist threats and the impact of potential terrorism scenarios. Improving public education may serve an ancillary goal: to replace the focus on terrorism fears, which we know is a common and expected response (Perry & Lindell, 2003), with a focus instead on human resilience, which we will discuss in Chapter 6.

In September 2009, a task force from the U.S. Department of Homeland Security Advisory Council (2009) released a report condemning the color-coded alert system. They stated that a national terrorism alert system is needed and that the current system has functioned "reasonably well" (p. 1). However, they concluded that the alert system needs an overhaul and does a poor job in communicating useful information to the general public: "at its best, there is currently indifference to the Homeland Security Advisory System and, at its worst, there is a lack of public confidence in the system" (p. 1). For a national terrorism alert system to function, the public must take the system seriously. Thus, the task force argued, "this lack of public confidence must be remedied" (p. 1).

The task force recommended a rethinking of the color-coded alert system (Homeland Security Advisory Council, 2009). Among their recommendations were (1) a more geographically narrow alert system, to avoid elevating the alert system for the whole nation; (2) more specific information about terrorism threats, including the type of threat and the credibility of the source; and (3) information about the government's plans to mitigate the threat as well as protective steps the general public can take. The task force also recommended reducing the number of alert levels from five to three: guarded, elevated, and high alert. This would, they contended, enhance public confidence in the alert system. It should also be taken into account that since the implementation of the system, the alert level has never been lowered to low (Green) or guarded (Blue).

Towards the end of 2010, the media began speculating that the Department of Homeland Security was preparing to terminate the current system and instead was considering a two-level system (Bennett, 2010). On January 27, 2011, the Secretary of Homeland Security, Janet Napolitano, announced that a new terrorism alert system would replace the color-coded alert system in the near future (Ryan & Thomas, 2011). In the new system, referred to as the National Terrorism Advisory System, there are two tiers: "elevated threat" and "imminent threat." Any elevation in the alert system will carry with it specific information about the potential threat, actions taken to ensure public safety, and response recommendations. Moreover, in the new alert system the threats can be limited to certain sectors (e.g., law enforcement, malls, mass transportation, etc.) or the general public. This change in the alert system was, in part, based on the findings of the task force.

RISK APPRAISAL AND THREAT DISSEMINATION

As we have highlighted above, for a national terrorism alert system to be effective we must understand the emotional effects, both negative and positive, it may have on citizens. As risk appraisal theory stipulates, different emotions may affect individuals' responses to risk and threats differently (Smith & Ellsworth, 1985; Lerner & Keltner, 2001). Research has demonstrated that individuals' negative emotions are often associated with pessimistic risk assessments, whereas positive emotions are more often related to optimistic assessment of risk and threat (Johnson & Tversky, 1983), although sometimes negative emotions can trigger optimism (Lerner & Keltner, 2001).

Two emotions that have received extensive attention by appraisal theorists are fear and anger. Fear is associated with appraisals of uncertainty and situational control, whereas anger is related to appraisals of certainty and individual control (Lerner & Keltner, 2001). Thus, in other words, fear and anger may evoke opposite responses in individuals, one being positively and optimistically-valenced and the other being negative and pessimistic. This finding alone is of critical importance when thinking about constructing and disseminating information about terrorism threat. That is, depending on what the message conveys and how it is conveyed, a national terrorism alert system can have major consequences on citizens' responses to the threat.

In the aftermath of 9/11/2001, Lerner, Gonzalez, Small, and Fischhoff (2003) examined the differential effects of fear and anger on the perceived risk of terrorism in a representative sample of 973 Americans. In the study, participants were given vignettes that were experimentally manipulated to induce fear or anger emotions related to the 9/11/2001 attacks. Thereafter, the participants were asked to judge the likelihood that (1) future terrorist events would occur in the United States, (2) they would experience risky events and precautionary actions, and (3) the average

American would experience risky events and precautionary actions. The participants were also asked to evaluate four potential government policies.

The results showed major effects for both fear and anger and significant differences between the two emotions. First, the authors found that the emotion primes (the vignettes) increased the target emotion (fear or anger). Second, and perhaps not too surprisingly given the close proximity in time to the 9/11/2001 attacks (all data were collected within 4 months of the attacks), anger was found to be the most dominant emotion across the experimental conditions. Third, the male participants were found to be more optimistic than the female participants, with the latter group exhibiting larger overall risk estimates. Last, and most importantly, induced anger was associated with reduced risk estimates and plans for precautionary measures, whereas induced fear correlated with an increase in risk estimation and plans for precautionary actions. In other words, the findings suggested that anger triggered greater optimism and fear triggered more pessimism. The study also demonstrated that fear and anger predicted diverging government preferences: participants who were in the induced-anger condition, compared to those in the induced-fear condition, were more likely to support a vengeful deporting policy and less likely to support a conciliatory contact policy.

Through the lens of risk appraisal theory and Lerner and colleagues' study, it is not hard to see how government messages can be manipulated to evoke a certain public response, and how messages put out by a national terrorism alert system may have potential harmful effects. Messages and reports put forth by TV, radio, newspapers, or other media outlets may have similar effects. Therefore, it is important that any threat dissemination, whether through a national alert system or the media, takes into account the emotional effects it may have on the general public, as well as politicians. It is also important for the public to be educated in how to respond to the dissemination of threats at different levels, such as the different levels in the Homeland Security Advisory System.

THE EFFECT OF PERCEIVED THREAT AND THE EXPERIENCE OF ANXIETY

The emotional experiences of fear or anger are not the only psychological reactions that have been studied with regards to psychological reactions to terrorism and the influence it may have on policymaking. Huddy, Feldman, Taber, and Lahav (2005) examined the perception of threat and the experience of anxiety in a large sample of American adults from October 2001 to March 2002. The survey, which was administered via phone interviews, asked questions about the perceived threat of future terrorist attacks, terrorists' use of biological or chemical weapons in future attacks, and an individual's concern that he or she, or a friend or relative, would be affected by the terrorist strike. Participants were also asked what effects the 9/11/2001 attacks had on their personal safety and security and whether they experienced anxiety symptoms when thinking about 9/11/2001. Other questions related to views on military action against terrorists, approval of President George W. Bush, involvement in the world, surveillance of Americans (and Arabs), restrictions on immigration, and civil liberties.

The results were what most people would expect: that most Americans perceived a high level of threat for future terrorist attacks, and many were concerned that this would be a biological or chemical attack. Many Americans were concerned that they, or a friend or relative, would be affected by a future terrorist attack. Paralleling the larger clinical literature on this issue, this study also demonstrated that a minority of people expressed considerable increased anxiety in response to the 9/11/2001 attacks—again suggesting there may be a subset of people who are more at risk for negative outcomes. More importantly, the study findings showed that as perceived threat increased, so did the support for military action against terrorism, curtailment of civil liberties, increased surveillance, and stricter immigration restrictions for Arabs. Conversely, high levels of anxiety were associated with less support for military action, increased American isolationism, and increased disapproval of President George W. Bush's performance.

This study provides further support for the power that lies within the messages being communicated by the government: the perception of a high threat for terrorism would likely facilitate public support for aggressive policies by the government. This has been shown by several research studies both in the United States (Herrmann, Tetlock, & Visser, 1999) and elsewhere (Friedland & Merari, 1985). As Huddy and colleagues (2005) stated, "The Bush administration seemed aware of this link and issued terrorist alerts into the early months of 2002, perhaps helping to explain why the perceived risk of terrorism remained relatively high throughout the study period." However, Huddy and colleagues (2005) also pointed out that there is a fine line in disseminating these threats in the context of such high anxiety and fear, as the end result may be reduced public support for the government and its actions. Other studies have also argued that the rhetoric from politicians and White House officials matters in terms of getting public support for aggressive and military measures of response, although this may be influenced by political awareness (Drury, Overby, Ang, & Li, 2010).

Fischer, Greitemeyer, Kastenmüller, Frey, and Oßwald (2007) tested the notion that perceived terror threat can influence people's opinion of what government responses would be appropriate. They examined whether people's perceptions of what punishments for crimes would be appropriate (the crimes were unrelated to terrorism) would vary based on induced terror salience, experimentally measured by (1) distance in days from the London 2005 terrorist attack; (2) various levels of manipulated newspaper vignettes about expected terror risk, and (3) responses to pictures depicting terror acts versus neutral pictures. Their findings showed that higher terror salience increased the likelihood that participants would assign stronger punishment to people violating criminal laws, even though the violations were unrelated to terror. The authors showed that carefully inducing a terror threat can have a significant public influence on the perception of what a socially accepted reaction to the threat would be on the part of citizens.

In a study from Israel, Friedland and Merari (1985) found that although terrorism produced expected high levels of fear and worry, the effects were counterproductive to what was intended: instead of producing desired changes in attitudes, most people became supportive of "extreme counterterrorist measures." This study demonstrated that terrorism, and the threat of terrorist attacks, can be used as a powerful tool of political influence on citizens.

DOES DISTANCE FROM TERROR TARGET INFLUENCE THE PERCEPTION OF THREAT?

Another factor that needs to be taken into account is the distance people live from the epicenter of a potential terror target. Obviously, people living in certain geographical regions that are *not* primary targets of terrorism may feel less fear and sense of threat due to the lower risk of an attack. However, the closer one gets to the epicenter of a terror target (e.g., New York City), the higher the likelihood for psychological stress reactions. This research was documented at length in Chapter 2.

Fischhoff, Gonzales, Small, and Lerner (2003) found that judgments of terror risks, but not routine risks (e.g., getting the flu, being a victim of a violent crime, and dying from any cause), were associated with the distance that a participant lived from the World Trade Center. Those who lived within 100 miles of the World Trade Center perceived higher terror-related risk (e.g., being hurt in a terror attack, trouble sleeping because of terrorism, traveling less because of the fear of terrorism, screening mail carefully due to fear of bioterrorism, and taking antibiotics for anthrax) compared with those living further away. Similarly to the Eisenman and colleagues (2009) and the Boscarino and colleagues (2006) studies discussed above, Fischhoff and colleagues (2003) found that certain subgroups are less sensitive to terror risks, particularly if they live further away. Fischhoff and colleagues found that lower risk perception was associated with being male, adult, white, and Republican.

With respect to the issue of communicating threat information, these findings are significant for several reasons. First, they indicate that specific communications should be targeted differentially to specific communities and regions that may vary as a function of both threat and sense of risk. Second, the study again highlights the fact that groups vary along a myriad of continuums in terms of how they perceive threat, and may be more or less vulnerable psychologically to this threat. As a result, they may be prone to different types of reactions and response when threat communications are disseminated. The bottom line is that a general message for everyone may not be the best method for disseminating threat information, and that messages should be tailored to the specific region and population for which they are intended.

CHANGES IN PUBLIC PSYCHOLOGICAL RESPONSES TO TERRORISM THREAT OVER TIME

With the extensive media coverage of crisis events, has the public response to the ongoing terrorism threat changed compared to prior to 9/11/2001 and with respect to other national disasters? Smith and Rasinski (2002) compared people's reactions to the 9/11/2001 attacks with that of another American tragedy: the assassination of President John F. Kennedy in November 1963. Like the 9/11/2001 attacks, the assassination profoundly affected the citizens of the United States as well as the international community.

Smith and Rasinski (2002) demonstrated the similarities in public responses to these two incidents. Around 75% of Americans felt that their daily activities were disrupted, and many people felt four or more stress and anxiety symptoms, including crying, nervousness, trouble sleeping, upset stomach, increased smoking, headaches, increased heartbeat, forgetting things, and losing their temper more often. People felt more angry (angry that someone could do this) after the 9/11/2001 attacks than after the Kennedy assassination, but more ashamed (that this could happen in the United States) after the Kennedy assassination than after the 9/11/2001 attacks. Although this may reflect differences in the type of attacks, it may also reflect a generational shift in the psychological reactions in the general public.

TYPE OF THREATS AND INFORMATION BEING DISSEMINATED: ARE WE PREPARED FOR FUTURE ATTACKS?

The key question has become whether we are better prepared now for a possible terrorist attack than we were before 9/11/2001. We raise this question in light of numerous recent reports that terrorism is still likely to occur in the United States. For example, in a national survey in the summer of 2008, CNN found that 35% of Americans believed a terrorist attack would occur in the United States in the next few weeks of when they were assessed (Silverleib, 2008). (Chapter 4 presented multiple other scientific and polling studies that have reported similar results.) Although this number actually represented a decline compared with a previous CNN survey, the high number of Americans believing that an attack is imminent indicates that terrorism, and the threat of terrorist attacks, continues to be a primary concern for many citizens.

Authorities have also argued that it is likely that terrorists will attempt to get their hands on and use chemical, biological, radiological, or nuclear weapons (also referred to as weapons of mass destruction). For example, in 2009 the U.S.

Commission on the Prevention of Weapons of Mass Destruction Proliferation and Terrorism stated that it was likely that terrorists would deploy a nuclear or biological weapon within the next 5 years somewhere around the globe (Associated Press, 2008). Following on this, Carpintero-Santamaría (2010) stated in an editorial that there is a good possibility that nuclear and radioactive materials may end up in the hands of terrorists, and that they will attempt to use these materials to make "radiological dispersion devices" (so-called dirty bombs).

With reports like these, the method for developing and disseminating communications to the public becomes of paramount importance. As we have already discussed, the dissemination of terrorism threat communications can have severe consequences on the general public, depending on the content of the message. Inappropriately phrased and presented messages can enhance negative psychological outcomes within the population (as discussed in Chapters 2 and 4) and can decrease the likelihood that people will make the sorts of preparations that are recommended (see Boscarino et al., 2004, 2006). This latter finding runs contrary to the intention of many of these communications. Messages may have paradoxical and even counterproductive effects that deserve further study by those in charge of developing them.

Following on this and in a more global sense, most U.S. federal agencies, as well as the international community, were surprised by the 9/11/2001 attacks, despite some anticipation of terrorism manifest around the turn of the millennium. Consequently, one could argue that the response to 9/11/2001 was very much developed in the moment, and some have argued that it was inadequate. Similarly, United States counterterrorism and law enforcement agencies were poorly prepared for the anthrax letter attacks, as well as the shoe bomb plot. While we have no desire to enter into this debate, the issue of preparation and response are now front and center as we plan for future acts of terrorism.

This also raises the question of whether national and international communities, and the various emergency and responder agencies, are prepared for future acts of terrorism—particularly with respect to the threat posed by weapons of mass destruction falling into the hands of terrorist groups. The answer to this is of course that we will never know until another attack takes place. However, it is clear that national and international responder agencies have learned from previous attacks, and 10 years after 9/11/2001 they are better prepared for the ever-evolving terrorist threat (Mueller, 2010). An essential part of this process, however, is that any threat of terrorism conveyed by authorities to the public is based on thorough and adequate information.

SUMMARY

Federal agencies' and departments' ability to communicate terrorist warnings effectively to the public and the government can be extremely beneficial to a country's preparedness for strikes. However, as we have discussed in this chapter, communicating warning, or threat dissemination, can also have several unwelcome outcomes and can induce various emotional states in citizens. It is thus important that any terrorist threat be carefully evaluated and examined before dissemination, as the consequences can be disastrous in any number of ways, from inducing fear and severe distress all the way to producing apathy and lack of preparedness.

The U.S. Department of Homeland Security Advisory System is the national terrorist alert system that was developed and established in the aftermath of 9/11/2001. Although the intentions of this national terrorist alert system are to create a common language that both the government and the general public can understand, and to facilitate appropriate decisions to threats of terrorism, it is questionable whether this system ever really served the intended goal—for many of the reasons we discussed above. That being said, we view the evolution of this system as positive and reflecting an effort by those managing it to further refine the method. Evidence for this includes moving away from assigning threat conditions to an entire country to focusing on particular regions and industries. As a result, the public can better differentiate contexts where there may be more threat, and plan accordingly.

In 2009, a task force from the U.S. Department of Homeland Security Advisory Council released a report that also questioned the effectiveness of the then-current color-coded alert system (Homeland Security Advisory Council, 2009). They concluded that the current system needed a thorough overhaul, and that it needed to be better at communicating useful information to the public, including providing more specific information about new threats. On Jan. 27, 2011, it was announced that the original alert system would be replaced with a new terrorism alert system,

With regards to the effectiveness of a terrorist alert system, one of the unwarranted consequences can be the exacerbation in stress, anxiety, and emotional states in the public. As noted above, Kramer and colleagues (2003) found that elevations in the Homeland Security Advisory System were associated with increased reports of physiological arousal, anxiety, and depression in disaster-relief workers in New York City after 9/11. Eisenman and colleagues (2009) further demonstrated in a large study conducted in Los Angeles that certain vulnerable subgroups of the population are more susceptible to overestimating threats of terrorism. These groups, such as the mentally ill, those who are disabled, and several non-White ethnic groups, are more likely to experience higher levels of worry. Other studies have supported the notion that there are vulnerable subgroups of the population who are more susceptible to threats of terrorism (Boscarino et al., 2006; Omer et al., 2007).

Research also shows that depending on the threat being communicated, different emotional states may be induced. In the aftermath of 9/11/2001 Lerner and colleagues (2003) examined the effects of induced fear and anger on the perceived risk of terrorism. They found that induced anger was associated with reduced estimates of terrorism risk and greater optimism, whereas induced fear was related to increased estimates of risk and greater pessimism. It is not difficult to extrapolate from this that warning messages may have powerful influences on the public and policymaking. Those crafting the messages should incorporate these data into their approach and should construct messages so as to facilitate a sense of control, predictability, and order.

These data are also important when considering how people think about and make decisions with respect to the issue of terrorism. In a study on psychological reactions to terrorism threat and policymaking, Huddy and colleagues (2005) found that as perceived threat increased, so did the support for military action against potential terrorists, surveillance of the public, curtailment of civil liberties, and stricter immigration restrictions for Arabs. Similarly, Fischer and colleagues (2007) demonstrated that people's perceptions of socially acceptable responses to threats of terrorism can depend on the level of induced threat. Given these and many other studies presented in Chapter 4, it is clear that the methods employed by governments and officials have a direct impact on the general population in specific ways and affect decisions about who to vote for, which policies to support, and how to engage the political process.

One of the important questions in today's world, with everything we have learned since the 9/11/2001 attacks, is whether we are better prepared for detecting and responding to potential terrorist attacks. With the copious research that has been dedicated to the topic, we are certainly better informed, and we know much more about the advantages and disadvantages with threat dissemination. However, one thing is clear in this world of ever-evolving terrorist threats: it is important that we continue to empirically study all the various factors involved in terrorism. This will promote improved knowledge and better preparedness for future threats of terrorism.

REFERENCES

Aguirre, B. E. (2004). Homeland Security warnings: Lessons learned and unlearned. *International Journal of Mass Emergencies and Disasters, 22*(2), 103–115.

Antonius, D., & Sinclair, S. J. (2009). In the wake of terrorist attacks: attitudes, the role of media, and identity. *Behavioral Sciences of Terrorism and Political Aggression, 1*(2), 81–83.

Associated Press. (2008). Panel: Biological attack likely by 2013. Retrieved Dec. 2, 2008, from http://www.msnbc.msn.com/id/28006645/.

Bennett, B. (Nov. 25, 1010). Terror alert system on its way out. *Los Angeles Times.* Available at http://articles.latimes.com/2010/nov/25/nation/la-na-color-coded-alerts-20101125

Boscarino, J. A., Adams, R. E., & Figley, C. R. (2004). Mental health service use 1-year after the World Trade Center disaster: implications for mental health care. *General Hospital Psychiatry, 26*(5), 346–358.

Boscarino, J. A., Adams, R. E., Figley, C. R., Galea, S., & Foa, E. B. (2006). Fear of terrorism and preparedness in New York City 2 years after the attacks: implications for disaster planning and research. *Journal of Public Health Management and Practice, 12*(6), 505–513.

Carpintero-Santamaría, N. (2010) The incidence of illegal nuclear trafficking in proliferation and international security. *Behavioral Sciences of Terrorism and Political Aggression.* Advance online publication. Available at http://www.tandfonline.com/doi/abs/10.1080 /19434472.2010.512156#preview

de l'administration Française. (2010). Sécurité: le plan vigipirate. Retrieved Nov. 30, 2010, from http://www.service-public.fr/actualites/001793.html.

Drury, A. C., Overby, L. M., Ang, A., & Li, Y. (2010). "Pretty prudent" or rhetorically responsive? The American public's support for military action. *Political Research Quarterly, 63*(1), 83–96.

Eisenman, D. P., Glik, D., Ong, M., Zhou, Q., Tseng, C. H., Long, A., et al. (2009). Terrorism-related fear and avoidance behavior in a multiethnic urban population. *American Journal of Public Health, 99*(1), 168–174.

Fischer, P., Greitemeyer, T., Kastenmüller, A., Frey, D., & Oßwald, S. (2007). Terror salience and punishment: Does terror salience induce threat to social order? *Journal of Experimental Social Psychology, 43*(6), 964–971.

Fischhoff, B., Gonzalez, R. M., Small, D. A., & Lerner, J. S. (2003). Judged terror risk and proximity to the World Trade Center. *Journal of Risk and Uncertainty, 26*(2/3), 137–151.

Friedland, N., & Merari, A. (1985). The psychological impact of terrorism: a double-edged sword. *Political Psychology, 6*(4), 591–604.

Goltz, J., Russell, L., & Bourque, L. (1992). Initial behavioural response to a rapid onset disaster. *International Journal of Mass Emergencies and Disasters, 10,* 43–69.

Grant, B. F., Stinson, F. S., Dawson, D. A., Chou, S. P., Dufour, M. C., Compton, W., et al. (2004). Prevalence and co-occurrence of substance use disorders and independent mood and anxiety disorders: results from the National Epidemiologic Survey on Alcohol and Related Conditions. *Archives of General Psychiatry, 61*(8), 807–816.

Herrmann, R. K., Tetlock, P. E., & Visser, P. S. (1999). mass public decision to go to war: a cognitive-interactionist framework. *American Political Science Review, 93*(3), 553–573.

Homeland Security Advisory Council. (2009). *Homeland Security Advisory System: Task Force Report and Recommendations.* Retrieved Dec. 07, 2010, from http://www.dhs.gov/ xlibrary/assets/hsac_final_report_09_15_09.pdf.

Huddy, L., Feldman, S., Taber, C., & Lahav, G. (2005). Threat, anxiety, and support of antiterrorism policies. *American Journal of Political Science, 49*(3), 593–608.

Johnson, E. J., & Tversky, A. (1983). Affect, generalization, and the perception of risk. *Journal of Personality and Social Psychology, 45*(1), 20–31.

Johnson, N. R., Feinberg, W. E., & Johnston, D. M. (1994). Microstructure and panic: The impact of social bonds on individual action in collective flight from the Beverly Hills Supper Club Fire. In R. R. Dynes & K. Tierney (Eds.), *Disasters, collective behavior and social organization* (pp. 168–189). Newark: University of Delaware Press.

Kearon, T., Mythen, G., & Walklate, S. (2007). Making sense of emergency advice: Public perceptions of the terrorist risk. *Security Journal, 20*(2), 77–95.

Kramer, M. E., Brown, A. D., Spielman, L., Giosan, C., & Rothrock, M. (2003). Psychological reactions to the national terror-alert system. *The Id: Graduate Faculty, Psychology Society Bulletin, 1*(1), 67–70.

Lachlan, K. A., Spence, P. R., & Seeger, M. (2009). Terrorist attacks and uncertainty reduction: media use after September 11. *Behavioral Sciences of Terrorism and Political Aggression, 1*(2), 101–110.

Lerner, J. S., Gonzalez, R. M., Small, D. A., & Fischhoff, B. (2003). Effects of fear and anger on perceived risks of terrorism: a national field experiment. *Psychological Science, 14*(2), 144–150.

Lerner, J. S., & Keltner, D. (2001). Fear, anger, and risk. *Journal of Personality and Social Psychology, 81*(1), 146–159.

McDermott, R., & Zimbardo, P. G. (2007). The psychological consequences of terrorist alerts. In B. Bongar, L. Brown, Beutler, L., J. Breckenridge, & P. Zimbardo (Eds.), *The psychology of terrorism* (pp. 357–370). Oxford: Oxford University Press.

Mueller, R. S. (2010). *Statement before the Senate Committee on Homeland Security and Governmental Affairs.* Retrieved Dec. 7, 2010, from http://www.fbi.gov/news/testimony/nine-years-after-9-11-confronting-the-terrorist-threat-to-the-u.s.

Obama, B. H. (2008). *Obama remarks on confronting terrorist threats (transcript).* Retrieved Dec. 07, 2010, from http://www.washingtonpost.com/wp-dyn/content/article/2008/07/16/AR2008071601474.html

Omer, S. B., Barnett, D. J., Castellano, C., Wierzba, R. K., Hiremath, G. S., Balicer, R. D., et al. (2007). Impact of Homeland Security Alert level on calls to a law enforcement peer support hotline. *International Journal of Emergency Mental Health, 9*(4), 253–257.

Pena, C. V. (2002). Homeland Security Alert System: Why bother? Retrieved Nov. 30, 2010, from http://www.cato.org/pub_display.php?pub_id=4205.

Perry, R. W., & Lindell, M. K. (2003). Understanding citizen response to disasters with implications for terrorism. *Journal of Contingencies and Crisis Management, 11*(2), 49–60.

Pyszczynski, T., Solomon, S., & Greenberg, J. (2003). *In the wake of 9/11/2001: The psychology of terror.* Washington, D.C.: American Psychological Association.

Ryan, J., & Thomas, P. (2011). Color-coded terror alerts retired by Department of Homeland Security. Retrieved Jan. 27, 2011, from http://abcnews.go.com/News/color-coded-terror-alerts-retired-department-homeland-security/story?id=12780975.

Silverleib, A. (2008). Poll: Terrorism fears are fading. Retrieved Dec. 2, 2008, from http://www.cnn.com/2008/POLITICS/07/02/terrorism.poll/.

Slovic, P., Fischhoff, B., & Lichtenstein, S. (1980). Facts and fears: Understanding perceived risk. In R. C. Schwing & W. A. Albers (Eds.), *Societal Risk Assessment.* New York: Plenum Press.

Smith, C. A., & Ellsworth, P. C. (1985). Patterns of cognitive appraisal in emotion. *Journal of Personality and Social Psychology, 48*(4), 813–838.

Smith, T. W., & Rasinski, K. A. (September/October 2002). Assassination and terror: Two American tragedies compared. *Public Perspective,* 34–38.

Strik, J. J., Denollet, J., Lousberg, R., & Honig, A. (2003). Comparing symptoms of depression and anxiety as predictors of cardiac events and increased health care consumption after myocardial infarction. *Journal of American College of Cardiology, 42*(10), 1801–1807.

Tierney, K., Lindell, M. K., & Perry, R. W. (2001). *Facing the unexpected: Disaster preparedness and response in the United States.* Washington, D.C.: Joseph Henry Press.

United Kingdom Home Office. (2010). *Current threat level.* Retrieved Nov. 30, 2010, from http://www.homeoffice.gov.uk/counter-terrorism/current-threat-level/.

U.S. Department of Homeland Security. (2008). *Homeland Security Presidential Directive 3: Homeland Security Advisory System.* Retrieved Nov. 29, 2010, from http://www.dhs.gov/xabout/laws/gc_1214508631313.shtm#content.

U.S. Department of Homeland Security. (2009). *Citizen Guidance on the Homeland Security Advisory System.* Retrieved Nov. 29, 2010, from http://www.dhs.gov/xlibrary/assets/citizen-guidance-hsas2.pdf.

U.S. Department of Homeland Security. (2010). *Homeland Security Advisory System.* Retrieved Nov. 29, 2010, from http://www.dhs.gov/files/programs/Copy_of_press_release_0046.shtm.

U.S. Department of Justice. (2010a). *Amerithrax investigative summary.* Retrieved Dec. 7, 2010, from http://www.justice.gov/amerithrax/docs/amx-investigative-summary.pdf.

U.S. Department of Justice. (2010b). *Amerithrax investigative summary and errata* (updated version). Retrieved Dec. 7, 2010, from http://www.justice.gov/amerithrax/docs/amx-investigative-summary2.pdf

Wells, K. B., Golding, J. M., & Burnam, M. A. (1989). Chronic medical conditions in a sample of the general population with anxiety, affective, and substance use disorders. *American Journal of Psychiatry, 146*(11), 1440–1446.

Willis, H. H. (2006). *Analyzing terrorism risk.* Retrieved Dec. 2, 2008, from http://www.rand.org/content/dam/rand/pubs/testimonies/2006/RAND_CT265.pdf.

6 Coping with Terrorism
The Psychology of Resilience

In the somber time that followed what to the most of the world was a surreal experience, resembling more a scene from a Hollywood movie, it was not the expected chaos that ruled. Rather, it was help—it seemed as if everyone wanted to travel to the south part of Manhattan to help. This tiny area became a symbol of "the big melting pot" . . . where everyone, no matter their background, came together to help.

Antonius (2002)

The above quote is a translation of a Norwegian newspaper editorial written by one of the authors (DA) in the days after the Sept. 11, 2001, attacks. It provides a glimpse into this author's sense of how people came together to help one another in the immediate aftermath of the terrorist strike in New York City, and the comradeship and coping that took place. This very significant moment in time became an occasion where everyone, no matter their ethnic background or economic status, put their differences aside and came together to display strength and resilience in the face of the terrorist attacks that had taken place. For many residents of New York, it became critically important to show the attackers, the terrorists, that despite the devastation and the fear they had caused, people's spirit to live on as normal remained unbroken.

This ability to cope with stress and adversity during periods of catastrophe and crisis is a unique phenomenon in humans. Despite the physical and emotional/psychological devastation that catastrophic events (e.g., earthquakes, wars, and terrorism) can cause in entire populations, the psychological resilience inherent in humans makes us capable of not only surviving, but also effectively coping with the severe stress and adversity, and moving on with our daily lives without much interference.

As illustrated by the quote above, psychological resilience was in full display in New York City after 9/11/2001. "Ground Zero," where the Twin Towers had once stood, became the symbol for not only the terrorist attacks but also the exceptional collective resilient spirit of New Yorkers and the thousands of emergency workers who came from across the United States to assist in the search for survivors and clean-up efforts. Despite the constant media reminders of the destruction caused by the terrorists, and despite the numerous reports of new and pending terror attacks, the general American public was determined to clean up after the attacks and continue with their daily lives as normal. In Manhattan, despite the proximity to Ground Zero, it was remarkable how fast people and daily life returned to what can only be characterized as a somewhat normal state:

Daily life in the West Village [just north of Ground Zero], and the rest of Manhattan, is beginning to look like pre-Tuesday [September 11] again. People are once again eating outside at the restaurants, the taxis are once again racing through the streets. . ., people are once again talking loudly on their cell phones, and there is once again the never-ending noise that characterizes New York City. However, it seems like an illusion: Only a thousand meters down from where I live, called *Ground Zero*, are emergency personnel still working on getting under control the sporadic fires and removing the rubble in hopes of still finding survivors in the ruins of what was once the tallest skyscrapers in New York City. All bridges, tunnels, and boats that transport millions of people to and from Manhattan each and every day are guarded by the police or the army. Memorial places and walls have appeared in all neighborhoods in Manhattan, and the news are each day filled with sad stories about people who have been affected by the tragedy. (Antonius, 2002)

This quote is from the same Norwegian newspaper editorial and illustrates the scene in Manhattan only few days after the 9/11/2001 strike as perceived by one of the authors (DA). It also serves to illustrate once again the remarkable and powerful, and sometimes overlooked, psychological resilience that humans possess and that they can turn to when faced with serious stress and trauma. In this chapter, we will review the trauma literature and how it relates to terrorism, paying particular attention to how people cope with and manage stress and fears related to terrorism on an ongoing basis. Moreover, in this context, we will focus on the concept of psychological resilience and people's ability to cope with ongoing threat, and we will provide some suggestions about how to best create and build resilience, especially for people who may be considered "at risk." Lastly, we will briefly discuss some relevant neurobiological findings pertaining to the issue of risk and resilience, and underlying biological factors that may influence these outcomes.

WHAT IS PSYCHOLOGICAL RESILIENCE?

What is it that defines psychological resilience? Why is it so important for human functioning? In the study of loss and trauma, much of the research has focused on the individuals and groups who suffer negative psychological and physical consequences, for which they often need some sort of pharmacological or psycho-therapeutic treatment. However, as most people are exposed to at least one traumatic event during their life, and many, as in the above example from Manhattan, can move on with their daily lives in a relatively efficient manner, some researchers have also begun to focus on the psychological factors that promote resilience and adaptation following traumatic events. This brings up an important distinction between resilience and recovery (Bonanno, 2004), and the fact that being psycho-logically resilient is not simply being able to recover after having experienced significant trauma. With recovery, a person is affected by the traumatic event to the point of exhibiting symptoms of elevated distress and/or psychopathology (e.g., anxiety, depression, post-traumatic stress disorder, etc.), with the added expecta-tion that he or she will return to a pre-trauma level of functioning after several months or years. Resilience, on the other hand, is the ability of people to maintain a stable equilibrium in the aftermath of traumatic events, and at points even use the traumatic experience as a means of growth and opportunity.

As Bonanno, Brewin, Kaniasty, and La Greca (2010) pointed out in a recent publication on the topic, individuals vary considerably in their response to trau-matic events. However, within this heterogeneity, several response patterns appear to stand out. First, there are individuals who have chronically elevated stress and anxiety symptoms, which often do not dissipate over time. Second, there are people who initially show low levels or an absence of psychopathological symptoms but then develop them later—in a delayed symptom onset pattern. Third, there are groups of people who initially demonstrate high levels of symptoms but then show a full recovery; this probably accounts for the majority of people in the population, as is demonstrated by much of the longitudinal research presented in Chapter 2. Fourth, there are individuals who show psychological resilience and a healthy adjustment to the experienced stress. Of course, within these four categories there are likely to be other subcategories that may be driven by extraneous variables such as psychiatric illness, distance from the point of disaster, prior exposure to disasters, and other factors, as we discussed in Chapter 5. Furthermore, psychological resilience is also characterized as being inherently heterogeneous, with no one single resilient personality type (Bonanno, 2005). In fact, academics seem to differ substantially in their definition of resilience (Norris, Stevens, Pfefferbaum, Wyche, & Pfefferbaum, 2008).

As it turns out, in most people psychological resilience is at play daily as it moderates our emotional responses to normal stressors. Research has shown that in dealing with chronic, daily stress, those with lower levels of resiliency traits (i.e., the low-resilient individuals) have trouble regulating their negative emotions (e.g., nervousness, being scared, irritability), whereas positive emotions (e.g., enthusiasm, excitement, being proud, etc.) are more common in those with higher levels of resiliency traits (i.e., the high-resilient individuals). High-resilient individuals are also better at using their experience of positive emotions in recovering from the daily stress (Ong, Bergeman, Bisconti, & Wallace, 2006). This affective relationship, between positive and negative emotional processes and a person's psychological response to his or her negative emotions, may be an important pathway to understanding resilience and the ability to maintain a stable equilibrium. Supportive evidence has come from neurobiological research, which shows that a resilient affective style and psychological well-being has distinct neural correlates with fast neural recovery to negative and stressful events (Davidson, 2004). The neurobiology of coping and resilience, as it relates to stress and trauma, will be discussed more towards the end of this chapter.

PSYCHOLOGICAL RESILIENCE IN THE AFTERMATH OF 9/11

Research that examines resilience following terrorist attacks is naturally limited because there have (historically) been relatively few incidents compared to other forms of crises and disasters—thus yielding lower base rates, which makes it difficult to study in naturalistic settings. However, the 9/11/2001 attacks provided an opportunity to investigate psychological resilience and related factors, and in the years since the attacks several studies have been published on the topic. Perhaps most prominent are the research studies conducted by Bonanno and colleagues (Bonanno, Rennicke, & Dekel, 2005; Bonanno, Galea, Bucciarelli, & Vlahov, 2006, 2007), who focused on psychological resilience and its predictors following the 9/11/2001 attacks.

In one of their studies, in which they explored predictors of psychological resilience, Bonanno, Rennicke, and Dekel (2005) examined the personality feature "self-enhancement." Self-enhancement refers to the notion that some people have unrealistic views of themselves and overly positive biases in favor of themselves, and that this can be adaptive and can actually promote well-being (Bonanno, 2004). Self-enhancement has both rewards, in the form of higher self-esteem, as well as costs, such as narcissistic tendencies and behaviors. In the event of a traumatic experience such as a terrorist attack, researchers have speculated that people with higher levels of self-enhancement may demonstrate more positive outcomes.

This is exactly what Bonanno and colleagues (2005) found in a sample of individuals who were in or near the World Trade Center during the 9/11/2001 strike. Those subjects who scored high on self-enhancement assessment were more psychologically resilient to the trauma experience and also reported more overall positive affect in follow-up interviews, compared to people lower in self-enhancement. However, those who were characterized as self-enhancers also demonstrated a cost to their behavior: 18 months after 9/11/2001 their friends and relatives characterized them as showing decreased levels of social adjustment and honesty.

One may speculate that this is related to the narcissistic features present in the self-enhancers and their overly favorable perception of themselves. As described above, these features increase their ability to cope with severe traumatic events, which may be perceived favorably by others in the immediate time after a terror attack—potentially as a sign of psychological strength. However, over time, these same narcissistic features may begin to evoke unfavorable impressions in others as the overly self-involved characteristics become more present. This is an interesting area of research that warrants further study,

In another study of resilience among 2,752 residents living in the New York City area in the aftermath of 9/11, Bonanno, Galea, Bucciarelli, and Vlahov (2006) examined the prevalence of post-traumatic stress disorder symptoms. The authors defined resilience for the purpose of this study as having no symptoms or only one symptom of PTSD, and they found that of the total sample approximately 65% met criteria for resilience during the first 6 months following the attacks. In exploratory analyses the authors examined the presence of resilience when it was defined as including up to two PTSD symptoms; this increased the percentage to 73%. Bonanno and colleagues also reported some demographic differences: men demonstrated higher levels of resilience than women (71% vs. 60%); age was related to resilience (those who were older showed more resilience); Asians showed the highest level of resilience (82%); higher income was associated with more resilience; higher education was related to higher resilience; and unmarried couples demonstrated the lowest levels of resilience.

In a follow-up study with the same population, Bonanno, Galea, Bucciarelli, and Vlahov (2007) used more advanced statistical methods to explore the prevalence of sociocontextual demographic factors and their predictive validity in explaining psychological resilience in the aftermath of 9/11. They found that psychological resilience was uniquely predicted by gender, age, ethnicity, education, absence of depression and substance use, lower income loss, social support, fewer chronic diseases, fewer recent life stressors and past traumatic events, and less direct impact of the attacks. Not only are such findings informative for researchers, but such data may also be important for decisions regarding the disaster emergency relief, and they may have widespread implications for where to focus public attention (and where to focus less attention) and implement intervention strategies in the aftermath of terrorist attacks and other disasters.

Bonanno and his colleagues' excellent work on psychological resilience demonstrates an important fact that often has been neglected in scientific research and more generally in the media; that is, most people are actually extremely psychologically resilient and can cope with disasters such as terrorism much better than we expect. As we will discuss later in this chapter and have alluded to earlier, this may serve certain evolutionary advantages.

Other research since 9/11/2001 has examined the various factors that may contribute to psychological resilience. For example, Butler, Koopman, Azarow, Blasey, Magdalene, and colleagues (2009) conducted a longitudinal study in which they examined psychological resilience (for the purpose of this study, resilience was defined as higher well-being and lower distress) in 1,281 individuals within the first few months after 9/11 and then again after 6 months. The findings demonstrated that those who showed higher resilience in the months after 9/11 had lower levels of emotional suppression, denial, and self-blame, as well as fewer negative worldview changes (they had a less pessimistic outlook on their future). Moreover, Butler and colleagues found that individuals who exhibited less negative worldview changes, some positive coping mechanisms (i.e., seeking emotional support and less self-blame), and strong social support also showed better psychological well-being or less distress at the 6-month follow-up.

These findings support other longitudinal research on psychological coping styles after the 9/11/2001 attacks showing that active coping and acceptance are related to decreased global distress (Silver, Holman, McIntosh, Poulin, & Gil-Rivas, 2002). Conversely, ineffective coping styles such as denial, giving up, and self-distraction are associated with higher distress (Silver et al., 2002). Similarly, research has shown that a higher level of social support in the 6 months before 9/11/2001 was related to better psychological coping, as measured by significantly fewer symptoms of PTSD and depression in individuals living south of 110th Street in Manhattan (Galea et al., 2002). In a study examining positive (and negative) outlook changes following 9/11/2001 in a British sample, respondents who viewed the terrorist attacks as an attack on their own values and beliefs were more likely to report positive changes (e.g., valuing friends and family more) than negative changes (e.g., greater anxiety) (Linley, Joseph, Cooper, Harris, & Meyer, 2003). Overall, the findings by Butler and colleagues, as well as other researchers, emphasize the importance of effective coping styles and having networks of supportive family and friends following exposure to and working to overcome traumatic events. As will be discussed below, this finding is consistent with the overall trauma literature.

Fredrickson, Tugade, Waugh, and Larkin (2003) conducted a prospective study on psychological resilience in which they assessed different emotional responses in 46 college students before and after 9/11/2001. They found positive correlations between resilience and the following positive emotional terms: interested/alert/curious, glad/happy/joyful, hopeful/optimistic/encouraged, sexual/desiring/flirtatious, proud/confident/self-assured, and content/serene/peaceful. Conversely, the authors also showed that psychological resilience correlated negatively with angry/irritated/annoyed and sad/downhearted/unhappy.

Moreover, Fredrickson and colleagues were able to demonstrate, using mediational analyses, that positive emotions, such as those described above, experienced in the wake of the terrorist attacks accounted for the association between trait resilience (as measured before 9/11/2001) and later development of depressive symptoms and increases in psychological resources (after 9/11/2001). In other words, those who exhibited higher trait resilience prior to the attacks were buffered from depression by the experience of positive emotions, and they appeared to thrive as a function of these positive emotions (sometimes referred to as positive post-traumatic growth in psychological resources, which we will discuss later in this chapter).

PSYCHOLOGICAL RESILIENCE IN THE AFTERMATH OF TERRORISM IN ISRAEL

The study of psychological resilience in the aftermath of terrorism is certainly not distinct to the 9/11/2001 strikes. Researchers have examined psychological resilience in people living in areas other than the United States, including regions that have been affected by terrorism. One country of particular interest to researchers has been Israel, as well as the whole Middle East region, which has battled terrorism threats and acts of terrorism both domestically and internationally for decades. This line of research may be particularly relevant as a means of comparing the effects of the 9/11/2001 strikes.

Hobfoll, Canetti-Nisim, and Johnson (2006) studied terrorism exposure and coping styles in 905 adult Jewish and Palestinian citizens of Israel. Although this study did not focus on psychological resilience *per se*, the findings showed that among those who had been exposed to terrorism and who reported higher rates of social support, there were fewer reports of PTSD symptoms and depression symptoms. This result is similar to other studies examining the effects of social support on coping mechanisms after terrorist attacks (Benight et al., 2000) and other types of disasters (Norris & Kaniasty, 1996; Brewin, Andrews, & Valentine, 2000).

Hobfoll and colleagues also found that Palestinian participants were more likely to have higher rates of psychopathology than Jewish participants, although this finding should be considered in light of the fact that Israel was where the study was conducted. That is to say, environmental and contextual factors likely explain this discrepancy.

Palmieri, Canetti-Nisim, Galea, Johnson, and Hobfoll (2008) explored resiliency and PTSD rates among Jewish and Arab citizens of Israel who had been exposed to terrorism and rocket attacks by Hezbollah following the Al Aqsa Intifada. The Al Aqsa Intifada, also known as the Second Intifada, was, in brief, a period of approximately 5 years (from 2001 to 2006) in which the Palestinian–Israeli violence intensified and several thousand people were killed. Immediately after the Al Aqsa Intifada, during a period of about 1 month, several thousand rockets fell in Northern Israel, causing severe psychological and physical distress to the inhabitants.

To study the impact of risk and resilience factors in people living in these regions, Palmieri and colleagues conducted a large-scale phone survey of 1,200 people. Psychological resilience was examined through questions about positive changes, self-efficacy, satisfaction, and social support and their impact on the development of PTSD symptoms. None of these factors emerged as resilience factors. The authors speculated that the lack of resilience factors they found may be due to the closeness in time to the rocket attacks: the study was carried out in the 2 months immediately after the attacks (the attacks ended on Aug. 14, 2006, and the study began on Aug. 15, 2006). Therefore, there may not have been enough time to allow protective factors to develop. An alternative explanation may be that the study did not adequately account for heterogeneous effects in the population, and that the analyses should have been stratified from the beginning. It may also simply be that the people living in this region represent a different psychosocial population from those living elsewhere.

To study coping and resilience *during* a period of terrorism, Hobfoll, Canetti-Nisim, Johnson, Palmieri, Varley, and Galea (2008) carried out a study while the Al Aqsa Intifada was taking place. They examined the association between psychological resilience and PTSD in Jewish and Arab citizens in Israel during a 2-month period in 2004 when threats of rocket strikes and attacks by Palestinian militants were common. They evaluated the positive changes and the social support that ensued during this period. They referred to the positive changes as "traumatic growth," operationally defined as "resource gains in intimacy and sense of meaning resulting from trauma" (p. 10) (e.g., feeling closer to friends and others, feeling more meaning with one's own life, and having higher self-confidence).

Hobfoll and colleagues (2008) found that in those exposed to terrorism, traumatic growth and social support were associated with a higher risk of developing probable PTSD. This finding may at first appear surprising, but it may also reflect an interrelationship between these factors in which those experiencing more psychological distress are more likely to seek higher traumatic growth as a coping mechanism (e.g., seeking friendships and looking for a meaning with their life), but at the same time these people are also equipped with a more supportive social network. These findings may also reflect differences in coping styles and psychological resilience during periods of terrorist attacks and terrorism threat, compared to in the aftermath of attacks, when only the threat of terrorism is still present.

Hobfoll, Palmieri, Johnson, Canetti-Nisim, Hall, and Galea (2009) also conducted a longitudinal study on psychological resilience and distress during the Al Aqsa Intifada in 2004 and 2005. They were able to establish a resilience trajectory, where 13.5% of the study participants described some initial symptoms of traumatic stress but then become relatively asymptomatic. Those who exhibited greater psychological resilience reported less psychosocial resource loss and were more likely to be Jewish (as compared to Arab). Hobfoll and colleagues (2009) also found that those demonstrating higher levels of psychological resilience had a higher socioeconomic status and had more supportive friends and less traumatic growth.

Traumatic growth, often referred to as post-traumatic growth, is a debated topic. We will discuss this psychological construct further in the next section, including describing in more detail what the construct is and presenting contrasting perspectives from different research groups, including Hobfoll and colleagues (2009) and Bonanno and colleagues (2007).

POST-TRAUMATIC GROWTH

An area that has received less empirical study and perhaps more debate is that of post-traumatic growth. This psychological construct refers to the positive psychological changes some people experience in the aftermath of a challenging life event (Tedeschi, Park, & Calhoun, 1998; Tedeschi & Calhoun, 2004), such as a traumatic interaction (e.g., terrorist attack). In other words, this term refers to the notion that some people have positive reactions to a traumatic experience. This positive reaction does not, of course, come as a direct result of the traumatic experience. Rather, it occurs only through a complex cognitive process in which there is a personal struggle to try to understand and cope with the traumatic experience.

Few studies have investigated post-traumatic growth in the aftermath of terrorist attacks, and the results have been inconsistent. Val and Linley (2006) studied post-traumatic growth (using a measure of post-traumatic growth that captures positive experiences following a traumatic event) and positive and negative changes in 153 individuals in Madrid after the March 11, 2004, terrorist attacks. They found that post-traumatic growth and positive changes were associated with extroversion, but not depression and anxiety. Laufer and Solomon (2006) examined post-traumatic growth using a longer version of the measure of post-traumatic growth that Val and Linley (2006) used in a large sample of Israeli adolescents, approximately 70% of whom had been exposed to one or more terrorist incidents. They found a positive correlation between post-traumatic growth and post-traumatic symptoms. Although counterintuitive, this finding may be seen in the context of Hobfoll and colleagues' (2008) report on traumatic growth, which we discussed above. Those experiencing higher levels of psychological distress (post-traumatic stress symptoms) may also be more likely to seek out positive experiences (post-traumatic growth) as a way of coping with the situation. Both of these studies also found that the females reported more psychological growth (Laufer & Solomon, 2006) and positive change (Val & Linley, 2006), and Laufer and Solomon also found that the younger adolescents who had experienced more serious traumatic incidents earlier in their life reported more post-traumatic growth.

More recent work by Hobfoll and colleagues (2007) has questioned the beneficial role of post-traumatic growth. Their research from New York post-9/11/2001, as well as in Israel during periods of violence and terrorism, have generally shown that post-traumatic growth is related to psychological distress, as well as more right-wing political attitudes and support for retaliatory violence. However, in one of their studies, Hobfoll and colleagues discovered some contrasting results with regards to post-traumatic growth. They (Hall, Hobfall, Palmieri, Canetti-Nisim, Shapira, and others, 2008) studied a group of settlers in Gaza who had to move out of their homes and the region as part of the Israeli government's policy of disengaging from Gaza in 2005. Those who reported higher post-traumatic growth exhibited less psychological distress. The authors speculated that this may be related to the higher level of involvement and action that these settlers were engaged in, compared to the more passive experience of being witness to and even victims of terrorism. The settlers physically had to move based on their government's policy change, which they may have judged a betrayal from the government's previous promises that they could settle in Gaza. The authors further speculated that higher post-traumatic growth may serve as a protective factor against PTSD symptoms; this appears to mirror findings in other trauma-exposed populations (Frazier, Conlon, & Glaser, 2001).

The latter findings on post-traumatic growth by Hobfoll and colleagues are intriguing and suggest there may be heterogeneity in the way post-traumatic growth can be experienced, similar in ways to psychological resilience, and this heterogeneity may depend on or be associated with the level of cognitive and physical engagement in the terrorist experience. In extending these findings to our previous writings about those living south of 14th Street during and after the 9/11/2001 attacks in Manhattan, it may be that a subgroup of those residents (who experienced the attacks indirectly and lived in the area that eventually was closed off for the general public) developed different patterns of psychological symptoms and post-traumatic growth, and their pattern of psychological resilience may also have been different.

However, other researchers have questioned some of the premises on which the research is based. There often appears to be an insufficient distinction made between post-traumatic growth and resilient outcomes (Westphal & Bonanno, 2007). Westphal and Bonanno (2007) argued that post-traumatic research fails to take into account that "resilient outcomes may provide little need or opportunity for posttraumatic growth" (p. 425). They called for a broader understanding of the processes involved in resilient outcomes, which need to be understood within the framework of heterogeneity of pathways and trajectories, as well as individual differences.

SOME CULTURAL AND RELIGIOUS CONSIDERATIONS IN PSYCHOLOGICAL RESILIENCE

Culture and religion, as we have alluded to previously in this chapter, are likely to have an important effect on the development of psychological resilience and the way an individual reacts to and copes with severe traumatic experiences, such as terrorist attacks. We have described how different ethnic groups in the aftermath of the

9/11/2001 attacks displayed varied levels of psychological resilience. We have also discussed how Jewish citizens of Israel demonstrated different levels of psychological resilience from their Arab counterparts. Developing a better understanding of cultural and religious differences when studying the psychological resilience in humans faced with traumatic events not only is important for researchers and academics, but may also have major implications on public policy, as disaster interventions and rebuilding efforts need to account for such diversity. Unfortunately, only limited research has focused on cultural and religious factors in psychological resilience. Below we discuss some of this research.

In a theoretically oriented paper, Hernández (2002) discussed collective and community resilience in Colombia, and more broadly in Latin America, a region that has seen decades of political persecution and social turmoil, and where acts of terrorism have been widely used by various groups as a method to instill fear in the population in an attempt to force political and social changes. Hernández argued that in Latin America the establishment of social relationships through community networks is a key feature in psychological resilience to traumatic events. Moreover, Hernández pointed out that psychological resilience, as well as recovery from the trauma related to political violence, is in Latin America embedded into the ethos of communities rather than individuals (although one may argue that there are likely to be individual differences as well). This article is primarily theoretical and does not present empirical data on resilience in Latin America, although such research studies are increasingly warranted to better understand these issues.

Focusing on a different part of the world and a different ethnic population, Moscardino, Axia, Scrimin, and Capello (2007) conducted a study in the aftermath of the school siege in Beslan, Russia, in 2004. This is one of the few studies that investigated psychological resilience in children who have been directly exposed to terrorism, while concurrently examining the children's caregivers' reactions. In the Beslan school siege, 32 Chechen terrorists took hostage over 1,100 children and adults. Of the more than 700 children who were kept hostage, most if not all were reportedly kept without food and water for over 50 hours, as they watched friends, relatives, and teachers being beaten and even murdered. Three days into the siege, Russian Security Forces stormed the building with heavy artillery, resulting in a fierce gun battle with the terrorists and several explosions. In the end, more than 350 of the hostages were killed, more than 150 of them children (several hundred are still considered missing or unidentified).

Moscardino and colleagues used a thematic approach and examined the narratives from 17 caregivers who had at least one child who survived the school siege. Their findings demonstrated the strong cultural and religious values present in many residents of Beslan, many of whom are of Ossetian ethnicity. When asked how their children coped during the traumatic experience, the caregivers emphasized in their narratives factors such as heroism, courage, and revenge, which are consistent with traditional Ossetian cultural norms and values. The authors also reported that some children turned to their religious faith during the siege and were observed holding on to their orthodox crosses: "the orthodox cross forms part of an Ossetian's identity; losing the cross was a major source of distress for these children" (p. 1785).

With regards to resilience and being able to live with the fear of future terrorist attacks, the study showed that the caregivers in general emphasized the need to reaffirm positive and culturally shared values. This is similar to what Hernández postulated in her account of resilience factors that are important in Latin America. Moscardino and colleagues highlighted the importance of "affection and connectedness" (p. 1785) between children and parents as important factors in building psychological resilience to trauma in children. Similar reports on the importance of a strong bond between children and parents have also come out of research examining children and caregivers in the United States (Kirkley & Medway, 2003).

Undoubtedly, cultural and religious factors come into play for many people when an act of terrorism occurs. Sometimes the terrorist act may be perceived as a direct attack on one's culture or religion. This sense of being attacked for one's culture, ethnic background, and/or religion may produce a heightened sense of protection—the need to protect one's group culture and religious belief. In fact, as is discussed in Chapter 3, terror management theory provides a nice theoretical framework for why this is so, and specifically why so many people seek proximity to their culture and in-group values as a means of transcending this sense of threat (Pyszczynski, Solomon, & Greenberg, 2003). However, more research is needed to thoroughly understand the effects of culture and religion on the development of psychological resilience, and how this differs across various cultures and religions.

The reports and research on cultural and religious influences do point out the importance of the social environment in the development of resilience following acts of terrorism. Other researchers have studied community resilience more broadly. For example, Norris, Stevens, Pfefferbaum, Wyche, and Pfefferbaum (2008) highlighted the adaptive capabilities of a community network in coping with adversity after a disaster, and equated such community adaptation to population wellness. They argued that effective community resilience is based on the following adaptive capacities: economic development, social capital, information and communication, and community competence. They also emphasized that simply showing social support is not enough to promote resilience; rather, successful adaptation to the aftermath of a disaster such as a terrorist attack also involves "healthy patterns of behavior, adequate role functioning, and satisfactory quality of life" (p. 144). One may argue that culture and religion (or spirituality) are major parts of this. In the next section, we will discuss further community resilience.

BUILDING PSYCHOLOGICAL RESILIENCE IN AT-RISK POPULATIONS TO HELP COPE WITH TERRORISM

In an attempt to strengthen psychological resilience in the public, the American Psychological Association put together a task force on Promoting Resilience in Response to Terrorism (APA, 2004) following the 9/11/2001 attacks. The group produced a set of fact sheets for psychologists, describing how they can help their patients become more resilient in coping with stress related to terrorism, as well as other disasters. The fact sheets provide information on how to help different populations (e.g., children, adults, those with mental illness, and people of different ethnicities) who have experienced traumatic events. There are even fact sheets for an often-overlooked population: those who are elderly (APA, 2011b). We have previously described how those who are younger may be at higher risk for developing PTSD symptoms. Conversely, older age may serve as a protective factor against developing psychopathology after a terrorist attack; those who are elderly may exhibit higher levels of psychological resilience on average to traumatic events. However, those who are elderly may also face problems after traumatic events that other populations do not experience in the same way. For example, they may have problems taking advantage of available resources in the aftermath of a terrorist attack. They may have a different pattern of response to severe stress than other populations. In their fact sheets, the APA highlights seeking education and normalization, maintaining a routine, taking good care of oneself, engaging in pleasurable activities, finding support in other people, developing a plan of how to solve any potential problems, and trying to find meaning and purpose with one's life during and after a disaster as ways to promote resilience in those who are elderly (APA, 2011b).

The fact sheets are primarily meant as a resource for individuals and families. However, according to the APA, they can also facilitate community resilience. The APA has also developed a website listing articles on how to build resilience and how to recover from disasters and terrorism (APA, 2011a). This website was developed to provide further help to the public, as well as academics and other professional groups.

Few studies have investigated psychological factors and resilience-building in American military and civilian personnel serving abroad. Speckhard (2002) surveyed American military and civilian personnel in Brussels, Belgium, in the aftermath of the 9/11/2001 attacks. Based on her findings, she provided suggestions for how to promote resilience to threats of terrorism in Americans living and working abroad. Among her suggestions were having stress debriefing sessions by experienced clinical staff, and normalizing heightened arousal states in individuals affected by the terror threat. Speckhard also talked about the importance of putting threats into perspective, and coming to an acceptance of the perceived threat as being part of one's life. Being able to limit rumors of threats within the workplace and organization can also be important, as well as having well-organized and effective communication and notification systems. Speckhard raised other important factors as well, such as the ability to be engaged in helping efforts, having a sense of community and social support, and having access to religious and spiritual services.

Pfefferbaum, Reissman, Pfefferbaum, Klomp, and Gurwitch (2007) provided a framework for examining and building community resilience in relation to terrorist attacks. They highlighted the fact that terrorism's primary target actually is the community rather than the individual. Thus, the development of community resilience is of the utmost importance in high-risk regions. They listed seven factors that are important in establishing community resilience: connectedness, commitment, and shared values; participation; structure, roles, and responsibilities; resources; support and nurturance; critical reflection and skill-building; and communication. They emphasized that to truly develop community resilience, it is also important to understand the complex interaction between biological, behavioral, physical, and socio-environmental factors that exist within and between individuals, including the individual characteristics, the nature of the traumatic event and the exposure in the person, and the capability of recovery in the immediate social environment. Lastly, they stressed the importance of having people from various sectors in the community—business, education, government, health, or elsewhere—understand their roles in times of disasters, such that community resilience can most effectively be promoted.

A country's ability to effectively and appropriately respond to terrorism, as well as to effectively communicate threats of terrorism, may also have a significant impact on building resilience in people. In Chapter 5 we discussed the color-coded terrorism alert system in the United States and highlighted the importance of federal departments and agencies, as well as local authorities, being able to effectively communicate threats of terrorism while also being sensitive to how people might respond. We also discussed the potential problems with the alert system, which have been pointed out by both scholars and politicians. Related to this, Longstaff and Yang (2008) emphasized the importance of a country's communication system in building resilience. They analyzed a number of crises, including several terrorism attacks, and concluded that trust is one of the most important variables in effective communication in communities. They argued that for a local population to be able to return to normal life after a disaster, such as a terrorist attack, it must have access to information that is trustworthy. Residents will then be able to act promptly and to adapt in a confident manner to the situation.

NEUROBIOLOGY OF PSYCHOLOGICAL RESILIENCE AND STRESS REACTIONS

We will now briefly turn to the neurobiology of resilience. The neural circuits and genetic factors underlying stress reactions have been widely studied. More recently, with the advances in neurobiological research techniques, studies on the neurobiology underlying resilience have become more in focus. Today we are much better informed about the neural and genetic correlates of psychological resilience in people who are faced with stressful situations compared to just one decade ago. Here we will only briefly review some of the findings as they pertain to our previous discussions.

We have previously discussed studies in which levels of cortisol, a steroid hormone, have been used as a biomarker for stress severity in people exposed to trauma. Cortisol is particularly important for controlling reactions to stress and is released into the bloodstream upon activation of the hypothalamic-pituitary-adrenal (HPA) axis (Kemeny, 2003). Short-term increased levels of cortisol have been shown to serve as a protective factor and to promote healthy adaptation. In contrast, excessive and sustained high levels of cortisol have been related to negative effects on brain regions such as the hippocampus and the amygdala—regions involved in the processing of memory and emotions—as well as being associated with a variety of health problems. Thus, optimal function of the HPA axis and proper release and reduction of cortisol are important to effectively cope with traumatic experiences and to promote resiliency in individuals (for an excellent review on this and the neurobiology of resilience, see Feder, Nestler, & Charney, 2009).

Several other neurobiological systems are also important for processing stressful events, such as the noradrenergic, serotonergic, and dopaminergic systems. All of these neurobiological systems affect neurons in different brain regions, including the hippocampus and amygdala, as well as the prefrontal cortex. Moreover, these brain regions are consistently implicated in stress responses. Davidson (2004) argued that higher levels of psychological resiliency are a function of prefrontal activation and effective modulation of activation in the amygdala, facilitating faster recovery from negative emotional and stressful events. This may not be surprising as the prefrontal cortex is highly involved in complex cognitive behaviors and decision-making and sorting out conflicting thoughts. The amygdala, on the other hand, is involved in emotional processing and reactions (LeDoux, 2003).

A number of genes have also been implicated in resilience, such as HPA axis-, serotonin-, and dopamine-related genes (for a review, see Feder, Nestler, & Charney, 2009). Recent research has particularly focused on brain-derived neurotrophic factor (BDNF), which is central in the generation of new neurons (neurogenesis) and may be particularly vulnerable to stressful experiences. Recent animal research has shown that severe stress in early life (e.g., the mother being severely abusive to her offspring in the first few weeks after birth) changed the BDNF gene expression in the prefrontal lobe of the offspring (Roth, Lubin, Funk, & Sweatt, 2009). This altered gene expression was carried over to the next generation, suggesting a generational effect of the severe stress. Conversely, offspring with mothers who are more attentive and caring may be more resilient to stress (see Liu, Diorio, Tannenbaum, Caldji, Francis, et al., 1997). These findings suggest that so-called epigenetic changes (the inherited changes in gene expression, caused by the stress in this case) may be involved in determining vulnerability to stress and psychological resilience. There is some support on this from human research on psychopathology and early maternal exposure; several neurodevelopmental disorders have been associated with pregnant women's exposure to severe stress, such as war and other types of disasters (for a review see, Bale et al., 2010).

Although we have only briefly discussed the neurobiology of resilience as it relates to trauma and stress, this is a highly important area of research that is growing exponentially. This field is continuously improving our understanding of the underlying neural circuits, the associated genes, and the epigenetic effects. Neurobiological research is of the utmost importance in laying the groundwork for new models of coping with the threat of terrorist attacks and building psychological resilience in those who are more at risk for such disasters.

SUMMARY

In this chapter we have defined psychological resilience and discussed research studies and findings pertaining to this construct and terrorism-related trauma. Most psychological and psychiatric research on terrorism attacks has focused on the development and treatment of psychopathological symptoms and disorders, such as PTSD. In this chapter we emphasized that in the aftermath of a terrorist attack, most people, in fact, appear to recover relatively quickly from psychopathological symptoms, and many exhibit psychological resilience. In other words, many people exhibit protective factors that prevent them from developing sustained psychopathological symptoms of stress, depression, and other disorders.

Bonanno and colleagues have published several papers on psychological resilience in people following the 9/11/2001 attacks. They argued that people exposed to terrorism can be categorized into at least four groups (Bonanno et al., 2010): (1) individuals who have chronically elevated stress and anxiety symptoms; (2) people who initially show low levels or an absence of psychopathological symptoms, but then develop them later; (3) people who initially demonstrate high levels of symptoms, but then show a full recovery; and (4) individuals who show psychological resilience and a healthy adjustment to the experienced stress. In one of their studies they found that approximately 65% of a large sample of New York City residents met criteria for resilience during the first 6 months after 9/11/2001 (Bonanno et al., 2006). However, they also pointed out that there is heterogeneity within the latter group (Bonanno, 2005).

Bonanno and his group have studied the predictors of psychological resilience in people exposed to the 9/11/2001 attacks. They found that several factors predicted the level of psychological resilience, including gender, age, ethnicity, education, absence of depression and substance use, lower income loss, social support, fewer chronic diseases, fewer recent life stressors and past traumatic events, and less direct impact of the attacks (Bonanno et al., 2007). They also examined self-enhancement, the overly positive bias of oneself, and found that this construct was related to better psychological resilience in people who were in or near the World Trade Center on 9/11/2001 (Bonanno et al., 2005).

Other research on psychological resilience in the aftermath of the 9/11/2001 strikes has demonstrated an association between resilience and less denial, self-blame, and negative worldview changes (Butler et al., 2009) and more active coping and acceptance (Silver et al., 2002). Fredrickson and colleagues (2003) showed that the level of positive emotions in a relatively small sample of college students assessed before the 9/11/2001 strikes accounted for the relationship between psychological resilience before the strikes and later development of psychopathological symptoms.

Research focusing on terrorism in Israel, and coping styles and resilience among people living there, have shown that social support may be another important factor in the development of a resilient style (Hobfoll et al., 2006), although the data on this are inconsistent (Hobfoll et al., 2008; Palmieri et al., 2008). There is evidence suggesting ethnic differences; being of Jewish background was related to better coping and resilience in Israel specifically (Hobfoll et al., 2006, 2009).

A topic related to psychological resilience is post-traumatic growth. This psychological construct refers to the positive psychological changes that some people may experience in the aftermath of a disaster. The research findings on post-traumatic growth following terrorist attacks have been inconsistent. Some studies, but not all, have found an association between post-traumatic growth and the development of psychological distress and PTSD symptoms (Laufer & Solomon, 2006; Hall et al., 2008). Some researchers also question the premises that research on post-traumatic growth is based on, and whether it actually is a self-standing psychological construct.

Two other factors that often are overlooked in research on psychological resilience are culture and religion. Both of these may have a significant impact on the ability to effectively cope with the trauma related to a terrorist attack, and in this chapter we presented some evidence for this in Latin American (Hernández, 2002) and Russian (Moscardino et al., 2007) culture. These factors demonstrate the importance the social environment may have in resilience.

With regards to strengthening psychological resilience in the public, a few independent reports provide some guidelines. However, possibly the best material has come from the APA, which put together a task force on Promoting Resilience in Response to Terrorism in the aftermath of the 9/11/2001 attacks. The APA has published fact sheets for psychologists that provide guidelines for how to help patients become more resilient in coping with stress related to terrorism and other disasters. The APA also has online resources available for both experts and the public on how to cope with traumatic events.

Lastly, we briefly discussed underlying neurobiological factors of resilience, including the importance of the HPA axis as a protective factor in controlling reactions to stress. We also discussed important brain regions, such as the prefrontal cortex, the hippocampus, and the amygdala, as well as genetic links (brain-derived neurotrophic factor), and how these may be implicated in stress reactions to traumatic events, such as terrorism attacks.

Overall, this line of research is important for a number of reasons. First, when all of the attention is directed at understanding why and how people react negatively to terrorism, one may easily miss how people remain resilient in the face of this threat. It is not enough to identify risk factors for negative outcomes, and further work is needed to better understand why some if not most people exhibit positive outcomes following tragedy. In doing so, we increase our chances of promoting recovery and resilience in a preventive way, as opposed to responding and managing negative outcomes following an act of terrorism. Finally, there are many layers of factors that place people in a position of either strength/resilience or vulnerability/weakness. These range from one's biology all the way to the communities and countries where people live. As we unpack this complexity, we make ourselves more prepared to promote health and well-being in any number of ways, and thereby reduce the number of people who are adversely affected.

The events of 9/11/2001 were horrific. It was a painful day for most living in the United States. However, a lot of good came of that day, and the human spirit was on full display. Thus, while fear and distress plagued many people much of the time, it was also a time marked by incredible kindness, empathy, and courage. In a way, it was a proud moment for us—as both a country and members of the human race. While the central focus of this book has been fear, we would argue here that 9/11/2001 was perhaps most significant in terms of the positive human growth and profound sense of connection that ensued—on an infinite number of levels. As a result, we feel it is most appropriate to finish off this book with a discussion about resilience and what makes us human, as opposed to what lurks under our beds.

REFERENCES

American Psychological Association. (2004). *APA releases fact sheets on resilience to help people cope with terrorism and other disasters.* Retrieved Jan. 10, 2011, from http://www.apa.org/news/press/releases/2004/02/resilience-facts.aspx

American Psychological Association. (2011a). *Disasters and terrorism.* Retrieved Jan. 10, 2011, from http://www.apa.org/helpcenter/disaster/index.aspx

American Psychological Association. (2011b). *Fact sheet: Fostering resilience in response to terrorism: For psychologists working with older adults.* Retrieved Jan. 10, 2011, from http://www.apa.org/pi/aging/older-adults.pdf

Bale, T. L., Baram, T. Z., Brown, A. S., Goldstein, J. M., Insel, T. R., McCarthy, M. M., et al. (2010). Early life programming and neurodevelopmental disorders. *Biological Psychiatry, 68*(4), 314–319.

Benight, C. C., Freyaldenhoven, R. W., Hughes, J., Ruiz, J. M., Zoschke, T. A., & Lovallo, W. R. (2000). Coping self-efficacy and psychological distress following the Oklahoma City bombing. *Journal of Applied Social Psychology, 30*(7), 1331–1344.

Bonanno, G. A. (2004). Loss, trauma, and human resilience. *American Psychologist, 59*(1), 20–28.

Bonanno, G. A. (2005). Resilience in the face of potential trauma. *Current Directions in Psychological Science, 14*(3), 135–138.

Bonanno, G. A., Brewin, C. R., Kaniasty, K., & La Greca, A. M. (2010). Weighing the costs of disaster: Consequences, risks, and resilience in individuals, families, and communities. *Psychological Science in the Public Interest, 11*(1).

Bonanno, G. A., Galea, S., Bucciarelli, A., & Vlahov, D. (2006). Psychological resilience after disaster: New York City in the aftermath of the September 11th terrorist attack. *Psychological Science, 17*(3), 181–186.

Bonanno, G. A., Galea, S., Bucciarelli, A., & Vlahov, D. (2007). What predicts psychological resilience after disaster? The role of demographics, resources, and life stress. *Journal of Consulting and Clinical Psychology, 75*(5), 671–682.

Bonanno, G. A., Rennicke, C., & Dekel, S. (2005). Self-enhancement among high-exposure survivors of the September 11th terrorist attack: resilience or social maladjustment? *Journal of Personality and Social Psychology, 88*(6), 984–998.

Brewin, C. R., Andrews, B., & Valentine, J. D. (2000). Meta-analysis of risk factors for post-traumatic stress disorder in trauma-exposed adults. *Journal of Consulting and Clinical Psychology, 68*(5), 748–766.

Butler, L. D., Koopman, C., Azarow, J., Blasey, C. M., Magdalene, J. C., DiMiceli, S., et al. (2009). Psychosocial predictors of resilience after the September 11, 2001 terrorist attacks. *Journal of Nervous and Mental Disease, 197*(4), 266–273.

Davidson, R. J. (2004). Well-being and affective style: neural substrates and biobehavioural correlates. *Philosophical Transactions of the Royal Society London: Biological Sciences, 359*(1449), 1395–1411.

Feder, A., Nestler, E. J., & Charney, D. S. (2009). Psychobiology and molecular genetics of resilience. *Nature Reviews Neuroscience, 10*(6), 446–457.

Frazier, P., Conlon, A., & Glaser, T. (2001). Positive and negative life changes following sexual assault. *Journal of Consulting and Clinical Psychology, 69*(6), 1048–1055.

Fredrickson, B. L., Tugade, M. M., Waugh, C. E., & Larkin, G. R. (2003). What good are positive emotions in crises? A prospective study of resilience and emotions following the terrorist attacks on the United States on September 11th, 2001. *Journal of Personality and Social Psychology, 84*(2), 365–376.

Galea, S., Ahern, J., Resnick, H., Kilpatrick, D., Bucuvalas, M., Gold, J., et al. (2002). Psychological sequelae of the September 11 terrorist attacks in New York City. *New England Journal of Medicine, 346*(13), 982–987.

Hall, B. J., Hobfoll, S. E., Palmieri, P. A., Canetti-Nisim, D., Shapira, O., Johnson, R. J., et al. (2008). The psychological impact of impending forced settler disengagement in Gaza: Trauma and posttraumatic growth. *Journal of Traumatic Stress, 21*(1), 22–29.

Hernández, P. (2002). Resilience in families and communities: Latin American contributions from the psychology of liberation. *Family Journal: Counseling and Therapy of Couples and Families, 10*(3), 334–343.

Hobfoll, S. E., Canetti-Nisim, D., & Johnson, R. J. (2006). Exposure to terrorism, stress-related mental health symptoms, and defensive coping among Jews and Arabs in Israel. *Journal of Consulting and Clinical Psychology, 74*(2), 207–218.

Hobfoll, S. E., Canetti-Nisim, D., Johnson, R. J., Palmieri, P. A., Varley, J. D., & Galea, S. (Writer) (2008). The association of exposure, risk, and resiliency factors with PTSD among Jews and Arabs exposed to repeated acts of terrorism in Israel. *Journal of Traumatic Stress, 21*(1), 9–21.

Hobfoll, S. E., Hall, B. J., Canetti-Nisim, D., Galea, S., Johnson, R. J., & Palmieri, P. A. (2007). Refining our understanding of traumatic growth in the face of terrorism: Moving from meaning cognitions to doing what is meaningful. *Applied Psychology, 56*(3), 345–366.

Hobfoll, S. E., Palmieri, P. A., Johnson, R. J., Canetti-Nisim, D., Hall, B. J., & Galea, S. (2009). Trajectories of resilience, resistance, and distress during ongoing terrorism: The case of Jews and Arabs in Israel. *Journal of Consulting and Clinical Psychology, 77*(1), 138–148.

Kemeny, M. E. (2003). The psychobiology of stress. *Current Directions in Psychological Science, 12,* 124–129.

Kirkley, K. O., & Medway, F. J. (2003). Promoting children's resilience and coping following September 11, 2001. *School Psychology International, 24*(2), 166–181.

Laufer, A., & Solomon, Z. (2006). Posttraumatic symptoms and posttraumatic growth among Israeli youth exposed to terror incidents. *Journal of Social and Clinical Psychology, 25*(4), 429–447.

LeDoux, J. (2003). The emotional brain, fear, and the amygdala. *Cellular and Molecular Neurobiology, 23*(4–5), 727–738.

Linley, P. A., Joseph, S., Cooper, R., Harris, S., & Meyer, C. (2003). Positive and negative changes following vicarious exposure to the September 11 terrorist attacks. *Journal of Traumatic Stress, 16*(5), 481–485.

Liu, D., Diorio, J., Tannenbaum, B., Caldji, C., Francis, D., et al. (1997). Maternal care, hippocampal glucocorticoid receptors, and hypothalamic-pituitary-adrenal responses to stress. *Science, 277,* 1659–1661.

Longstaff, P. H., & Yang, S. (2008). Communication management and trust: Their role in building resilience to "surprises" such as natural disasters, pandemic flu, and terrorism. *Ecology and Society, 13*(1), [online].

Moscardino, U., Axia, G., Scrimin, S., & Capello, F. (2007). Narratives from caregivers of children surviving the terrorist attack in Beslan: issues of health, culture, and resilience. *Social Science & Medicine, 64*(8), 1776–1787.

Norris, F. H., & Kaniasty, K. (1996). Received and perceived social support in times of stress: a test of the social support deterioration deterrence model. *Journal of Personality and Social Psychology, 71*(3), 498–511.

Norris, F. H., Stevens, S. P., Pfefferbaum, B., Wyche, K. F., & Pfefferbaum, R. L. (2008). Community resilience as a metaphor, theory, set of capacities, and strategy for disaster readiness. *American Journal of Community Psychology, 41*(1–2), 127–150.

Ong, A. D., Bergeman, C. S., Bisconti, T. L., & Wallace, K. A. (2006). Psychological resilience, positive emotions, and successful adaptation to stress in later life. *Journal of Personality and Social Psychology, 91*(4), 730–749.

Palmieri, P. A., Canetti-Nisim, D., Galea, S., Johnson, R. J., & Hobfoll, S. E. (2008). The psychological impact of the Israel-Hezbollah War on Jews and Arabs in Israel: the impact of risk and resilience factors. *Social Science & Medicine, 67*(8), 1208–1216.

Pfefferbaum, B. J., Reissman, D. B., Pfefferbaum, R. L., Klomp, R. W., & Gurwitch, R. H. (2007). Building resilience to mass trauma events. In: *Handbook of injury and violence prevention* (pp. 347–358). Springer.

Pyszczynski, T., Solomon, S., & Greenberg, J. (2003). *In the wake of 9/11/2001: The psychology of terror.* Washington, D.C.: American Psychological Association.

Roth, T. L., Lubin, F. D., Funk, A. J., & Sweatt, J. D. (2009). Lasting epigenetic influence of early-life adversity on the BDNF gene. *Biological Psychiatry, 65*(9), 760–769.

Silver, R. C., Holman, E. A., McIntosh, D. N., Poulin, M., & Gil-Rivas, V. (2002). Nationwide longitudinal study of psychological responses to September 11. *Journal of the American Medical Association, 288*(10), 1235–1244.

Speckhard, A. (2002). Inoculating resilience to terrorism: Acute and posttraumatic stress responses in U.S. military, foreign & civilian services serving overseas after September 11th. *Traumatology, 8*(2), 103–130.

Tedeschi, R. G., & Calhoun, L. G. (2004). Posttraumatic growth: conceptual foundations and empirical evidence. *Psychological Inquiry, 15*(1), 1–18.

Tedeschi, R. G., Park, C. L., & Calhoun, L. G. (1998). *Posttraumatic growth: Positive changes in the aftermath of crisis.* Mahwah, NJ: Lawrence Erlbaum Associates.

Val, E. B., & Linley, P. A. (2006). Posttraumatic growth, positive changes, and negative changes in Madrid residents following the March 11, 2004, Madrid train bombings. *Journal of Loss and Trauma: International Perspectives on Stress & Coping, 11*(5), 409–424.

Westphal, M., & Bonanno, G. A. (2007). Posttraumatic growth and resilience to trauma: Different sides of the same coin or different coins? *Applied Psychology, 56*(3), 417–427.

7 Implications and Conclusion

"As fear increases into an agony of terror, we behold, as under all violent emotions, diversified results."
Charles Darwin

In his brilliant volume on emotions, *The Expression of the Emotions in Man and Animals* (1872), Charles Darwin discussed in detail and quite elegantly the emotional expression of fear in humans. He vividly illustrated the physical manifestations of someone who is experiencing fear, including how somatic senses are amplified, heart palpitations increase, the skin pales, muscles shiver, the hair stands straight, breathing gets heavier, and the mouth becomes dry. He went on to describe the elevations in physical symptoms when fear becomes horror before concluding that eventually the "mental powers fail" (p. 292). One may argue that Darwin painted a poignant picture of the potential fear trajectory for someone who is experiencing a threatening event, such as an impending terrorist attack. At first, when one's cognitive processes fully recognize the threat of an imminent terrorist attack, the physical manifestations of fear become apparent. Then, eventually, after a prolonged and sustained elevation of these physiological symptoms, a person's mental state is subsequently affected, resulting in psychological distress.

Darwin's description of fear, although more than 100 years old, is quite consistent with how today's scientists view fear: as a complex psychophysiological emotional experience that interacts with biological (internal) and environmental (external) influences, resulting in alterations in mood, temperament, motivation, and personality. Over time, the chronic experience of fear can morph into serious psychological distress that eventually may develop into a mental disorder.

But why do people become fearful in the first place? Why do people exhibit these complex psychophysiological symptoms when they are feeling threatened, such as in the aftermath of a terrorist attack or when anticipating future terrorism? Why do people go through this process that can be so emotionally draining and have such severe physical and psychological consequences? These are crucial questions that many scientists and academics have attempted to answer. Various theories have been postulated, most of them focusing on the so-called flight-or-fight reaction—that if we perceive a threat, our body will prepare us for action in either a fight to the death or a desperate flight to survive. This evolutionarily rooted and adaptive role of fear, as an organism survival mechanism, was also recognized by Darwin (1872, p. 308):

"Men, during numberless generations, have endeavoured to escape from their enemies or danger by headlong flight, or by violently struggling with them; and such great exertions will have caused the heart to beat rapidly, the breathing to be hurried, the chest to heave, and the nostrils to be dilated. As these exertions have often been pro-longed to the last extremity, the final result will have been utter prostration, pallor, perspiration, trembling of all the muscles, or their complete relaxation. And now, whenever the emotion of fear is strongly felt, though it may not lead to any exertion, the same results tend to reappear, through the force of inheritance and association."

Recent research using state-of-the-art methods to study emotions in humans have found further support for the evolutionary importance of fear. In a study published in *Nature Neuroscience*, Susskind, Lee, Cusi, Feiman, Grabski, and Anderson (2008) explored the expression (production) of the fear response. They examined facial expressions of fear and disgust and found that the production of fear expressions enhanced their participants' visual field and increased their nasal inspiratory capacity (whereas disgust decreased these sensory perceptions). These findings, they argued, support the notion that fear (as well as other emotions) serves an egocentric evolutionary role. That is, fearful expressions are not arbitrary configurations of social communication, but instead they function to increase preparedness for perception and action by enhancing a person's sensory systems.

In other words, whether it is the experience of fear, the expression (or production) of fear, or the anticipation of fear, the emotion serves an evolutionarily adaptive function that increases the likelihood for the organism's survival. As we have argued throughout this book, the fear associated with terrorism threats reflects this inherent human survival instinct as well. A central thesis of this volume is that the events of Sept. 11, 2001, and the threat of terrorism that ensued, primed an inherent survival mechanism in people in which fear was the driving force that motivated people to find protection and security. Developing a deeper understanding of what underlies human reactions to terrorism and the important role fear plays in the context of terrorism threat is, in fact, the primary reason why we set out to write this book.

Through our discussions in Chapters 1 through 6, we hope that this book has provided the readers—whether academics working in the field of terrorism research or laypeople just interested in developing a better understanding—with in-depth knowledge of the current state of psychological research on terrorism, and perhaps more importantly has advanced people's understanding of the psychology associated with terrorism fears—as distinct from discrete psychological disorders, which have been the focus of most of the research in this arena. As we proposed in the beginning of this book, we believe that *the psychology of fear is truly the underlying psychology of terrorism itself.* Although this may have been to some a bold statement when it was first read, we hope that by now, at this final stage of the book, this statement has substantially more meaning to our readers—particularly after having read and digested the research we presented, as well as our discussions of this research, and after taking into account the evolutionary perspective of fear as discussed above.

We presented and discussed current research on the psychological impact of terrorism in Chapter 2 and argued that most of this research has focused on discrete diagnostic/clinical constructs (as defined in the APA's DSM-IV-TR) exhibited in people post-9/11/2001. Impressive large-scale studies have demonstrated increased rates of symptoms related to PTSD (Galea, Resnick, Ahern, Gold, Bucuvalas, Kilpatrick, et al., 2002; Schlenger, Caddell, Ebert, Jordan, Rourke, et al., 2002; Silver, Holman, McIntosh, Poulin, & Gil-Rivas, 2002), depression (Galea et al., 2002), and stress and anxiety (Schuster, Stein, Jaycox, Collins, Marshall, et al., 2001) in people following the 9/11/2001 attacks. These rates, according to the research, generally declined over time (e.g., Silver et al., 2002). However, as we discussed in Chapter 2, by focusing on the better-known conventional clinical constructs, researchers may be missing what is arguably an even more significant concern: the underlying fear that is present in the population at large as a consequence of the elevated terrorism threat levels. Fear is, after all, the *primary psychological weapon underlying acts of terrorism.*

Targeting people's fear—whether through actual terror strikes or by the threat of attacks—is destructive in ways that may not be immediately apparent but, over time and through repeated exposure to threatening stimuli, may have severe negative effects on both individuals and whole societies. As mentioned above and further addressed in Chapter 3, fear of terrorism is linked to humans' inherent survival instinct. The events of 9/11/2001 primed this inherent survival mechanism and fear drove people to find protection and security—in other words, fear elicited a drive to live in the face of potential extinction. Terror management theory (Pyszczynski, Soloman, & Greenberg, 2003; Pyszczynski, Motyl, & Abdollahi, 2009) provides a framework for understanding how mortality salience, or fearing death, leads people to seek proximity/connection to culture as a means of transcending these anxieties. Terror management theory stipulates that being aware of one's own mortality increases one's need for security and probability of survival; when faced with the fear of terrorism, people are more likely to seek goals with a positive valence, rather than a negative valence, to decrease their own perceived risk of extinction. However, in the case of terrorism threat, the experience of fear in anticipation of some terrible event is often prolonged through the constant media exposure or politicians' tendency to continuously remind the public about the threat. This prolongation of the experience of fear may eventually, as we discussed in Chapter 4, have such a negative impact that people will alter their daily behaviors and routines, as well as their beliefs regarding political issues and their trust in the government.

Moreover, this notion that fear, when examined over time, may be associated with both positive and negative emotional components that may affect people's decision-making capacity in distinct ways at different points in time, as well as whether people will pursue goals with positive or negative valences, is a concept that has received limited attention in the scientific community. However, this idea is an important aspect of risk appraisal and relative risk appraisal theories, which we discussed in Chapter 5. Risk appraisal theory argues that negative emotions are typically associated with pessimistic risk assessments, whereas positive emotions are more often related to optimistic assessment of risk and threat (Johnson & Tversky, 1983). However, negative and positive emotions are dynamic and influenced by situational factors. Extending this to issues of terrorism, Marshall, Bryant, Amsel, Jung, Cook, and Neria (2007) proposed the term *relative* risk appraisal to capture what they believe is the psychological function behind our more conventional models of subjective behavioral responses to terrorism (e.g., PTSD, anxiety disorders, depression, etc.). Marshall and colleagues argued that one's interpretation and understanding of this ongoing threat is influenced by a multitude of factors. Fear in particular may play a significant role in terms of how this risk appraisal process unfolds, and is heavily influenced by factors including media exposure, dire public statements made by government officials, and continued elevations in the government's color-coded terror alert system. All of these factors contribute to a pattern of vicarious exposure for many living outside the areas immediately affected by terrorism, and contribute to a more global and acute sense of worry and distress.

As we discussed in Chapter 6, psychological resilience to traumatic events (such as terror attacks and other disasters) is the healthy adjustment to the experienced stress. As it turns out, the vast majority of people who are affected by terrorism, either directly or indirectly, do not go on to develop chronic psychopathological symptoms such as PTSD, anxiety, or depression. Instead, they show high rates of psychological resilience, which may suggest that psychological resilience is part of a complex fear–survival equation. As we stated in Chapter 6, psychological resilience is the ability to maintain a stable equilibrium following a traumatic event and to be able to use the experience as a means of growth and opportunity. Within resilience, there is also considerable heterogeneity (Bonanno, 2005), but one particularly important factor may be self-enhancement (Bonanno, Rennicke, & Dekel, 2005), which may help people to maintain a positive outlook and promote well-being during hard times. Although speculative, one may argue that in the context of ongoing terrorism threat the experience of fear in small and appropriate doses may actually facilitate psychological resilience, which then serves to increase one's motivation for security and protection, and ultimately survival of the individual.

Neurobiologically, there is some evidence to support this. The amygdala, the brain region most commonly associated with fear, is part of the limbic system that commonly is considered the oldest brain system, developed to serve the primary function of fight or flight (LeDoux, 2003). When faced with a threat such as an impending terrorism attack, the amygdala will project fear to the prefrontal cortex, the brain center involved in decision-making, and an appropriate response will be determined. With respect to the issue of psychological resilience, some degree of fear response may result in a healthier trajectory. However, if the connectivity between the amygdala and prefrontal lobe is disturbed and the modulation of the amygdala activation is impaired—such as after severe and/or prolonged exposure to terrorism threats—the result may be serious psychological damage, evident in symptoms of a mental disorder. Thus, the influence of terrorism fears on behaviors, as a function of changes in fear over time, is an area of research that warrants more study, both from a behavioral and a neurobiological perspective.

We began our book by discussing the definition of terrorism and presented different sides in the larger debate on how to define this act of violence. We converged on Jackson's definition that "Terrorism is violence or its threat intended as a symbolically communicative act in which the direct victims of the action are instrumentalized as a means of creating a psychological effect of intimidation and fear in a target audience for a political objective" (Jackson, 2011, p. 123). Over the course of this book we have focused on the psychological aspects of fear within the context of terrorism acts and threats. We have presented research on the consequences—psychiatric and medical—to people exposed to terrorism acts or threats. We have also discussed how priming people's fears about impending terrorism threats (e.g., through a national terrorism alert system) may serve the unwanted intent of frustrating and even deterring people rather than preparing them for a potential act of terrorism. One may even speculate that at certain critical times, governments and authorities purposely want to induce fear in the public to gain some political advantage; indeed, the term "terrorism" was allegedly popularized during the French Revolution's Reign of Terror (Hoffman, 1998), a period in which conflict between political parties resulted in violence by the state against civilians with the purpose of instilling fear in the public and preventing counter-revolution. In this volume, we have also presented research on psychological resilience that demonstrates that even though there may be negative consequences related to terrorism threat and prolonged fear in some people, an astonishingly high proportion of people are resilient to the fear-related stress.

Before we move on to discuss the implications of our findings, it is important to remind the reader about the several prominent research trends that have emerged on the psychological impact of terrorism. This body of research is important in that it has demonstrated that when a terrorist attack occurs (1) the incidence of psychiatric disorders increases immediately following the strike; (2) the psychological impact is more significant the closer you get to the epicenter of the attack; and (3) there is a general reduction in this psychological distress over time, following the initial spike. However, as we have repeatedly argued, the actual numbers of people affected by terrorism may in fact be skewed as a function of the models used for evaluating psychological impact—where constructs such as fear do not exist and receive no focus. In our opinion, this is ironic given that many would argue the goal of terrorism is to instill terror and fear and not necessarily discrete DSM-IV-TR constructs.

One definition of fear is "a feeling of agitation and anxiety caused by the presence or imminence of danger" (The Free Dictionary, 2011). This definition highlights the subtleness of fear: it is a feeling—actually an emotion—that may be difficult to quantify in the larger clinical picture when examining the consequences of terrorism and the threat of such actions. Nonetheless, however, fear can have severe consequences that go beyond what is directly measurable by our current diagnostic manuals (e.g., the DSM-IV-TR, American Psychiatric Association, 2000). Fear is, we contend, what underlies the psychology of terrorism.

IMPLICATIONS

What can be learned from the existing research on the psychological impact of terrorism? Where should the field of terrorism research go from here? These are two equally important questions to consider when discussing the implications of the research we have presented and discussed throughout this volume. First and foremost, we have shown that there has been a substantive amount of research on the psychological impact of terrorist acts and threats, which may help inform those who are tasked with responding to the general public following a terrorist attack. This research may in itself, and if seriously considered, provide the groundwork for future research and the foundation on which to build future disaster communication and management.

Chapter 5 focused on the art and science of threat dissemination and current models for communicating warning. For example, we provided an in-depth view into the U.S. Department of Homeland Security Advisory System. This color-coded alert system was implemented in the aftermath of the 9/11/2001 attacks, and although the concept and purpose were laudable, this system has since its inception drawn much criticism. This scrutiny has, in part, focused on the notion that the alert system may actually have the unintended function of *increasing* terrorism fears and anxieties in those directly affected, as well as the general public (Peña, 2002; Kramer, Brown, Spielman, Giosan, & Rothneck, 2003; McDermott & Zimbardo, 2007). In retrospect—hindsight being 20/20, of course—it is easy to argue that the Homeland Security Advisory System was not built on proper methodology (e.g., Aguirre, 2004) and was instead rushed into use in an attempt to satisfy the public's fear (and anger) over new terror attacks following the 9/11/2001 strikes. In developing a more effective terrorism alert system, one should as a first step take into account the research that is now available on the psychological impact of terrorism threat.

For example, as we have described in this book, there is considerable heterogeneity in people's response to terrorism and terrorism threat. When disasters occur or threaten societies, some fear is actually a common response among people. But in contrast to what might be popular thinking, most people respond to this fear in a rational and constructive manner (Goltz, Russell, & Bourque, 1992; Johnson, Feinberg, & Johnston, 1994). This rational approach towards potential threats, which is supported by evolutionary theory, is crucial and should be taken into account in the development of a new national terrorism alert system. The experience of fear actually mobilizes people to gain more information about the threat (such as through media outlets) and to take action to ensure their safety. Conversely, when this experience of fear is acute and prolonged, such as through an ongoing elevated terrorism threat alert level and with constant media reminders of the potential threat (e.g., New York City after 9/11/2001), people may instead over time demonstrate adverse reactions, from panic and outright avoidance to indifference and apathy.

As if this research was considered, on January 27, 2011, the Department of Homeland Security announced a new terrorism alert system to replace the old color-coded system (Ryan & Thomas, 2011). This alert system is allegedly less complicated than the old system, and any elevation in threat alert levels comes with very specific information that is designed to help people. At this point, and until implementation, the jury is still out as to whether this system actually will be more effective. However, based on early reports and descriptions of the system, it appears that this new terrorism alert system is built on a more informed foundation of terrorism threat.

In essence, policymakers and government officials must become more aware of and integrate more carefully what we know about people psychologically in the face of threat. Understanding basic principles, such as how anger may reinforce a sense of control and optimism, while fear decreases this experience, is one simple finding that has enormous implications for how warnings should be constructed and disseminated (Lerner et al., 2003). Fostering a sense of control and agency within these messages by presenting basic steps for preparedness and focus may subsequently decrease fear and/or apathy. In contrast, disseminating messages that are vague and nondescript—as many have been post-9/11/2001—may only serve to reinforce fear and apathy.

Warning messages should also be specific and void of histrionics. In the aftermath of 9/11/2001, there are numerous examples of government officials discussing what they deemed to be "credible" and "imminent" threats that caused them to lose sleep at night. In the absence of specific usable data, these kinds of statements serve to (1) reinforce fear and (2) reduce a sense of control in the general population. For those at increased risk for psychopathology, these kinds of statements also stoke the flames of psychological distress. At a minimum, they do nothing productive and further miss the intended goal of moving the population towards some goal (e.g., preparation, vigilance).

Governments and policymakers also need to pay closer attention to how various subgroups within the population may respond differently to these threats, and how not all messages may be interpreted in the same way across groups. The United States government has moved to disseminating messages focused on specific regions (e.g., New York City, high-profile targets such as the Super Bowl) and/or industries (e.g., the airline and mass transit sector). In a similar vein, the messages themselves should be crafted with the many subgroups of people in mind, where some will be more susceptible to negative outcomes and others to positive outcomes. For example, what steps can people in these specific areas take to protect themselves in the ways that the government intends?

Secondly, we have in this volume emphasized the shortcomings of current psychological models for understanding the impact of terrorism, the majority of which tend to use a conventional psychopathology framework that focuses on diagnostically clinical symptoms or disorders (e.g., anxiety disorder, depression, PTSD, and other mental disorders as listed in the DSM-IV-TR, American Psychiatric Association, 2000). Instead, new empirically supported and theoretically rooted models must be developed that take into account the multitude and dimensional aspect of all relevant factors (e.g., one's support system, external level of threat, proximity to the event, etc.) and differences in outcome (e.g., level of fear, resilience, clinically significant psychopathology, etc.). One such model is the above-mentioned relative risk appraisal theory, which highlights the important fact that "human perception is an active, multidimensional process" (Marshall et al., 2007, p. 304).

Multidimensional models, such as Marshall and colleagues' relative risk appraisal theory, can help better inform health care workers, first responders, and others (e.g., those who may be directly affected of a terror attack) about the dynamics of terrorism threat and provide more accurate information about people who are at greater risk for poor outcomes. Thus informed, preventive strategies and interventions may be implemented earlier and reduce the risk of more severe mental health problems. Recent neurobiological research has focused on finding biomarkers that may identify at an early stage those who may be more vulnerable to developing severe stress reactions (e.g., PTSD: Miller, Wolf, Fabricant, & Stein, 2009; Jovanovic,

Norrholm, Blanding, Davis, Duncan et al., 2010), as well as those who are more likely to be resilient (for a discussion on this, see for example Yehuda & Flory, 2007). As suggested by some (e.g., Marmar, 2009), finding biomarkers that identify those at higher risk for severe stress reactions to trauma may also inform novel strategies for stress inoculation and resilience building. Whether focusing on new behavioral, cognitive, or biological methodology, being better informed through research is crucial, and it may help promote greater health, recovery, and psychological resilience in people following acts of terrorism, as well as during times in which the threat of terrorism is high.

Lastly, it is important to acknowledge that despite recent advances in research, it is obvious that we can further improve our knowledge about the psychological impact of terrorism acts and threats, as well as the underlying psychology of terrorism fears. In this book, we have focused on a variety of theoretical models, including relative risk appraisal theory, terror management theory, and cognitive-behavioral theory. However, to further advance the field, it is important that research continue to test these and other models, as well as develop new testable models for the psychological impact of terrorism. Such new models must incorporate into their theoretical frameworks individual differences in emotional reactions and behavioral responses, and the potential heterogeneous outcomes. For example, we have described how emotional reactions to terrorist strikes and the threat of impending attacks can vary from fear in one person to anger in another. The level of severity of emotional reactions also varies, and in some people fear may eventually become anger. People's emotional reactions are also closely linked to their feelings of pessimism and optimism, which subsequently may affect their decisions as whether to engage in behaviors of positive or negative valence. This, in turn, can dictate outcome (e.g., chronic psychopathology vs. recovery vs. resilience).

New models on the psychological impact of terrorism also need to consider more recent frameworks for assessing the multitude of factors underlying fear. For example, the Terrorism Catastrophizing Scale (Sinclair & LoCicero, 2007) was developed and validated with the purpose of assessing fears specifically related to terrorism. It is designed to quickly assess level of fear and provide some framework for structuring care moving forward. It also provides for a system of benchmarking different groups of people along a common metric, and identifying those more at risk for negative outcomes. And it does so without being rooted within existing diagnostic frameworks for psychopathology.

Understanding how people are differentially affected by terrorism, the role of fear as distinct from discrete diagnostic constructs, and the manner by which fear leads people to make different, but important, changes in their decisions is also of critical importance for the general medical and mental health communities. On a very basic level, we as medical professionals must be able to identify people at greater risk faster. Quickly assessing factors such as one's social supports and level of engagement with others, past history of mental health problems, proximity to areas affected by terrorism, and cultural factors that may place one at greater risk and affect an individual's ability to understand the nature of the threat are all of critical importance.

New models should also take into account critical psychophysiological and neurobiological, and situational and environmental factors. Today we know that the environment may affect the neurobiological processes that underlie emotions and behaviors, and that changes in our neurobiological makeup can influence our sensitivity to the environment. Only through the thorough examination and study of old and new theoretical models may we begin to uncover the deeper psychology of terrorism fears, and its true impact on individuals and societies.

CONCLUDING REMARKS

When we started this endeavor—to write a book on the psychology of terrorism fears—we began with the assertion that there was a significant gap in the scientific literature in terms of how people are affected by terrorism in a myriad of ways. As psychological scientists, we were both struck by how narrow the scope of this science has been, focusing on discrete criteria for conventional psychological disorders, as well as how an individual's experience of fear and terror had essentially been left out of this study. Further, the vast majority of this research has been set up retrospectively, focusing on how people are affected by past acts of terrorism. Little attention has been paid to how people are affected by the ongoing threat of future terrorism (a prospective focus)—and how something as simple as fear is essentially proof that terrorism is effective.

We would argue that in a fundamental way, we as a scientific community have missed the point as a function of limiting the focus in this way. That being said, we have begun to see evidence of a shift in this perspective. As discussed in Chapter 4, Somer and colleagues (2005) were the first we know of who have taken on the task of trying to better understand how people are affected by ongoing terrorism threat, and how best to manage these fears in a healthy and adaptive manner. They evaluated Israeli citizens who were calling into a telephone hotline because of worries they have about future terrorism. This shift in zeitgeist is compelling and deserves further study.

As McDermott and Zimbardo (2007) pointed out, we have gotten to a point where an act of terrorism is no longer a prerequisite for this phenomenon to manifest. Rather, because we now have a convoluted system of terror alert warning systems and a network of officials who make statements about the threat of terrorism that vary in terms of their usefulness, we now have an adequate infrastructure set up to terrorize ourselves. We no longer need Al Qaeda to do this for us, as it could be argued that we do a good job of it ourselves. It does not have to be this way, however, because we also know a lot about what makes people resilient and strong in the face of threat. We also know much more than we have in the past about how different approaches to managing and responding to this threat affects people in both positive and negative ways.

This book is our attempt to address this scientific gap in knowledge and to uncover and present the science that has been published on the psychological impact of fear specifically. In our opinion, the most significant psychological factor in thinking about terrorism, one that underlies all terrorism acts and threats, is terrorism fear. Although we have presented voluminous research on the psychological impact of terrorism, we contend that the field of terrorism research is still only in its infancy in terms of understanding how political violence affects individual people, groups, and whole societies. Improving this understanding through empirical research and discourse is critical to further advance our knowledge in this area. Such knowledge can help lay the groundwork for the development of new preventive interventions to reduce the real psychological impact of terrorism, as well as to inform policymakers and lawmakers.

REFERENCES

Aguirre, B. E. (2004). Homeland Security warnings: Lessons learned and unlearned. *International Journal of Mass Emergencies and Disasters, 22*(2), 103–115.

American Psychiatric Association. (2000). *Diagnostic and statistical manual of mental disorders-Fourth edition-text revision.* Washington, D.C.: American Psychiatric Association.

Bonanno, G. A. (2005). Resilience in the face of potential trauma. *Current Directions in Psychological Science, 14*(3), 135–138.

Bonanno, G. A., Rennicke, C., & Dekel, S. (2005). Self-enhancement among high-exposure survivors of the September 11th terrorist attack: resilience or social maladjustment? *Journal of Personality and Social Psychology, 88*(6), 984–998.

Darwin, C. (1872). *The expressions of the emotions in man and animals.* London: John Murray.

Galea, S., Resnick, H., Ahern, J., Gold, J., Bucuvalas, M., Kilpatrick, D., et al. (2002). Posttraumatic stress disorder in Manhattan, New York City, after the September 11th terrorist attacks. *Journal of Urban Health, 79,* 340–353.

Goltz, J., Russell, L., & Bourque, L. (1992). Initial behavioural response to a rapid onset disaster. *International Journal of Mass Emergencies and Disasters, 10,* 43–69.

Hoffman, B. (1998). *Inside terrorism.* London, UK: Victor Gollancz Ltd.

Jackson, R. (2011). In defence of terrorism: finding a way through a forest of misconceptions. *Behavioral Sciences of Terrorism and Political Aggression, 3*(2), 116–130.

Johnson, E. J., & Tversky, A. (1983). Affect, generalization, and the perception of risk. *Journal of Personality and Social Psychology, 45*(1), 20–31.

Johnson, N. R., Feinberg, W. E., & Johnston, D. M. (1994). Microstructure and panic: The impact of social bonds on individual action in collective flight from the Beverly Hills Supper Club Fire. In R. R. Dynes & K. Tierney (Eds.), *Disasters, collective behavior and social organization* (pp. 168–189). Newark: University of Delaware Press.

Jovanovic, T., Norrholm, S. D., Blanding, N. Q., Davis, M., Duncan, E., et al. (2010). Impaired fear inhibition is a biomarker of PTSD but not depression. *Depression and Anxiety, 27*(3), 244–251.

Kramer, M. E., Brown, A. D., Spielman, L., Giosan, C., & Rothrock, M. (2003). Psychological reactions to the national terror-alert system. *The Id: Graduate Faculty, Psychology Society Bulletin, 1*(1), 67–70.

LeDoux, J. (2003). *The emotional brain: The mysterious underpinnings of emotional life.* New York: Simon and Schuster.

Lerner, J. S., Gonzalez, R. M., Small, D. A., & Fischhoff, B. (2003). Effects of fear and anger on perceived risks of terrorism: a national field experiment. *Psychological Science, 14*(2), 144–150.

Marmar, C. (2009). Mental health impact of Afghanistan and Iraq deployment: Meeting the challenge of a new generation of veterans. *Depression and Anxiety, 26,* 493–497.

Marshall, R. D., Bryant, R. A., Amsel, L., Suh, E. J., Cook, J. M., & Neria, Y. (2007). The psychology of ongoing threat: Relative risk appraisal, the September 11 attacks, and terrorism-related fears. *American Psychologist, 62,* 304–316.

McDermott, R., & Zimbardo, P. G. (2007). The psychological consequences of terrorist alerts. In B. Bongar, L. Brown, Beutler, L., J. Breckenridge, & P. Zimbardo (Eds.), *The psychology of terrorism* (pp. 357–370). Oxford: Oxford University Press.

Miller, M. W., Wolf, E. J., Fabricant, L., & Stein, N. (2009). Low basal cortisol and startle responding as possible biomarkers of PTSD: The influence of internalizing and external comorbidity. *Post-Traumatic Stress Disorder, Part 4, 1*–17.

Peña, C. V. (2002). Homeland Security Alert System: Why bother? Retrieved Nov. 30, 2010, from http://www.cato.org/pub_display.php?pub_id=4205.

Pyszczynski, T., Motyl, M., & Abdollahi, A. (2009). Righteous violence: Killing for God, country, freedom, and justice. *Behavioral Sciences of Terrorism and Political Aggression, 1,* 12–39.

Pyszczynski, T., Solomon, S., & Greenberg, J. (2003). *In the wake of 9/11/2001: The psychology of terror.* Washington, D.C.: American Psychological Association.

Ryan, J., & Thomas, P. (2011). Color-coded terror alerts retired by Department of Homeland Security. Retrieved Jan. 27, 2011, from http://abcnews.go.com/News/color-coded-terror-alerts-retired-department-homeland-security/story?id=12780975.

Schlenger, W. E., Caddell, J. M., Ebert, L., Jordan, B. K., Rourke, K. M., Wilson, D., Thalji, L., Deniis, J. M., Fairbank, J. A., & Kulka, R. A. (2002). Psychological reactions to terrorist attacks: findings from the national study of Americans' reactions to September 11. *Journal of the American Medical Association, 288,* 581–588.

Schuster, M. A., Stein, B. D., Jaycox, L. H., Collins, R. L., Marshall, G. N., Elliott, M. N., et al. (2001). A national survey of stress reactions after the September 11, 2001 terrorist attacks. *New England Journal of Medicine, 345,* 1507–1512.

Silver, R. C., Holman, E. A., McIntosh, D. N., Poulin, M., & Gil-Rivas, V. (2002). Nationwide longitudinal study of psychological responses to September 11. *Journal of the American Medical Association, 288,* 1235–1244.

Sinclair, S. J., & LoCicero, A. (2007). Anticipatory fear and catastrophizing about terrorism: Development, validation, and psychometric testing of the Terrorism Catastrophizing Scale (TCS). *Traumatology, 13,* 75–90.

Somer, E., Tamir, E., Maguen, S., & Litz, B. T. (2005). Brief cognitive behavioral phone-based intervention targeting anxiety about the threat of an attack: A pilot study. *Behaviour Research and Therapy, 43,* 669–679.

Susskind, J. M., Lee, D. H., Cusi, A., Feiman, R., Grabski, W., & Anderson, A. K. (2008). Expressing fear enhances sensory acquisition. *Nature Neuroscience, 11*(7), 843–850.

The Free Dictionary (2011). Retrieved Feb. 4, 2011, from http://www.thefreedictionary.com

Yehuda, R., & Flory, J. D. (2007). Differentiating biological correlates of risk, PTSD, and resilience following trauma exposure. *Journal of Traumatic Stress, 20*(4), 435–447.

Index